Praise for *Happy Parents Happy Kids*

"She's done it again! Ann Douglas has written yet another must-read book for Canadian parents. Based on interviews with dozens of real moms and dads, *Happy Parents Happy Kids* is an engaging, timely, and comprehensive look at parenting culture today, offering insights and strategies that parents can use to create happier, healthier families. If you buy one parenting book this year, *Happy Parents Happy Kids* should be it."

—KIM SHIFFMAN, Editor-in-Chief, *Today's Parent*

"As a parent of two kids with more than ordinary needs, I wish I'd had a book like this when I was just getting started. It took a long time for me to figure out that sometimes, it's the parents who need to change, not their kids. This book helped me see that too."

—BRIAN GOLDMAN, MD, author of *The Power of Kindness*

"In *Happy Parents Happy Kids*, Ann Douglas has written the quintessential handbook for parenting in the digital age. She's covered every conceivable angle and topic, and gives practical, compassionate, non-judgmental, and research-based advice. Buy a copy (or two) for every expecting, new, or veteran parent you know."

—RICHARD MONETTE and the Active for Life team

"Ann Douglas has written another wonderful book: the perfect book, in fact, for our times. Parents everywhere who are struggling with the anxiety of parenting will benefit immeasurably from the stories that are told and the way they are told. *Happy Parents Happy Kids* delivers exactly what the title promises."

—DR. STUART SHANKER, author of *Self-Reg* and founder of The MEHRIT Centre

"This is a magnificent book. Ann Douglas has gone inside the lives of so many of us as parents and captured the joys, the challenges, and most importantly the 'what to do about it' dilemmas. She tackles head-on the issues of our day: distracted parenting, anxious guilt-ridden parenting. She states the subject, provides the evidence and so importantly makes practical, 'I can do this' suggestions. There are so many terrific messages here; we are not meant to travel th' is parenting journey alone. Find your village, aspire for healthy living; love your kids, love yourself. LOVE this book."

—JEAN CLINTON, child psychiatrist

"An essential guide to navigating the minefields in early twenty-first century parenting, Ann Douglas's latest delivers insights, empathy, and practical ways to shift from surviving to thriving."

—ARMINE YALNIZYAN, economist

"In an age of peak parental anxiety, *Happy Parents Happy Kids* is a tonic for what ails us. As a parent of two near-teen boys, I loved this book's combination of witty tone and wise advice. I feel better equipped for the most important job I have: being a great Dad."

—RICK SMITH, co-author of *Slow Death by Rubber Duck*

"Just as rising inequality is disrupting work, community life, and much else in Canada, it is disrupting parenting and childhood. So Ann [Douglas] wisely disrupts parenting advice. Rather than fueling the anxiety and fear that we tend to parent with in such times, Ann's advice stokes optimism. She trusts us and invites us to trust the kids. We're okay. Our social policies that support decent paid work and family obligations need to be better. It's time to raise Canada, not just our children."

—LISA WOLFF, Director, Policy and Research, UNICEF Canada

"Finally, a parenting book for real parents—a book that recognizes that we don't have to be perfect and neither do our kids. If you're looking for a parenting book that will leave you feeling calmer and more confident—as opposed to more anxious and more guilty —this is the book for you. Yes, parenting is tough, but you have what it takes to get through this—and this kind and encouraging book helps to point the way."

—CLAIRE KERR-ZLOBIN, Founder and CEO of Life With a Baby

"Once again, Ann Douglas shares insights on navigating the complex world of parenting in *Happy Parents Happy Kids*. Ann has the unique ability to combine the latest research with down-to-earth advice. An important read for parents and grandparents interested in being the best they can be."

—NORA SPINKS, CEO, the Vanier Institute of the Family

Happy Parents Happy Kids

ANN DOUGLAS

Happy Parents Happy Kids

Collins

Happy Parents Happy Kids
Copyright © 2019 by Ann Douglas.
All rights reserved.

Published by Collins, an imprint of HarperCollins Publishers Ltd

First edition

HarperCollins books may be purchased for educational, business,
or sales promotional use through our Special Markets Department.

HarperCollins Publishers Ltd
Bay Adelaide Centre, East Tower
22 Adelaide Street West, 41st Floor
Toronto, Ontario, Canada
M5H 4E3

www.harpercollins.ca

Library and Archives Canada Cataloguing in Publication
information is available upon request.

ISBN 978-1-4434-2575-9

Printed and bound in the United States of America
LSC/C 9 8 7 6 5 4 3 2 1

For every parent who ever trusted me enough
to share their story

Author's Note

The parent stories in this book are based on detailed conversations and/or correspondence with the parents who were interviewed for this book. In all cases, permission was obtained to quote these parents and to share their families' experiences. In some situations, identifying details were changed to protect the privacy of the individuals involved. In other cases, pseudonyms were provided at the family's request. I have edited and paraphrased some comments in the interests of clarity, while still honouring the spirit and intention of the original comments.

Medical Disclaimer

This book is designed to provide you with general information about parenting and health, so that you can be a better-informed health consumer and parent. This book is not intended to provide a complete or exhaustive treatment of this subject; nor is it a substitute for advice from the health practitioners who know you and your child best. Seek medical attention promptly for any medical or psychological concern you or your child may be experiencing. Do not take any medication without obtaining medical advice. All efforts were made to ensure the accuracy of the information contained in this publication as of the date of writing. The author and the publisher expressly disclaim any responsibility for any adverse effects arising from the use or application of the contents herein. While the parties believe that the contents of this publication are accurate, a licensed medical practitioner should be consulted in the event that medical advice is desired. The information contained in this book does not constitute a recommendation or endorsement with respect to any company or product.

Contents

Introduction • 1

1. Parenting in an Age of Anxiety • 7
2. Work-Life Imbalance • 31
3. The Why of Distracted Parenting • 55
4. The Truth about Parenting • 75
5. The Thinking Part of Parenting • 95
6. How to Boost Your Enjoyment of Parenting • 119
7. How to Tame the Anxiety, Guilt, and Feeling of Being Overwhelmed • 143
8. The Guilt-Free Guide to Healthier Living • 163
9. Parenting as a Team Sport • 209
10. Parenting Strategies That Work for You and Your Child • 233
11. Finding Your Village • 249

Acknowledgements • 273
Notes for Readers Who Want to Know a Little More • 277
Index • 295

Introduction

A funny thing happened on the way to writing this book. I almost ended up not having a book to write!

Okay, the situation wasn't quite *that* dire, but it was pretty dire in the early days, as I found myself scrambling to find parents who were willing to be interviewed for a book about being the happiest, healthiest parent possible—and raising the happiest, healthiest kid. Here's how things played out time and time again during the earliest stages of my book research: I'd approach some parents, tell them about the book, and ask them if they'd be willing to be interviewed. The parents would initially express great enthusiasm for the project, telling me that there was a tremendous need for just such a book, and that, in fact, they couldn't wait to rush out and pick up a copy for themselves.

And then, boom, the parents would turn down my request for an interview.

It wasn't that they didn't *want* to help, they were quick to explain; it was just that they didn't feel *qualified* to help. Yes, they were parents, but it's not like they were especially *good parents*. In fact, truth be told, they believed they were pretty much *doing it all wrong*. They simply didn't have any business being interviewed for a book about parenting. You understand?

1

The first few times this happened, I shrugged my shoulders and moved on. But then it kept happening. And I started to wonder how it could be that the most educated generation of parents ever was experiencing such a collective crisis in confidence. This was my first clue that things were going to be a little different when it came to writing this book. My gut instincts were telling me that something about parenting had changed. It was the first time in all my years of interviewing parents (twenty years, fifteen books) that I'd ever encountered this kind of resistance and fear.

Oh yeah, fear! That reminds me: I need to tell you about the fear . . .

If you've read any of my previous books, you know that the parent stories aren't just part of the book; they *are* the book. So, it's not as if I'm a newbie when it comes to interviewing parents—finding them, recruiting them for interviews, and establishing the kind of trust that allows people to speak frankly and openly about their experiences.

But this time around, something felt different. Parents were much more cautious. Some even seemed to be afraid of the possible consequences of speaking frankly about their experiences. They worried that someone might figure out that they were *that mom* who expressed resentment and profound disappointment about the way her marriage evolved after baby, or *that dad* who lamented the impact of parenthood on his career. One parent was so afraid that her identity might be revealed that she pretty much entered the witness protection program, setting up a separate email account and creating a unique online identity for herself for anything even remotely touching upon the book interview process. Yep, her fear ran that deep.

Around the same time that all that was happening, I began to notice a growing trend: a really nasty tendency to name and shame parents—and kids—online. I quickly concluded that most of us mere mortal parents are just one moment of inattention or parenting bad luck away from being forever known as that shamefully awful parent who did such and such a thing, with accompanying photos and video if it happened to be a particularly hellishly unfortunate day. This is not to imply that parents haven't been on the receiving end of harsh societal judgment since pretty much the beginning of time, and certainly since long before the smartphone ever came along. But because there was no permanent and instantly retrievable record of your least proud moment of parenting, there was always the hope that other people's memory of the incident would fade over time. Of course, there's no such luck in the age of Google.

So, I'm not surprised that parents are a little more reluctant to bare their souls in an age of instant judgment and even quicker retribution. Add to this the fact that our expectations of ourselves as parents continue to notch up ever higher, and you've got the ingredients for a perfect storm—a perfect tsunami, actually—of parental anxiety, guilt, and feeling overwhelmed. It makes perfect sense, then, that parents today are a bit warier about speaking frankly and openly (at least under their real names) than they were when I first started writing books about parenting twenty years ago. The stakes seem so much higher nowadays—frighteningly so, in fact.

It was this realization that got me thinking: Why is everything so high stakes? Does parenting actually have to be this hard? Why is it so hard? Is there something we can do to make it a little easier—to boost our enjoyment of parenting and ditch some of the anxiety, guilt, and feelings of being overwhelmed along the way? This book is my attempt to answer those questions.

How This Book Is Organized and Who This Book Is For

So, now that I've told you *how* the book came about, I suppose I should tell you a bit more about *what* the book is about and who it is for. For starters, I'll give you a snapshot of what you'll find as you begin to make your way through its various parts.

The first few chapters in the book get right down to the nitty-gritty, zeroing in on the reasons why so many of us are feeling stressed, overwhelmed, and—of course—guilty. I talk about what's fuelling our anxiety as parents, and the impact that has on ourselves and our kids; why work-life imbalance is such a huge and growing problem, and why work-life guilt is so pervasive and so misplaced; and how technology is impacting family life in far-reaching ways, and what we can do to turn the situation around (in realistic, non-guilt-inducing ways). Finally, I challenge the prevailing notion that parenting is, by definition, an exercise in misery. Spoiler alert: it isn't parenting that's making us miserable; it's all the stuff that gets in the way of parenting.

In the heart of the book, I talk about the all-important role you have to play in making things better for yourself and your kids. Not only are you your kids' role model (but no pressure, okay?), you also have the ability to set the emotional tone for the family. Yes, *it starts with you:* how you feel about parenting, how you think about parenting, what strategies you use to manage your moods, minimize stress, increase your energy level, and safeguard your physical and mental health, and how you encourage your kids to do the same. It's also about choosing the right parenting strategies—parenting strategies that work for parents *and* kids as opposed to parents *or* kids—and nurturing your relationship with your child's other parent and/or your partner. This section of the book is all about boosting your enjoyment of parenting and becoming the happiest, healthiest family you can be—in other words, getting more of the good stuff and less of the annoying stuff that can just plain wear a person down.

The final chapter recognizes that while it starts with you, it certainly doesn't end with you. After all, if it takes a village to raise a child, it takes a village to support that child's parent. This part of the book is all about tapping into support from that village—or building that village from scratch, if need be. It's also about imagining a world that would actually make things better for kids and parents, and figuring out what it would take to make that happen. It's about making the shift from thinking of parenting as a personal problem and embracing the idea that raising up the next generation of citizens is both a hefty responsibility and an exciting opportunity that we should embrace collectively. So, yes, it may start with you, but it can't end with you, not if we're going to make things better in a meaningful way—a way that improves the quality of life for every parent and every kid in the village.

As for who this book is for, that part's easy. It's for pretty much anyone who's a parent. It doesn't matter if you're brand new to the world of parenting or if you're a more seasoned veteran—someone with many years, and possibly even decades, of parenting under your belt. It doesn't matter if you have a single kid or a houseful of kids; if you're living on easy street or struggling to get by on an impossibly tight budget; if you feel like you've basically got your parenting act together or if you're totally convinced that you do not. There's something in this book for you.

The book is peppered with the experiences of all kinds of parents at every conceivable stage of parenting who are grappling with both ordinary and extraordinary circumstances. What these parents have in common is their willingness to be incredibly honest about both the joys and the struggles that are parenting, in the hope of making things better for some other mom or dad.

Because this book is based on interviews with Canadian parents, it has a decidedly made-in-Canada flavour and feel. That's not to say that I don't dip across the border and around the world to highlight important research and other findings that are relevant to our lives as parents. But I run all that data through a maple syrup—infused filter to ensure its relevance to Canadian parents. I hope you'll find this perspective valuable and helpful.

Enjoy the book!

P.S. As always, I would welcome your input and comments for future editions of this book. You can contact me via my website at anndouglas.ca.

CHAPTER 1

Parenting in an Age of Anxiety

I feel like every interaction with the kids—every decision that we make as parents—has this huge weight associated with it. How is this going to impact them as they grow into adults? Is this the right thing to do? Will this set them on the right path?

—Katie, mother of three school-aged boys

If you've got kids, you've got worries. That's the way it's always been and the way it will always be. As a parent, you're asked to keep one eye on the future and the other eye on the here and now, to simultaneously care for the person your child is today and to nurture along the adult your child will eventually become. It can be a mind-blowing and dizzying task. And it seems to me that it's getting harder. It sometimes feels like we're being invited to play an *Alice in Wonderland*—type game called parenting—a game where no one actually bothers to explain how the game is played but where everyone is quick to judge if you happen to break any of the game's unspoken rules.

Part of the problem, of course, is that no one seems to understand the rules. We are, after all, living at a time when the world seems to pivot and shape-shift every time we check our news feeds. It's hard enough to make sense of our world as it is right now let alone to allow ourselves to imagine how very different our lives and our children's lives are likely to be in the not-so-distant future. And this, in a nutshell, is what's fuelling a lot of our anxiety as parents—the feeling that the future is intruding on our lives in the here and now, making everything about parenting feel impossibly high-stakes.

Parenting is, after all, the ultimate leap of faith. You're asked to sign up for an extended mission without knowing up front what the terms of engagement actually are—and knowing that the terms of engagement will be endlessly rewritten along the way. As sociologist Kerry Daly noted in *The Changing Culture of Parenting*, a think piece written for The Vanier Institute of the Family back in 2004, "The culture of parenting is one that is shaped by the challenges of an emergent future rather than a settled past." Is it any wonder then that we find the job of parenting so unsettling?

But something about this moment feels different. The future feels frighteningly close. We're being asked to prepare our children for a world that seems harsher and less forgiving, a world where the life scripts that seemed to make sense for recent generations (study hard, get a job, get married, buy a house, start a family) no longer seem to apply, where there are few, if any, guarantees. Add to that increasingly alarming (albeit sometimes alarmist) head-lines about our looming apocalyptic future—a world ravaged by climate change and controlled by artificial intelligence; a world where decades of social progress can be wiped away with a single stroke of a politician's pen—and you can see why so many of us are approaching peak parental anxiety. This isn't what we signed up for when we decided to become parents.

Anxiety is a perfectly rational response to the state of the world, a perfectly understandable response to an increasingly uncertain future. This chapter is all about understanding the roots of a key piece of that anxiety—economic anxiety—and fig-uring out how to manage that anxiety, for the sake of both ourselves and our kids. Because here's the thing: there's a growing body of evidence to show that the economy has a major impact on our parenting. And, yes, I'll be talking about that too.

A Multi-Layered Economic Anxiety Sandwich

Do you find yourself worrying about your ability to provide for your kids financially, or whether they'll be able to provide for themselves in years to come? (Or both. You're definitely allowed to answer "both" to this one.) If you find yourself worrying about your family's bottom line, you're certainly in good company. Economic anxiety has crept into the lives of growing numbers of parents—and it's spilling over into the lives of their kids too.

How could it not be so? There's so much to worry about: sky-high rental and housing prices, child-care fees that can feel like a second mortgage, soaring college and university tuition fees—and that's just for starters. Where the real anxiety sets in is when we talk about jobs. As American author and journalist Malcolm Harris noted in his recent book *Kids These Days*, "It's harder to compete for a good job, the bad jobs you hope to fall back on are worse than they used to be, and both good jobs and bad jobs are less secure. The intense anxiety that has overcome . . . childhood flows from a reasonable fear of un-, under-, and just plain lousy employment."

In the good old days, education used to be a guaranteed ticket to a really good job—the kind of job you could plan a future and build a life around. That simply isn't the case any longer. We're living in an era of increasingly precarious employment—a time when knowing when you'll be working and how much you'll be making a day or a week from now is fast becoming a luxury. Is it any wonder that 40 percent of workers now report that anxiety about their employment interferes with their personal and family lives on a regular basis?

The anxiety can be particularly intense for young people who are trying to establish a foothold in the job market so that they can launch themselves out of their parents' basements and into the world. It's increasingly difficult to find a job that actually pays the bills, even if you're a twenty-something who is highly motivated and highly qualified. It's a point that Toronto educational consultant Alex Usher made in a series of recent posts for his blog. Not only have employment rates for recent university graduates not fully recovered from the point at which they hit rock bottom (that was back in 2010), but wages paid to new graduates have continued to tumble. Income (in inflation-adjusted dollars) is continuing to fall slightly, as it has ever since the recession set in. "The decline differs somewhat by field of study, but the direction is unmistakable—down 10% since 2005 in Business, 17% in Humanities, and 21% and 23% in Education and Physical Science respectively," he noted. And it's not just jobs in certain niche fields, he stressed. Some fields that might seem to offer tremendous potential when it comes to income simply haven't been delivering on that front. In fact, if you compare the income earned by new graduates before and after the 2008 to 2009 global recession (which Usher does by comparing income reports two years post-graduation for students graduating in the years 2005 and 2014), you find income declines of 24 percent for students who studied food science and nutrition; 20 percent for students who studied kinesiology, life sciences, and agriculture; and 16 percent for law and dentistry. His takeaway message? The wage dip is pretty widespread: "If incomes in dentistry and humanities are falling at more or less the same rate, it's probably fair to conclude that whatever's going on with graduate salaries, it's economy wide, not confined to some mythical group of medieval historians pouring coffee at Starbucks."

But wait, it gets worse!

At least, for now, there are actual jobs to chase after. In the not-so-distant future, there may be fewer and fewer jobs available (for ourselves and our kids) because the robots are coming for our jobs. That's the word from economists and business analysts, who are trying to make sense of and plan for a world in which a greater number of workplace tasks are automated. The picture that they are painting is pretty bleak:

- A 2013 study by the University of Oxford Department of Engineering Science estimated that 47 percent of current jobs are likely to find their way onto the endangered species list. These jobs are vulnerable to automation and they're at risk of being eliminated within the next decade or two.

- A 2017 report by Deloitte and the Human Resources Professionals Association predicted that between 35 and 42 percent of current Canadian jobs will disappear, as a result of the growing reach of automation.

In other words, your kid isn't just going to be competing with a huge pool of other highly qualified kids for that ever-elusive first job. She could very well be competing with a robot too. Even if she doesn't go head to head with a robot right away, she is likely to end up doing so at some point over the course of her working career. How do you and your kid wrap your heads around that?

In many cases, we don't. We bury that anxiety because the problems that are fuelling it don't have easy answers. They certainly aren't anything we're going to be able to fix in a day or even a month—no matter how diligent our quest for answers on career websites or in self-improvement books. What we're left with is a nagging sense that something is wrong, and that the situation could get even worse.

After all, if kids are earning less and having a harder time than ever landing and keeping jobs, that means our financial responsibilities as parents to provide for our children will have to extend longer—well past the traditional financial finish line of parenting, when a newly minted graduate could be expected to land a good job and cross over into the heady world of financial self-sufficiency. That neat little script no longer applies to the current generation of young adults, and it certainly doesn't apply to their parents either. Parents today expect to shoulder financial responsibility for their not-yet-financially-independent kids for longer than ever before. A 2015 study by US student loan company Sallie Mae found, for example, that roughly two-thirds of parents expected to be supporting their children financially for up to five years after college graduation. That's consistent with the experience of significant numbers of Canadian parents as well: according to Statistics Canada, one-quarter of young adults ages twenty-five through twenty-nine lived with their parents in 2011. What's more, a growing number of Canadian parents (at least one in four, according to a 2017 TD Wealth Financial Planning study) are continuing to support their children (and, in some cases, their grandchildren) well into adulthood. This extended period of parental investment is taking its toll on parents' ability to squirrel away funds for their own retirement, which is, in turn, fuelling considerable anxiety on that front. (RRSP guilt season, anyone?) That same TD study noted that 58 percent of boomer-generation parents are stressed by the fact that providing for their kids well into adulthood is forcing them to dip into their own retirement savings—a financial cramping of style that has been dubbed the "déjà-boom" effect. Of course, these boomer parents were members of a financially fortunate generation that actually had the means and opportunity to build up a retirement nest egg while they were raising their kids. That's anything but a given for the current generation of young parents.

It's not just the boomer generation of parents who are acutely aware that junior may be looking to them for financial help for an extended period of time—assistance that they may or may not be in a position to provide. This new reality weighs heavily on the minds of anyone who is even flirting with the idea of becoming a parent. After all, a standard rite of passage in the lives of many would-be parents is an extended meditation on that ever-daunting question, "Can I actually afford to have kids?" According to a recent study of workers in Southern Ontario, as many as one in five millennial-aged workers are answering that question with a definitive no.

So, there are a lot of layers to this anxiety sandwich: worries about what the future has in store for our kids, what we can do to prepare them, and how we're going to pay for it all. There's no question that we have a lot to feel anxious about, including how all this anxiety is impacting our parenting.

How Anxiety Affects Our Parenting

Parenting doesn't happen in a bubble. We can't help but be affected by what's happening in the world beyond our front door. And when it comes to economic forces, the impact on our parenting can be quite dramatic.

Take, for example, the impact of living through a major recession. This was the focus of a recent study by a group of Portuguese researchers led by PhD student Gabriela Fonseca of the University of Coimbra, who surveyed the available research from around the world in order to identify the common threads in such experiences. They identified two types of effects that are relevant to the lives of parents.

First, living through a recession takes a toll on the couple relationship. Couples are less likely to communicate effectively and are more likely to experience conflict, leading to an increased likelihood of divorce. What they identified can best be described as a recipe for spousal disaster: men tend to become depressed, more hostile, and less warm, while women tend to become more anxious and less supportive.

Second, living through a recession affects the quality of parenting. Parents tend to be more anxious, more depressed, and less involved in parenting. They're also more likely to rely on harsher and more controlling parenting methods in response to increased pressure to raise competitive, market-ready kids. The researchers discovered an increase in the amount of spanking during the 2008 recession, for example.

A separate analysis conducted by Yale economist Fabrizio Zilibotti identified a similar increase in the amount of controlling and achievement-focused parenting in times of increasing inequality. He found that as income inequality rises (as has been the case in Canada for the past thirty to forty years), parents become less permissive and more controlling. "Socioeconomic conditions drive how much control or monitoring parents exercise on their children's choices," he explained in a press release related to his research.

It just makes sense. If you feel that the odds of success are increasingly stacked against your child, you're likely (consciously or otherwise) to ramp up the amount of pressure you place on your kid, nudging or even shoving him on to what you perceive to be the right path (that path being the path of least danger or greatest opportunity, depending on your family's circumstances). There's a solid body of research to show, for example, that raising a child in a more dangerous neighbourhood may necessitate a more controlling parenting style, simply because that's what's required to keep children safe. Likewise, if you feel that your family is losing ground financially, you may take on a second job in an attempt to halt the financial free fall—even if it means sacrificing time with your child.

So, while economic forces might seem to be completely separate and distinct from anything even remotely related to our parenting, they're actually anything but. As the economic stakes get higher, the pressure on parents and kids gets ever greater, and parents are more likely to decide that harsher and more controlling parenting is the best way to respond to the challenges posed by an uncertain future.

In addition to adapting our parenting in response to our own deep-rooted anxiety, we also pick up on and react to the endless barrage of media and social media messages about what it means to be a good parent these days. Let's talk about that next.

On Judging and Feeling Judged

Feel like you're developing a case of emotional whiplash as you try to make sense of all the conflicting messages you're being given about how you're supposed to be raising your kids? On the one hand, you're being told that you should be using kind and gentle parenting methods to nurture your kids along; on the other, you're being told that it's your job to make your kids behave. The non-stop messaging around this last piece is anything but subtle. Time and time again, you're told that you made the decision to have kids, so it's your job to raise them—and, by the way, you're doing it wrong.

Angie knows what it's like to be on the receiving end of these kinds of messages. Because there are so many conflicting norms about what it means to be a good parent, she is often left with the sense that she's managed to fall short on every conceivable parenting standard simultaneously: "It often feels to me like the person sitting on one side of me thinks that my child should have more freedom, while the person sitting on the other side just wishes to hell I would control my child more," she says.

If your child's struggles are more extreme, people's judgment tends to be more extreme as well. Or at least that's been Sandra's experience. She is the mother of ten-year-old twins who were born in Ethiopia and then adopted and brought to Canada at the age of one. Both of her children struggle with attention deficit hyperactivity disorder, with her daughter's symptoms being more pronounced. "Parent shaming comes from every direction," she laments. She resents the fact that random strangers feel compelled to comment on her daughter's outbursts, that they don't pause to consider the possibility that there could be something more to the story than just garden-variety bad parenting. "When someone really digs in with a shameful comment, I will usually just shoot back, 'She cannot help herself. She does not have impulse control,'" she says.

Just as some kids are more likely to be judged, so too are some parents. Lower-income parents, for example, are frequently subjected to harsh and unfair judgments about the quality of their parenting. It's a point that University of Bristol sociologist Esther Dermott made in a recent blog post: "The associations made between poverty and poor parenting are ideologically driven rather than based on evidence. Claims that families who are poor do not engage in good parenting practices are misplaced."

Of course, it's not just lower-income parents who report feeling judged. This feeling of being judged is rapidly becoming the norm, at least according to a recent University of Michigan study. The researchers found that nearly two-thirds of mothers (61 percent) had been criticized for their parenting decisions, with most of that criticism coming from members of their own family. (The judgy family members? The mother's spouse, her parents, and her in-laws, in roughly equal measures.)

Of course, we aren't just feeling judged. We're also doing our fair share of judging. A recent study conducted by ZERO TO THREE and the Robert Wood Johnson Foundation in the United States found that "parents of children ages 5 and younger feel *other* parents are not doing enough to nurture their children's healthy development." On the other hand, those very same parents are generally pretty satisfied with their own efforts on this front.

Trying to make sense of this apparent contradiction? Cognitive psychology to the rescue! While we're acutely aware of our own efforts and intentions when it comes to parenting (because we happen to live inside our own heads), we don't have the same front-row seats when it comes to witnessing the efforts and intentions of other parents. As a result, when they fall short in the parenting department—at least in our not-so-humble estimation—we chalk it up to bad parenting. But when we fall short of those very same standards, we're willing to cut ourselves some slack because we know that we intended to do better. It's worth making note of this particular cognitive error, if only to increase the likelihood that you'll (a) hit the judgment brakes and (b) hold off on making that snarky social media post the next time you feel compelled to call out what appears to be an incident of bad parenting.

Parent Shaming and Kid Shaming

Of course, the tendency to treat parenting as the ultimate spectator sport spills over into the media on a regular basis, fuelling sensationalistic stories about helicopter parents and bad parents, snowflake kids and narcissistic kids, ramping up the pressure on parents and kids in nasty and far-reaching ways.

HELICOPTER PARENTS

If there's one parenting narrative that has been amplified and celebrated by the media in recent years, it's the idea of the helicopter parent—that ever-present, overprotective parent who is constantly hovering in junior's vicinity. If you prefer to go with an analogous term that feels a bit more Canadian, you might opt for "curling parent" instead. As a 2016 CBC News article explained, curling parents endeavour to "[sweep] aside obstacles for their adult children" while leaving those children "unable to handle the rocks life throws at them." Helicopter parent, curling parent—whatever you choose to call it, we're talking about the same thing: the widespread belief that the current generation of parents is guilty of caring too much.

Before you start engaging in the parental soul-searching that the mere mention of the term "helicopter parent" seems to trigger, you need to know one all-important fact about helicopter parenting: it's a myth. Or, to be fair, the idea that helicopter parenting is the defining parenting style of our time is a myth. American author and journalist Alfie Kohn tackled the myth head-on in a September 2015 article for *Salon*—an article with a wonderfully feisty title, I might add: "Debunking the Myth of the 'Helicopter Parent': The Pernicious Cultural Biases behind a Collegiate Urban Legend." In this must-read article, Kohn makes the case that helicopter parenting is little more than a media-fuelled urban myth, one that is heavily reliant on judiciously hand-picked anecdotes about that one parent who did that one over-the-top thing that one time. You'd think this article would have spelled an end to helicopter-parenting news stories, but sadly, they merely mutated and began to appear in a slightly different form. The media was no longer solely fixated on helicopter parents wrapping their tiny tots in bubble wrap or clinging to the electronic umbilical cord when their darlings headed off to college; now they were showing up in the workplace too!

Yep. That's the most recent twist to a tale that just won't end. A recent article in *The New York Times* titled "When Helicopter Parents Hover Even at Work" is typical of this genre. Writer Noam Scheiber only managed to produce one piece of evidence in support of the "helicopter parents head to work" hypothesis. That key piece of data? A 2016 OfficeTeam study that reported that workplace helicopter parenting was "not unheard-of"— hardly evidence of the massive epidemic of helicopter parenting you might expect, given the alarmist headline. On this side of the border, a 2015 article in the *Financial Post* tried—and failed—to make a similar case. In an article titled "Leave Mom at Home: Why Canadian Business Owners Are Having Such a Hard Time Hiring," writer Dan Kelly reported that "more than a few" of the respondents to a Canadian Federation of Independent Business (CFIB) survey had reported parents showing up for their kids' job interviews. Then, in a related post the following year, the CFIB reported on "two actual scenarios" of helicopter parents intruding in their children's working lives, and "countless stories" of parents trying to interfere in the job interview or hiring process. So, should every cubicle desk issued to a millennial-aged new hire automatically be equipped with an extra chair for mom or dad? The rather underwhelming evidence to date suggests not.

On the one hand, it's easy to dismiss helicopter-parenting stories as merely silly or annoying. Unfortunately, they have a tendency to get inside your head. Whenever I speak to a group of parents, there's inevitably at least one parent in the crowd who will raise a hand and then make a comment along the lines of "You're probably going to think I'm a helicopter parent . . ." Almost inevitably, the story they feel compelled to preface with such a shame-filled disclaimer is, in fact, a story about really great parenting.

That's what disturbs me most about this whole helicopter-parenting phenomenon: the fact that it leaves parents feeling anxious and guilty for being a good parent. (I'll have a lot more to say about "good parenting" in Chapter 10, when I run through the best evidence on what actually encourages kids to thrive.) Unfortunately, the damage doesn't always stop there. Sometimes, fear of being labelled a helicopter parent causes parents to pull away from their kids or to parent in unnecessarily harsh ways. In some cases, parents have even turned to social media, seeking validation for these "tougher is better" approaches to parenting. I'm thinking of the mom in Ontario who forced her boys to walk two hours to school in February, wearing a sign that read like a pet-shaming meme: "Being bad and rude to our bus driver! Moms [sic] makin [sic] us walk." I'm also thinking about the dad in Virginia who forced his son to run to school after he was kicked off the school bus for bullying, and then broadcast the resulting video footage via Facebook Live. "He got actually kicked off the bus for three days because he was being a little bully, which I do not tolerate, cannot stand, and therefore he now has to run to school," the father explained in the video, seemingly oblivious to his own act of bullying. In a subsequent Facebook post, reflecting upon the attention the video had received, the father expressed his hope that his no-nonsense discipline style would "give inspiration around the world" because "parenting isn't always about being a friend it's about leading them into the future." There it is again: the future. The whole reason we supposedly need to be tough on kids in the here and now.

Not surprisingly, the media loves these "tough is better" tropes too. They're even willing to carry them into the world of puppy parenting. An August 2017 study published in the *Proceedings of the National Academy of Sciences* attracted a lot of media attention, largely on the basis of one key finding that just happened to support the idea of "tough is better" parenting. The researchers were trying to figure out what type of parenting leads to better guide dogs. Do you want a potential guide dog to be raised by a mama dog who is the canine equivalent of a helicopter parent, or is it better if she practises the puppy world equivalent of tough love? In case you're wondering what tough love looks like in the world of puppy parenting, it's about making your offspring work at getting fed: "When mothers nursed vertically, while sitting or standing, nursing was a more difficult, active, and effortful endeavor for puppies." You know how this story turns out, right? The whole reason that we ever heard about this study is because the researchers concluded that parental tough love leads to better guide dogs, or more specifically, dogs that were more likely to demonstrate the persistence, ingenuity, and problem-solving abilities required to make it through guide dog training. What we're talking about are puppies with grit—as opposed to less capable snowflake puppies.

Of course, the media doesn't limit itself to stories about helicopter parents and about parents finding very public ways to reject the whole idea of helicopter via tough-is-better parenting. It also tends to put the spotlight on parents who through sheer bad luck or momentary inattention found their children in unspeakably awful situations. Perhaps the best-known example is the story of the three-year-old boy who crawled through a barrier and fell twelve feet into a gorilla cage at the Cincinnati Zoo back in May of 2016. The internet reacted immediately, with people questioning the zoo's decision to shoot the gorilla, Harambe, in order to save the boy, and directing heated criticism toward the boy's mother, who was judged harshly for allowing herself to be momentarily distracted by other children at the time of the incident—a parenting sin that the majority of us mere mortal parents have been guilty of at one time or another, albeit with less dramatic results. Is it any wonder, then, that so many of us worry about being judged, or possibly becoming the internet's next bad parenting meme?

I've been on the receiving end of some of that judgment, although, thankfully, long before anyone had ever coined the term "helicopter parent." In those days, you were just a garden-variety bad parent. I remember trying to make sense of two conflicting comments lobbed at me in rapid succession by two different neighbours: the mom who called me to suggest that I might want to supervise my school-aged kids a little more closely while they were playing on the street, and the dad who called me out for sticking too close to my kids on Halloween and not giving them the freedom to have fun and "just be kids." At first, those comments stung. The fact that I can still remember them nearly two decades later tells you how much they stung. But in the end, I decided to ignore them. After all, if one person was telling me that I was overprotective and another person was telling me I was under-protective, it seemed to me that the most sensible thing to do was simply to average the two pieces of feedback and conclude that I was being just protective enough. I'd stumbled into the Goldilocks zone of parenting, if you will. How much harder it would have been if my perceived parenting sins were broadcast on social media. I was lucky to stumble through the muckiest parts of parenting at a time when the internet still knew how to forget.

SNOWFLAKE KIDS

A few paragraphs back, we were talking about snowflake puppies. Now let's talk about snowflake kids—the idea that we're raising up a generation of super-fragile, just-plain-useless kids. It's a criticism that's flung at young adults on a regular basis. In fact, it has pretty much become the go-to insult if you want to fling mud at a teenager or a millennial these days.

The stereotype doesn't sit well with Renee, the mother of a preteen daughter and a school-aged son. The reason? For her, it simply doesn't ring true. She vehemently challenges the idea that we're raising up a generation of kids who are fragile and weak. "This isn't a culture of victimhood that we're creating; it's a culture of empowerment," she insists. In recent months, she's watched her daughter participate in a Grade 8 equivalent of the #MeToo movement, pushing back against sexist comments and unwanted touching from boys. "It's amazing watching these kids," Renee says. She has so much respect for the fact that her daughter and her friends are willing to challenge behaviours that previous generations of girls simply learned to tolerate or work around. She is inspired by their willingness to insist on a better world. "Why shouldn't things be better for them? Why should they just put up with this stuff?" she asks.

Renee celebrates the kinds of people her children are becoming and how they're choosing to interact with other people in kind and respectful ways. "Sometimes, my daughter will read me the text exchanges she's had with her friends. I remember one such exchange where she and a friend were working through a misunderstanding that had turned into an argument. I have to tell you, there are adults who could have taken a lesson from these kids on how to fix things when something has gone wrong in a relationship. These kids are thoughtful and aware. The world's going to be in their hands in another twenty years' time, and you know what? I'm good with that."

NARCISSISTIC KIDS

Now let's tackle narcissism—or, more specifically, the idea that young people are increasingly self-centred, materialistic, and fame-obsessed. As it turns out, that happens to be a bogus claim as well.

In a 2013 article written for the journal *Emerging Adulthood*, developmental psychologist Jeffrey Jensen Arnett and other leading experts in the field took psychologist Jean Twenge to task for what they claimed were fundamental methodological errors in her research claiming that young people were increasingly narcissistic: "If she is wrong, then her errors are deeply unfair and damaging to young people, reinforcing the worst stereotypes that adults have about them and encouraging adults to vilify them. We believe she is wrong." They then went on to cite recent research from a national US survey of eighteen- to twenty-nine-year-olds, conducted in 2013. In that survey, 80 percent of young people agreed with the statement "It is more important to me to enjoy my job than to make a lot of money," while 86 percent said, "It is important to me to have a career that does some good in the world." Sure, things are different for this generation of young people: for economic reasons that are beyond their control, they're either living at home longer or boomeranging back in times of economic stress. But that doesn't mean it's their fault—or their parents' fault, to touch upon the helicopter-parent stereotype yet again. As Arnett noted in a recent article for *Aeon*, "Understanding that a new life stage of emerging adulthood is now typical between adolescence and young adulthood, and that it is a time when change and instability is the norm, will make it possible to ease up on the negative stereotypes and learn to appreciate their [young adults'] energy, their creativity, and their zest for life." And, I would argue, it will ease their parents' anxiety as well.

Anxiety Inc.

Here's something else to think about: parental anxiety isn't just taking its toll on our psyches; it's also taking its toll on our finances. Many parents are spending significant amounts of money to give their kids the competitive edge:

- An investigative report by Global News back in 2013 revealed a 60 percent increase in the use of private tutoring services in Toronto over a five-year period—services that may amount to four hundred dollars a month for a child receiving two hours of tutoring each week.

- A growing number of educational consultants and admissions counsellors are hanging out their shingles in Canada. Once an American phenomenon, it's now becoming increasingly common for well-heeled Canadian parents to pay hefty fees to private consultants who can boost their children's odds of being admitted to elite private schools and universities. It's all about resumé-building, starting in the early years of high school, with extracurricular activities being key. One education consulting firm notes on its website that its services include assessing the student's extracurricular record and suggesting ways to "maximize opportunities, including summer programs, internships and employment."

- Even parents of preschoolers are getting in on the action, turning to AI-powered smartphone apps for help in building a smarter and more future-ready kid. One child development app claims "to predict life outcomes and to show you what you can do today to maximize the lifelong potential of your child," while another app, this one a language learning app, promises to give your kid "a head start they'll retain all their lives" because "early talkers who start out ahead tend to stay ahead."

Elaine understands the pressure that many parents are feeling to ensure that their kids are able to measure up in an increasingly competitive world. She describes her family as "essentially your stereotypical stressed-out urban family"—in this case, two parents (both working professionals) and their two teenage daughters. She describes the world in which her kids are growing up as a bit of a pressure cooker: "Parents in our city are pretty Type A. When the kids were younger, there was a lot of pressure to have your kids in the right swimming lessons, Gymboree classes, and preschools, which, in turn, was followed up by pressure to enroll your kids in the right schools once they hit school age." She feels that the unrelenting emphasis on making the right choices every step of the way has resulted in her university-bound eldest daughter feeling tremendous pressure to choose the right program at the right university. "We're living in such an overachieving culture that getting accepted into a great program at a mid-ranked university feels like a failure to our teens," says Elaine, noting that this marks a major shift from what things were like when she was growing up, "when no one really cared about what university they would attend," and when the option of "just going out and getting a job" was still completely valid. Things are different now because job prospects are different now, and that fuels massive anxiety for parents and kids alike. Elaine explains, "The job market for young people is brutal and this may be why our kids and we as their parents feel so much pressure. Everyone wants (or wants their kid) to have some sort of competitive edge to help them get a job." In a world where every parent feels that pressure to help their kid get that edge, what qualifies as an edge continually ramps up ever higher. "I hear too many stories of young adults being devastated by the realities of the job market, and of university students who are in crisis because they didn't get all As. We definitely need to change this."

It's not just higher-income parents who are feeling the need to do everything in their power to give their kids that competitive edge. Kim, who admits to juggling no fewer than five jobs in an effort to keep her family afloat financially, has grappled with these feelings too. At one point, these feelings led to sky-high expectations for her two daughters. "My expectation was that my kids were going to be great, that they were going to be exceptional at everything," she confesses. That's a lot of pressure to put on a kid—something she fully recognizes now. But it was a hard-earned lesson for herself and her family. At one point, her eldest daughter, who was then in Grade 5, responded to that pressure by deciding to run away from home. "We actually had the police looking for her," Kim admits, recalling how painful and scary that experience was for the entire family. In the aftermath, she felt she needed to ease up on her expectations on her daughters, particularly around the issue of homework. "I have people who judge me, who think that I'm too hands off, but I'm actually not hands off at all. I check in with the girls about how things are going at school. I check on their grades. And I talk to their teachers. But I no longer make a big deal of things." It's an approach that's working for her and her kids. Things are calmer and happier at home as a result of Kim's more realistic expectations.

There's good reason to put the brakes on our rising expectations. A recent study of more than 41,000 Canadian, American, and British college students who graduated between 1989 and 2016 points to rising rates of perfectionism. As the study's authors, UK psychologists Thomas Curran and Andrew P. Hill, noted in a recent article in the *Psychological Bulletin,* young people are being asked to compete against one another "within increasingly demanding social and economic parameters" and that "perhaps to cope" they are demonstrating higher levels of perfectionism. Specifically, they "perceive that others are more demanding of them, are more demanding of others, and are more demanding of themselves." It's clearly a recipe for rising anxiety and unhappiness, the authors conclude. "Neoliberalism [the idea that everything that matters in our lives can be measured by economic activity and that the market should be given free rein] has succeeded in shifting cultural values so to now emphasize competitiveness, individualism, and irrational ideals of the perfectible self."

In a related article written for the *Harvard Business Review* in early 2018, Curran and Hill noted that some collective navel-gazing is definitely in order. Specifically, we need to consider "how we are structuring society and whether our society's strong emphasis on social comparison, and the sorting, sifting, and ranking that follows, is benefiting young people." Spoiler alert: the answer is no.

It's not that our kids are snowflakes; actually, they're being realists. They're acutely aware of the impossibly high standards that they're being measured by, and they're understandably anxious that, despite their best efforts, they simply won't measure up.

How to Tame the Anxiety

Now that we've come up with a fairly comprehensive list of reasons why parents and kids are experiencing so much anxiety, let's talk about what to do about it—how we can help our kids cope with that anxiety and how we can manage it ourselves. What follows are a few brief takeaway points that I want you to carry forward as you continue reading the book.

Accept that while much of this is beyond your control, some of it is *within your control.* You may not be able to rejig the economy or chase away the AI-powered robots on your own, but you *can* take steps to manage your day-to-day anxiety level. Work at feeling a little calmer a little more often, and help your kids to do the same. (Note: If you're not familiar with the concept of feeling calm, you'll find a crash course in Chapters 5 and 6. I'm a recent convert to the art of living less stressfully, and I'm eager to share what I've learned.)

Recognize that anxiety is a major cognitive drain. Think of it as an exercise in multi-tasking—and a not particularly enjoyable one at that. You're asking your brain to constantly switch tasks, to toggle between your most pressing worries and whatever it is you're actually trying to accomplish at any given time. The net result is a distracted and worn-down you. You'll want to check out the coping strategies that I map out in Chapters 5, 6, and 7.

Commit to parenting in a way that will leave your kids better equipped (as opposed to less well-equipped) to meet the challenges of the future. Allow yourself to be inspired by this challenge (which we'll be exploring at length in Chapter 10). The future needs your kid: a happy, healthy adult who is capable of navigating life's challenges and seizing upon the types of opportunities that we can't even begin to imagine today. It's kind of exciting, if you think about it. You have the opportunity to raise a child who is an all-star in areas where the robots simply can't compete. I'm talking about uniquely human skills like empathy, collaboration, and problem-solving. According to a 2017 Pew Research Center report, "Tough to teach intangibles such as emotional intelligence, curiosity, creativity, adaptability, resilience, and critical thinking will be most highly valued" skills in the world of the future. They're also the kinds of skills that contribute to quality of life beyond the workplace and that improve children's quality of life *while they are still children*—which brings me to my next point. You don't have to go out of your way to look for opportunities to help your child acquire these skills. They're built into the day-to-day curriculum called living. As social worker and family therapist Shelley Hermer likes to point out, "Every scraped knee, change in schedule, bad test result, and broken heart is an opportunity to develop all these things." And you, as your child's parent, are uniquely positioned to guide them in this learning.

Resist the temptation to fast-forward through your child's childhood as a means of coping with your own anxiety about the future. Specifically, try to avoid treating him like a mini-adult by asking him to shoulder worries and responsibilities that he shouldn't have to concern himself with quite yet.

Perhaps you spotted this Facebook post when it went viral: the post in which a mother shared her plans to start charging her five-year-old daughter rent. Specifically, the mother explained, she was asking her daughter to fork over a portion of her seven-dollar-a-week allowance as follows: "$1 for rent $1 for water $1 for electricity $1 for cable and $1 for food," a strategy that "prepares your child for the real world."

Kids are seizing upon that message, and what too many of them are hearing is that they can't afford the luxury of being a kid. Instead, they need to keep their eyes focused firmly on the future. I recently spotted a message on Twitter that captured this sentiment perfectly. It was a tweet from a teenager who was sharing a photo of the whiteboard in her twelve-year-old brother's room. On it, he had made two separate lists: a list of everything he thought he should be learning in school ("How to pay taxs [sic] and how to get a job") and a list of all the things he "didn't need or want to learn" at school but was being forced to ("mental maths, past events, dance, [Shakespeare], basketball, football, tennis, badmintin [sic], soccer, drama, and finaly [sic] roman numerals"). It was a pretty depressing set of lists.

Yes, it's important to prepare kids for the future, but not if it means sacrificing their one and only precious childhood along the way. Childhood is, after all, a limited time offer, a once-in-a-lifetime opportunity to grow in an unhurried way—or at least that's what it's supposed to be. In a recent essay for *The New York Times*, lawyer and father of two Ryan Park reflected on the tremendous pressure he felt to measure up to the sky-high expectations of his achievement-oriented immigrant parents during his growing up years. "Was the tradeoff between happiness and success worth it?" he asked himself. In the end, he concluded that it wasn't, and committed to raising his own two children to be "happy, confident, and kind," as opposed to "driven, dutiful, and successful"—his parents' recipe for successful parenting. You too have the opportunity to make that parenting shift.

Recognize that many of the problems that we are grappling with as parents are too big to solve on our own. Systemic problems require systemic solutions, after all. So look for opportunities to join forces with other people who share your desire to create a world that's kinder and friendlier to parents and kids. We can work together for policies that make life better, not harder for our families. I'm thinking about workplace protections that help to make precarious jobs a little less life-sucking and anxiety-producing. I'm envisioning updated family policy that reflects those very same workplace realities—like the fact that it can be near-impossible to qualify for parental leave benefits when you're juggling multiple part-time jobs. And I'm imagining groundbreaking economic policy that anticipates the loss of jobs through automation and offers a bold and reassuring path forward for our families—a roadmap to a happier, healthier, and less anxious place.

CHAPTER 2

Work–Life Imbalance

There is never enough time to get everything done for work and family, and it often feels like we aren't doing either particularly well.

—Elaine, mother of two teenage daughters

If I had been writing this book two decades ago, this chapter would have ended up with a slightly different title and a radically different focus and tone. You see, back then, I honestly believed that there was a secret formula for this elusive thing called "work-life balance," and that if you were smart enough and willing to work hard enough, you could find a way to keep all (or at least most) of the balls in the air.

In fact, I actually did write a book on this subject. If you root around in your favourite used bookstore, you might manage to dig up one of the few remaining copies of that 1999 book: *Sanity Savers: The Canadian Working Woman's Guide to Almost Having It All.* The book was my attempt to solve the work-balance equation for myself, to find a way to meet the needs of my growing family (four kids who were two, eight, ten, and eleven at the time) and my growing business (I was in the process of establishing my career as a pregnancy and parenting book author). The book consisted of strategies and checklists and time-saving tips designed to help other massively overloaded women to figure out how to squeeze forty-eight hours' worth of living into a twenty-four-hour day.

Flipping through that book two decades later, I can see that I was both fiercely optimistic and more than a little naive about what it would actually take to achieve anything even remotely resembling work-life balance. In fact, you'll be hearing about the extent to which I failed miserably in that mission when we get to the health chapter in this book and I talk about how, for the better part of two decades, I pretty much became the poster child for self-neglect. That ended up being my (non-) solution to work-life balance.

But back to this book and this chapter for a moment. When I sat down to write about work-life balance this time around, I kept thinking about a conversation I'd had with Kim, the mother of two teenagers, when I first started researching this book. Let's just say that Kim isn't exactly a fan of the whole idea of work-life balance—not surprising, given that she holds down no fewer than five different jobs. In fact, she argues that work-life balance doesn't actually exist, that it's kind of a made-up thing: "One of the things that's always pissed me off is the idea that there's such a thing as work-life balance. I call bullshit on that. There's no way. *There's no way!*"

That conversation with Kim got me thinking about what I've learned over the past two decades about work-life balance—and about all the mean-spirited and guilt-inducing messages that each and every one of us who is brave enough to attempt that balancing act receives on a regular basis. Instead of acknowledging how much the world of work has changed over the course of the past few decades—and how that's made it infinitely harder for parents—we continue to treat work-life balance as a problem that every family should be able to solve on its own. It's not about leaning in or trying harder. Most parents are trying plenty hard both at work and at home.

This chapter is my attempt to make sense of that reality. I'll be explaining why work-life imbalance is such a problem: the fact that there have been seismic shifts in the world of work and yet few corresponding workplace or social policy shifts to help us manage that load. I'll be delving into why work-life guilt is so pervasive and so misplaced. I'll be talking about how work-life imbalance impacts our lives as parents and our children's lives too, and what it will actually take to turn the situation around.

Why Work-Life Imbalance Is Such a Problem

It's not your imagination. The rules of the game—the work-life balancing game—have changed dramatically in recent decades. The game has gotten a whole lot harder. I'll explain why.

BOTH PARENTS ARE NOW WORKING, AND IN MOST CASES, THEY'RE WORKING FULL-TIME.
Let's hop in the time machine and take a quick trip back to 1976 and consider how very different things were for parents and kids back then. It wasn't just an era of his and her leisure suits and wood-panelled station wagons. It was also an era when having at least one parent at home with the kids full-time was still the norm. According to Statistics Canada, at that time, just one-third of households with children under the age of sixteen were dual-income households.

Fast-forward to the present—in this case, 2014, the most recent year for which Statistics Canada data is available—and you get a sense of just how drastically the situation has changed. The 1976 status quo has pretty much been flipped on its head, with more than two-thirds (69 percent) of Canadian households with children under the age of sixteen now reporting that both parents work outside the home. And here's an even more telling statistic: in more than half of such households in 2014, *both parents were working full-time* (as compared to just 24 percent in 1976).

Those numbers have more than doubled over the course of four decades—what amounts to a seismic shift in our collective work patterns. Not only has it become the new normal to have both parents working outside the home; it has become increasingly common to have both parents working on a full-time basis, which means that the majority of us parents are now routinely shouldering a massive, overwhelming load.

Of course, these kinds of statistics about the rise of the dual-income household can cause us to overlook another seismic shift in the landscape of parenting: the fact that the number of single-parent households in Canada more than doubled between 1976 and 2014, from 9 percent to 20 percent of households with children. It's also worth noting that, more often than not, mothers are the ones who continue to head up these single-parent households, although the number of fathers engaged in solo parenting has inched up a little over the past four decades, from 14 percent of single-parent households with children in 1976 to 19 percent by 2014.

What's leaving so many of us feeling exhausted and overwhelmed is the fact that there have been few corresponding workplace and social policy shifts to make it easier for us to manage what amounts to a massively increased load. There is still an unspoken expectation that someone is going to be available to do all the unpaid caring that raising a child demands, and that that someone, more often than not, will be mom. The fact that we still don't have anything even remotely resembling a universal child-care system in an era of almost universal dual-income parenting indicates how badly out of step our social policy continues to be, at least when it comes to responding to the realities of modern parenting.

What makes matters worse is the fact that existing social policies and workplace norms make it harder, not easier, for us to share care responsibilities fairly within our families. This makes life unnecessarily difficult for ourselves and our kids. Not only do these outdated policies and norms spark conflicts between partners (more about that in Chapter 9), they deprive children of the opportunity to have more than one actively involved caregiver and to grow up seeing themselves as both future workers *and* future caregivers (as opposed to just one or the other).

Imagine how different things would be if all individuals, regardless of gender, were supported in their roles as caregivers and financial providers (for example, if there was no such thing as the motherhood tax or the daddy bonus); if all families (not just higher-income families) could actually afford to take parental leave; if all parents were able to access and afford quality child care (as opposed to trying to make such a child-care arrangement appear out of thin air); and if all workers were encouraged to take advantage of flexible working arrangements at points in their lives when the work-life juggle tends to be most demanding—and without being penalized (most notably via the gender pay gap) for asserting their right to have a life outside of work.

But as much as introducing some or all of these policies would be a complete game-changer for our families, making our lives easier and better, they would still only solve part of the problem that is work-life imbalance. We'd still be left to grapple with a related issue: our collective obsession with a round-the-clock tetheredness to work.

OUR CULTURE OF "TOTAL WORK" HAS BEEN INTENSIFIED BY THE RISE OF MOBILE TECHNOLOGY.

Our work-life imbalance problems have been massively intensified by our collective willingness to embrace what philosopher Josef Pieper first described as a culture of "total work." Pieper coined that term back in the 1950s in an effort to sound the alarm bell about the way that work was well on its way to becoming the dominant force in our lives. The widespread use of technology has only served to accelerate that trend, increasing the amount of spillover between work and family life. Work is becoming harder and harder to escape—even in our supposedly non-working hours. "Most corporate jobs are 24/7 and come with the expectation that you'll be thinking about work or taking calls well into the evening," notes Alison, the mother of two school-aged children.

Families are feeling that pressure. The increased use of mobile technology, smartphones in particular, has coincided with a dip in the number of Canadians reporting that they feel "satisfied or very satisfied" with the amount of work-life balance they have been able to achieve. According to Statistics Canada, those numbers decreased from 78 percent in 2008 to 68 percent in 2016. It's worth noting that the first iPhone hit the store shelves in mid-2007, ushering in an era when smartphones would become ever-present in our lives, both at home and at work. By September 2017, 59 percent of the time Canadians spent online was being spent on mobile devices, according to comScore data published at the time. It could be sheer coincidence that the arrival of the world's most addictive hand-held device happened to coincide with a dip in work-life balance—or maybe it's not. (We'll be delving into this in greater detail in Chapter 3.)

TIME STRESS IS THE NEW NORMAL.
Forget about all the stereotypes about Canadians being polite or nice. If there's a dominant adjective to describe us these days, that adjective might very well be "time-stressed." That's the term used by Statistics Canada, who recently noted that nearly six in ten people who reported being dissatisfied with their work-life balance pointed to a lack of time for family life as the cause of their malaise.

Lynn can relate to those feelings. A first-time parent who describes her family as "tenuously straddling the line between middle and low income," she often thinks about how much easier her life would be if she had a little more time or a bit more money—or maybe even a little more of both: "If we had more resources to draw upon, we might hire people to help us clean our house, rake our leaves, and cook us food. We could pay a babysitter on a regular basis so that we could get a break." In other words, she and her partner could buy themselves *a little more time.*

Perhaps you've had some first-hand experience with the whole time-stress phenomenon—that creeping feeling of anxiety and dread that comes from the realization that there's simply not enough time to do everything that needs to be done over the course of a day. I know I've experienced it—repeatedly. It's a nasty by-product of the lack of downtime in an "always on" economy and an unwelcome side effect of punishing commuting times that can take a nasty bite out of your day.

It appears that no group of Canadians is completely immune to time stress—not men and not even people without kids. According to data drawn from Statistics Canada's 2014 general social survey, men and women are likely to report similar levels of time stress (34 percent of women as compared to 30 percent of men are less than satisfied). Ditto for people with and without children (33 percent versus 31 percent report feeling the crunch).

Of course, there are always ways to make a bad situation worse. According to Statistics Canada, commuting times have become a major source of misery in the lives of time-stressed Canadians. Not only has there been a 30 percent increase in the number of Canadians commuting to and from work since 1996, but the lengths of those commuting times have increased as well. The average nation-wide is now twenty-six minutes by car or forty-five minutes by public transit—travel times that are, of course, an absolute dream when compared to typical commute times in major metropolitan areas these days.

Researchers at the University of Waterloo who have studied the impact of commuting times on overall quality of life have found that lengthier commutes are associated with reduced life satisfaction, period, and an increased sense of time stress in particular. Commuting also takes its toll on relationships. Separation rates are higher in couples when one or both partners have to contend with a lengthy daily commute. And commuting takes its toll on health. Low energy, increased illness-related absences from work, and a greater likelihood of obesity are a few of the health by-products of lengthier commutes.

Physical activity appears to be a key piece in the commuter wellness puzzle. Commuters who are able to make the time to be physically active despite the amount of time out of their day that they lose to that commute are able to reduce the health-related toll of commuting. That's one of the reasons why Anthony, the father of two preteens, bikes to work: "A good deal of my stress gets dealt with every day. I commute back and forth to work by bicycle, and I find that's a great outlet for stress. I start the day fresh and relaxed and end the workday in the same way."

There are a couple of other commuter pro tips which may or may not apply to your situation. Turning commuting time into social time is a proven way to reduce the stress of commuting, so you might want to consider going to and from work with someone you care about. Another way to wrangle with the beast that is commuting is to negotiate for more flexible working hours so that you can steer clear of peak traffic, or for a bigger paycheque, so that you can pay other people to tackle yardwork or other household chores that would otherwise eat into your scarce and precious leisure time.

Why Work-Life Guilt Is So Pervasive— and So Misplaced

Start a conversation about work-life balance and it won't be long before someone spits out the word *guilt*—guilt about the work-related crisis that spilled over into what was supposed to be a relaxed family getaway, or about the family curveball that caused extra work for co-workers at a time when they could least afford to pick up the slack because it was already crunch season. The guilt flows easily in both directions, but it definitely flows in the work-intruding-on-family direction a whole lot more.

While 21 percent of Canadians aged fifteen through sixty-four who held down a job in 2016 told Statistics Canada that they "always" or "often" had difficulties fulfilling family responsibilities because of the amount of time they spent on their jobs, only 6 percent reported work-life spillover in the opposite direction, with family obligations getting in the way of work.

More often than not, it's women who bear the brunt of the work-life guilt. A 2017 study published in the *Journal of Child and Family Studies* reported that mothers experience significantly higher levels of "work-interfering-with-family guilt" and that this type of guilt tends to be a particular problem for mothers who work long hours, experience a lot of work-life conflict, and/or who lean toward more permissive parenting styles: "Perhaps mothers are more likely than fathers to feel that the experience of [work-interfering-with-family] conflict means that they have failed their children in some important way, or that it activates feelings of anxiety regarding not providing for children or not living up to societal, familial, or even personal expectations regarding work-life balance."

Even in 2018, there continue to be significant differences in the definition of what it means to be a good mom versus a good dad. But here's the thing: we aren't the guilty ones.

It's the system that is guilty.

It's the system that has failed us.

By "the system," I mean the tapestry of workplace and social policies that are supposed to make our lives easier or better but all too often don't. Consider the fact that the school day and the workday don't match up, to say nothing of the work- and school-year calendars; the fact that the supply of quality licensed childcare spaces falls far short of the demand for such spaces, leaving families in the lurch; or the fact that far too many government offices and medical services seem to assume that there's a parent at home during the day ready to function as a full-time appointment concierge.

Instead of rejecting those expectations of what it means to be a good mom on the basis that they're both unrealistic and out-dated, we have a tendency to swallow them whole, which leaves us with a belly full of guilt. And that, in turn, has a far-reaching impact on our parenting.

How Work-Life Imbalance Affects Our Parenting

You don't have to be a genius to connect the dots between work-life imbalance and less effective parenting. If you arrive home from work feeling stressed and depleted each and every night, you're simply not going to have the patience or energy required to engage with your kids in ways that you can feel good about.

There's a solid body of research to demonstrate that parents who struggle with high levels of work-life conflict are likely to be stressed, anxious, and depressed. They're also likely to be less healthy than their less stressed counterparts, which means that they're *less likely* to eat well and exercise regularly and *more likely* to turn to alcohol or drugs for stress relief (a particular issue for men). And they're more likely to be dissatisfied with their relationships with their partners and their kids. When work-life conflict is prolonged or extreme, parents end up being distant, inattentive, less sensitive, and less emotionally available to their kids.

Work can even have an impact on parenting *before* a parent returns to work after parental leave, notes Teresa Pitman, a mother of four, grandmother of ten, and author of numerous bestselling books about parenting. According to Pitman, worry about work can start to set in during even the earliest days of parenting, as parents begin to anticipate and prepare for their eventual return to work. They may worry about sleep schedules (when or whether baby naps, and how often baby is up in the night) and feeding issues (when to introduce a bottle or a cup). "They're thinking about what would make life easier for the daycare person down the road, and that becomes the top priority for the parents, as opposed to thinking about what might be best for themselves and their baby, what their baby really needs right now. It means that everything gets adjusted around work—and work isn't very friendly to babies and parents," says Pitman.

So, work has a habit of intruding on family life right from the beginning. And those intrusions tend to continue over time. You know how it goes. A work-related phone call or email message interrupts you when you're in the midst of a heart-to-heart conversation with one of your kids, or worry about work causes you to become distracted or impatient at the very moment your child needs you most. You may be physically present, but mentally, you're back at work. And once you realize that you've made that accidental mental leap, a tsunami of guilt sets in.

Here's something else you need to know about those nasty and intrusive work-related thoughts: they tend to be more of a problem for moms than they are for dads. Dads find it easier to leave work-related worries at work, particularly if they happen to be working long hours.

Sociologist Shira Offer explained this phenomenon in a recent article for the *Sociological Forum*, noting that dads who work long hours, which she defined as more than forty-six hours per week, may be particularly determined to protect their family time from work-related intrusions, including work-related thoughts, because their family time is in correspondingly short supply.

Those efforts are definitely worth it because kids *do* feel the impact when a parent works long hours. Children are particularly affected when those hours occur at times when children expect to be able to spend time with their parents (weekends, evenings, or nights), when parents don't have much flexibility about the hours they are required to work, and when the stress from high-pressure jobs spills over into family life. As Australian psychologist and public health researcher Lyndall Strazdins noted in a recent article for the

Child & Family Blog, "Childhood is at odds with many aspects of the evolving 24/7 economy."

Long hours aren't the only problem. Having a parent work unpredictable hours or a non-standard schedule can be similarly tough on kids, both because of the impact on day-to-day routines and because the parents themselves are more stressed. "The picture of workers with nonstandard schedules is unenviable," noted Magali Girard in an article for the *McGill Sociological Review.* "They are more stressed, perceive a lack of control in their lives, do not spend as much time with their children and partners as they would like, and are thus less satisfied with their family life and marital life." Mothers are disproportionately affected: "Nonstandard schedules are particularly difficult for mothers, undermining their emotional well-being, relationships with their partners, and general participation in family life," noted University of Texas at Austin doctoral student Kate C. Pickett in her 2015 doctoral thesis.

All this stress and disruption can take its toll on the parent-child relationship. Not only have parents' non-standard working hours been linked to increased behavioural problems in adolescents; they're also associated with increased stress and loneliness and poorer health in children of all ages.

What's ironic is that many parents seek out jobs with non-standard hours in an effort to maximize the amount of time they or their partner spend with their children. And yet "non-standard schedules are associated with stressors that might net out the potential benefits of additional time to invest in parenting," according to Pickett.

That's not to say that jobs with non-standard hours are never beneficial to families. They can, in fact, make life less stressful if the request for flexible or non-standard scheduling is initiated by the employee as opposed to being mandated by the employer, and if opportunities to work remotely from home are understood to be instead of (as opposed to in addition to) putting in a full day at the office. This latter scenario—being expected to be plugged in all evening on top of working all day—is a particularly detrimental and draining form of non-standard scheduling.

It's also easier to make non-standard hours work for you and your family if you're a part-time rather than a full-time worker. According to Pickett, "Part-time hours that can be conducted in the evenings and night may offer flexibility so that they do not disrupt family life in the way full-time evening and night work does."

Of course, no discussion about non-standard scheduling would be complete without a word about self-employment. Self-employment is often pitched as the ultimate solution to work-life balance issues because, hey, you can just make your business fit around your family, right? However, it frequently falls short of the miracle solution it promises to deliver. Sure, self-employment offers a lot of freedom—the freedom to work as long and as hard as you can. I say this from the vantage point of someone with more than twenty-five years of self-employment under her belt, which kind of begs the question: Where's my gold watch? I think it's important to acknowledge the reality that running your own business is actually a lot of hard work, and to consider the resulting impact on parenting. I think we need to talk more about this and to stop glamorizing the so-called gig economy, particularly given that so many new mothers gravitate toward self-employment, seeing it as a work-life balance miracle solution. The results can be less than miraculous for mothers, particularly those with multiple children. A recent study conducted by economist Kate Rybczynski of the University of Waterloo found that while a father's odds of thriving as an entrepreneur increased with each additional child, a mother's odds decreased correspondingly.

Even when the business is successful, the work-life juggling act can be exhausting. Karen, a self-employed writer and the mother of two preteens loves the flexibility that goes along with running her own business but says she could definitely live without all the added stress: "It's been great in terms of being with my children. But, at this point, I'm afraid to say no [to work]. I almost never say no to clients or work because my work situation is so precarious. In the six years that I've been working freelance and supposedly achieving this great work-life balance, I have never once taken a vacation where I didn't have to work. So, yeah, in one way it's been great, and in another way, it's like I'm never not working. My hours are flexible. I do have more control over my life. But, in this economy, I'm afraid to have the freedom that I really had envisioned for myself when I started freelancing."

The anxiety about precarious work that Karen describes is an increasingly common phenomenon. A 2015 McMaster University study concluded, for example, that more than half of workers in the greater Toronto area (GTA) work in temporary, contract, or part-time jobs. The phenomenon is hardly limited to the GTA. A 2013 study by the Organisation for Economic Co-operation and Development (OECD) concluded that roughly one in three Canadian workers are precariously employed. The impact on precariously employed workers and their families can be devastating and far-reaching. Not only do workers have to deal with unpredictable schedules and paycheques, but there's always looming uncertainty about the future. What's going to happen next week, next month, next year? And how will your family get by over the even longer term, in the absence of anything remotely resembling health benefits or a pension? An editorial published in the UK newspaper *The Guardian* in early 2018 spelled out the impact particularly bluntly: "Research last year found astonishingly that some jobs might be even worse than unemployment for one's health: people moving into poor-quality work were found to have the highest levels of chronic stress, higher than that recorded by jobless workers."

But wait; it gets worse. If precarious employment is characterized by periods of unemployment—if, for example, you're temporarily unemployed between contracts or temporarily laid off during your industry's off-season—the impact of those repeated periods of unemployment can be particularly devastating. Psychologist Ed Diener noted in a recent article for *Canadian Psychology*, "Even after reemployment, previously unemployed people do not always return to their pre-employment levels of [subjective well-being]." In other words, these types of experiences can be deeply scarring for precariously employed workers, which means they likely take their toll on their parenting efforts too.

What about negotiating for better working conditions? That tends to be a non-starter for most workers during tough economic times. According to the authors of the 2017 book *Work-Life Balance in Times of Recession, Austerity and Beyond*, workers are less likely to try to negotiate for work-life accommodations or even try to take advantage of existing work-life supports such as part-time work, flexible working arrangements, or family leave during times of recession and austerity.

What Is It Going to Take to Turn the Situation Around?

Let's shift the conversation back onto more positive ground by talking about what it's going to take to turn the situation around. What can we do to start to make that happen?

RESIST THE CULTURE OF "TOTAL WORK."
Commit to challenging the idea that a culture of total work is healthy or in any way life enhancing for anyone, and then look for opportunities to push back both at home and at work.

A crucial first step, of course, is to be crystal clear about what you want for yourself and your family, and to try to build your working life around that. Casey, the father of two young boys, is committed to playing a bigger role in his sons' lives than his father was able to play in his when he was growing up in Jamaica. He explains, "I come from a restaurant family culture. My dad ended up working twelve-to-sixteen-hour days, five to six days a week, so I don't really have a lot of childhood memories of my dad. He was working all the time to support us. This doesn't mean my dad was a bad dad. He did the best he could with the hand he had." Reflecting on what his father missed out on along the way made Casey realize that he wanted something more for himself, specifically, to be there as much as possible for his kids. He strives to make this happen in a realistic, manageable way: "I don't want to miss out on dinners, bath time, or story time," he explains. He works hard at honouring that commitment to himself and his family.

You'll also want to seize every opportunity you can to start shifting the culture at work. One powerful way to do this is by actually allowing yourself to completely disconnect from work when you're on vacation. This is a point that Katie Denis, chief of research and strategy for Project: Time Off, made in a recent article for the *Harvard Business Review*. She highlighted the devastating impact on workplace morale when workers are given the subtle—or not so subtle—message that they're actually expected to check in during their vacation time. "Every email sent by a vacationing employee is a tiny cultural erosion: a signal to other employees that time off isn't really time off."

Denis's article got me thinking about an autoresponder message I'd received a few years earlier after emailing Ottawa writer Shari Graydon one summer. The subject line in her email read, "I'm having a life; response may be delayed," and the message went on to explain that I wouldn't be hearing back from Shari for a little while: "Somewhere the sun is shining, and a patio or deck chair overlooking a lake or a vineyard is beckoning . . . I'll be back at my desk on August 2nd." Imagine the collective impact we'd have if we all sent out messages like that.

SPEND SOME TIME THINKING ABOUT WHAT MIGHT
ACTUALLY HELP TO MAKE THINGS BETTER.
Start out by pinpointing the underlying issue that needs to be resolved, for example, a hellishly long commute or long, erratic

work hours. Then brainstorm—perhaps with some input from another trusted person—any and all possible solutions, remembering to consider both the work and family variables in the work-family equation. You'll also want to consider whether this is a short-term problem that you can address via a temporary reallocation of resources (time, energy, or money) or whether you're dealing with a more permanent problem that's going to require a more permanent solution. Think about what that solution might be. Once you've generated a lengthy list of ideas, begin to zero in on what's possible, or what's possible for you right now.

For Karen, the freelance writer, that meant making the decision, along with her partner, to relocate themselves and their two young daughters from an expensive urban centre to a more affordable smaller community, where they wouldn't have to work as long or as hard to just get by. "We felt like we weren't achieving good work-life balance back in the city, that we were just spinning our wheels and nobody was happy. So, we decided to make a change."

For Alison, it meant shifting career gears entirely. A mom of two and an expat Canadian who was employed in the U.S. tech sector until recently, she didn't even try to talk with her employer about her desire for greater work-life balance because she knew that kind of conversation would be a complete non-starter at her workplace. "In today's start-up high-tech male-dominated environment, it isn't really an option to ask to work less. There is such an entrenched culture of working extreme hours that you find yourself driven to do that too," she explains. The culture worked for her for an extended period of time—and then suddenly, it didn't work anymore. She was hardly getting to spend any time with her kids: "Sundays and a few evenings a week, just long enough to help get them to bed." Both kids were struggling, one with a learning disability, the other with extreme anxiety. Her job had become more stressful, and she was tired of constantly putting her own health and well-being on the back burner. "I was worried about my health," she confesses. "I'm not fit and my family history isn't the greatest. I wanted a better and healthier second half of my life, and I couldn't see a way to get healthier if I stayed in my rat-race driven position, cool as it was." Ultimately, she decided that her best bet was to leave her corporate job behind and devote her energies and skills to building the family's contracting business.

Alison recognizes that she was fortunate to be in a position to pivot to a career Plan B, because not every stressed-out parent has that option. Germaine, a single parent and hospitality industry worker, has found that there are often no easy solutions for families like hers that are barely scraping by financially. "I have worked very hard to provide for my son," she explains. "I have gone without so he doesn't have to. Most recently, I've applied to take a second job part-time to supplement my income. This means less time with Samuel [her eleven-year-old son] and that hurts both of us. I hope that taking a second job will allow me to finally put some money away for his education. Every day, I worry that I am not doing enough to reach our goals. The stress of wondering where the money is going to come from keeps me awake at night. I hope that one day, we won't have to sacrifice as much and that we will be living a little more comfortably."

Do what you can to minimize the stress caused
by role conflict.
Role conflict occurs when a role that you care about collides with another important role, when your responsibilities at work get in the way of your responsibilities at home or vice versa. If you happen to work from home, you may find it particularly challenging to minimize this kind of conflict. Gordon, the father of two young girls, finds it mentally draining when he has to switch back and forth between work and family—something that happens on a fairly regular basis when you have two children

and two businesses living under the same roof: "I'll be working to a deadline on a project and then a little kid will show up in my office, asking if I can fix her toy. Of course, I want to chuck the work and go fix the toy and play, but I just can't right then. It's that feeling of being torn in two that's really the toughest thing to resolve—when you're doing one thing but being pulled to do something completely different."

Sometimes, role conflict is unavoidable, but at other times, it's within your control. It's a major source of work-life stress and guilt, so it's worth your while to try to find ways to minimize the problem whenever possible. Little things can make a big difference, like making a conscious choice to disable notifications on your smartphone so you aren't tempted to respond to work-related emails when you're playing with your kids at the playground. You'll feel less stressed and less distracted, and your kids will bask in the glow of your undivided attention, even when you think they aren't looking.

What follows are a few additional tips on reducing role conflict.

Try to minimize interruptions during your working day. The more you are able to maintain your focus and productivity while you're actually at work, the less work and worry you'll end up dragging home with you at the end of the day. "I don't want to be checking Facebook and wasting my work hours when I really need to be writing or researching," notes Nicole, the single parent of four school-aged children. A helpful strategy is to block off time in your schedule for periods of uninterrupted work, so that you can find and keep the focus necessary to take a mental deep dive. You might also want to find a way to signal to others that you're not available for certain blocks of time. This task could be handled rather elegantly by a desk light that automatically switches to red when you're in the zone and focused on your work—the brainchild of one University of British Columbia computer scientist.

Come up with strategies for escaping the world of work at the end of your working day. Try to download your worries before you head out the door, perhaps by making a quick note of the very first thing you have to do when you return to your desk in the morning. That will give the work part of your brain permission to take the rest of the night off as opposed to constantly prodding you to think about what you have to tackle first thing in the morning. Then go a step further by shifting your brain into family mode. Think of an activity you might enjoy with your preschooler or a funny story that you might share with your teenager. That way, by the time you leave work, you'll be starting to look forward to reconnecting with your kids.

Treat commuting time as role-switching time—when you allow your brain to make the switch from work mode to family mode. That way, when you walk through the front door, you'll already be back in the parenting groove. A 2016 working paper prepared for Harvard Business School offered a strategy that may work well in this situation. The paper actually talked about making the mental switch while travelling in the opposite direction—from home to work—but I think their strategy might be even more powerful when applied to the even more challenging work-to-home switch. They suggested that commuters treat the trip in to work as an opportunity to make the mental switch from home to work and to begin to focus on what they hope to achieve over the course of the day, a process they described as "goal-directed prospection"—in other words, thinking of your goals and using that as the launching pad to your day at work. I think that if focusing on your goals on the way to work can increase job satisfaction and reduce emotional exhaustion, focusing on your parenting goals on your way home could be the ticket to a more relaxed evening of parenting. Of course, there will be days when you simply don't have it in you to engage in that kind of heavy-duty thinking on your way home— and that's okay. Just cue up a comedy podcast and zone out guilt-free. It's all about having multiple strategies to draw upon on different days, so that you can switch your game plan accordingly after the day from hell.

Consider your physical environment. If you have to switch to work-related tasks when you're at home, try to limit those tasks to one specific spot in one specific room. What you want to do is avoid allowing work to put down roots in all areas of your home, something that can leave you feeling like you're living at work.

Make it quick. If you have to interrupt family time with a work-related task, try to dive in and dive out of your computer or smartphone quickly. You'll find it easier to do this if you remain purposeful—if you force yourself to focus on that one particular task. If you need to respond to a specific email message, use the search function in your email program to find it as opposed to scrolling through your entire inbox and thereby increasing the likelihood that you'll spot other emails that require your attention or that mentally drag you back to work.

Flag non-urgent work-related emails and set them aside to deal with in a single batch. Instead of allowing emails to disrupt and intrude on your entire weekend by dealing with them as they arrive, tackle them all at once on Sunday night (if you must) or first thing Monday morning (preferably).

Work through these issues with your partner, if you have one. Work-life conflict is a major source of resentment in many couple relationships. It can leave one or both of you exhausted by the end of the day, with little left to give to one another. These issues may not be easy ones to tackle, but they're important ones, for the health of your relationship and your kids. (More about this in Chapter 9.)

Reject productivity hacks that make you feel guilty or inadequate. Too often, one-size-fits-all productivity advice bumps up against the realities of life. Sure, it's a great idea to plan your life a week in advance—

if you have the luxury of knowing your schedule a week in advance. And, yes, keeping a time log can help you to find more time in your day—unless, of course, you're already completely maxed out. Sometimes the healthiest thing you can do when you encounter that kind of advice is to hit the delete key emphatically and unapologetically.

Recognize this for what it is: a life-cycle issue. It's a fact of life for humans: if you have relationships with other people, sometimes those people are going to need you, and sometimes their needs are going to spill over into the world of work. Life happens, and when you're part of a family, what happens to other family members can't help but affect you too.

The preschool years are a particularly tough time for parents trying to keep all the work-life balls in the air. Not only do young children require a lot of hands-on care, which can be exhausting in and of itself, but they also have a habit of absorbing and bringing home the daycare virus du jour. Is it any wonder, then, that the authors of the European Working Conditions Survey concluded, "Negative impacts on work-life balance are concentrated during the early phase of parenting, that is, when respondents have young, pre-school children."

That's not to say that the primary school years are easy ones for parents either. School hours are inflexible. Work hours may be inflexible too. Children aren't yet old enough to fly solo if the school day and workday happen to end at different times, or if they have to stay home for a couple of days while they're battling the flu.

This isn't something you should feel the need to apologize for, incidentally, the fact that you have a life and responsibilities outside of work. We all have to deal with this at some point—at least those of us who have people we care about. The best way to handle it is to simply acknowledge that it is happening and to be clear with your employer about what you need and whether the situation that you're dealing with can best be described as a temporary road bump or a longer-term detour. Stick to the basics: what's happening, how you're handling it, what your employer can expect, and how they can help. And, again, steer clear of the apologies and the guilt.

Join forces with other people who are concerned about work-life imbalance. Managing the massive problem that is work-life imbalance may start with you, but it can't end with you. You're not going to be able to solve this problem on your own. The good news is that you don't have to. You can join forces with other people who are just as passionate about these issues as you are, and work for change together.

Remind yourself that it's not all bad news. Work has been getting a bit of a bad rap in this chapter, but work doesn't have to be completely depleting. It can actually be life-enhancing too. If you enjoy your job and it's not too stressful, work can provide you with feelings of competence, the opportunity to develop new skills, a sense of achievement, and increased feelings of optimism and self-esteem. So, look for opportunities to get more of the good stuff from the world of work—the stuff that lifts you up instead of dragging you down. That can only do good things for your parenting.

CHAPTER 3

The Why of Distracted Parenting

The guilt around parental screen time can become another way to make us feel more profoundly ashamed that we are not the parents we had hoped we would be—it's not just that we're lackluster parents because we're scrolling and swiping, it's also that we're scrolling and swiping because we're bored in the company of our darlings.

—Pediatrician and mother Perri Klass, writing in
The New York Times

Ask a typical parent about her relationship with her smartphone and you're likely to unleash a tsunami of guilt fuelled by stories of smartphone sins.

Some of those stories are frightening and dramatic. "Last week, I almost killed my daughter," confessed writer Jenn Meer in a 2013 article for her parenting blog that detailed an incident in which her daughter nearly drowned in the bathtub while Jenn was momentarily distracted by an email.

Others are less dramatic but equally guilt-inducing for anyone who can relate to them—which, frankly, is most of us. "Like most addicts, I hit a rock bottom: it was noticing that not even my daughter's bath or bedtimes could escape a quick scroll of my social media feeds," confessed journalist Andrew MacDougall in a 2017 *Ottawa Citizen* article explaining his decision to unplug from social media.

It's hardly surprising that so many parents are stepping forward to confess their smartphone sins either quietly, in whispered conversations with equally guilty parents, or in a much more public way. The messages that parents have been receiving about the evils of distracted parenting have been relentless and hard-hitting. A 2015 article written by psychologist Richard Freed for *The Huffington Post* is typical of the tone taken by the legions of experts warning of the dangers of distracted parenting. Freed argued that "digitally-preoccupied parenting tears a wound in children's souls" and that these missed opportunities for parent-child connection inevitably result in future regret: "How many parents wish they could get back the moments they lost with their child?"

Now, don't get me wrong. I'm not saying that we shouldn't be talking about this issue. Distracted parenting is a growing problem for growing numbers of parents—which means it's a growing problem for growing numbers of kids too. But are messages designed to make parents feel incredibly guilty the answer? Is it possible that we need to dig a little deeper and consider the *why*, not just the *what*, of distracted parenting?

That's the approach I've chosen to take in this chapter. Yes, I'll be summarizing the research on what we're learning about the impact of distracted parenting, but in the context of what I consider to be the bigger issue: what it is about parenting that's causing us to turn to our phones for distraction, and what we can do about the problem.

The Truth about Distracted Parenting

Long before anyone ever invented the smartphone, there were distracted parents—parents who sought momentary escape from the hard work of parenting by taking a mental vacation.

For some parents, that simply meant allowing their minds to drift off to a world far removed from the day-to-day reality of diapers and dishes and other domestic detritus. For others, it meant escaping into a heartfelt conversation with another parent at the playground—a parent who was equally hungry for adult human contact. And for still others—for bookish parents like me—it meant seizing the opportunity to dive into the pages of a book whenever possible.

Children experienced the fallout of these types of distracted parenting—not every single time, but on a fairly regular basis. Toddlers seized the opportunity to wreak havoc with a crayon or to taste-test that crayon, and preschoolers attempted uncharacteristically risky manoeuvres at the playground and walked away with a few unwelcome bumps and bruises as a result of taking unexpected tumbles.

What was different about distracted parenting in the pre-smartphone era was both the extent of the distraction and the extent of the need for that distraction. Smartphones are uniquely distracting devices. In fact, that's their whole reason for being: they're designed to capture and keep our attention. And we, in turn, are extremely distractible. We are highly motivated to seek escape from the uncomfortable emotions that have become the backdrop to modern parenting: anxiety, guilt, and feeling overwhelmed.

Think about it. If you set out to design a device that would make it possible for parents to cope with these three powerful emotions, to say nothing of the countless other uncomfortable emotions that are baked into the experience of parenting, you would likely come up with something that looked a lot like a smartphone. In other words, you'd create a handy device that you could carry around in your pocket and that would serve up an enticing mix of connection, distraction, and instant validation. Is it any wonder, then, that so many of us find our devices so hard to resist?

The only way we're going to figure out how to resist our smartphones, and to deal with the underlying problem of distracted parenting, is by tackling the underlying issues that cause us to crave that distraction: the fact that parenting can be isolating, even lonely; the fact that the hard work of parenting can really wear a person down; and the fact that there isn't a whole lot of day-to-day validation in the life of a parent.

Because here's the thing: while allowing ourselves to be distracted by our smartphones appears to deliver up much-needed relief, it actually makes parenting harder and less enjoyable. That's because smartphones don't just respond to our anxiety, our guilt, and our feelings of being overwhelmed; they actually amplify those feelings as well.

As Nicholas Carr explains in his thought-provoking book *The Shallows: What the Internet is Doing to Our Brains*, "When our brain is over-taxed we find 'distractions more distracting' . . . it becomes harder to distinguish relevant information from irrelevant information, signal from noise."

The first step to breaking free of that nasty distraction feedback loop is to understand exactly what impact that technology is having on our brains, our relationships, and, more specifically, our parenting.

This Is Your Brain on Technology
Our love affair with technology is officially over. In fact, I think it's been over for quite some time. It's been a while since anyone waxed poetically, and completely uncritically, about technology as a universal force for good. This means that fewer of us are sporting a pair of rose-tinted glasses as we stare into our computer screens. (We're much more likely to be sporting blue-light-blocking yellow-tinted glasses instead.)

What's helped to unleash this backlash is our growing knowledge about the far-reaching impact of technology on both our brains and our lives. It's not just all the super-scary revelations about the ways that technology can be used to manipulate our social behaviours and political patterns; it's the way that technology can mess with our heads. We're more distracted and less able to deploy our attention in ways that work for us—to be productive, to think deep thoughts, and to truly connect with the people we love.

Here's a quick overview of some of the more noteworthy things we've been learning lately about the impact of technology in general and smartphones in particular.

Smartphones affect the quality of our thinking. Do you feel that engaging with a steady stream of text messages and tweets has whittled away at your attention span? It's not your imagination. As it turns out, the mere presence of a smartphone is cognitively draining. You don't have to be actually using the device for it to be taking a mental toll. A recent study by researchers at the University of Texas at Austin revealed that students whose smartphones were visible on their desks performed more poorly on cognitive tests than students whose phones were safely stashed outside the room—this despite the fact that the phones on the desks were placed face down, with all potentially distracting notifications turned off. The researchers concluded that when a smartphone is visible, your brain has to work at ignoring it, which takes a cognitive toll.

Of course, it's not your smartphone's job to simply lay passively, patiently waiting for you to decide that it's time to reengage. Your smartphone is designed to seek out and capture your attention as often as possible. It's the frequency of those interruptions that's at the heart of the cognitive drain problem, the repeated "task switching" from your smartphone to the rest of your life and back, over and over again. Each time you're interrupted, it takes time and effort to redirect your attention and completely regain your focus—an average of twenty-five minutes following each and every such interruption, according to figures cited by a Bank of England analyst in a recent interview with *The Globe and Mail*'s Eric Andrew-Gee. Likewise, a study of Microsoft employees concluded that it takes fifteen minutes to regain your focus after being interrupted by an email, and ten minutes after being interrupted by a text message. To make things worse, your brain begins to anticipate and, over time, to create its own interruptions. Your brain becomes so accustomed to being interrupted every few minutes by an on-screen notification or ping that it actually starts to interrupt itself. You'll find yourself feeling restless and distracted, and you'll respond to that distraction by taking a "little procrastination break," to borrow a phrase from Andrew-Gee. That not only leaves your increasingly restless brain craving still yet more distraction; it also leaves your brain less capable of deep, sustained thinking—something that, of course, has implications for the quality of your parenting.

Here's something else you need to know about those rather insidious self-interruptions: we tend to drastically underestimate how often we interrupt ourselves by turning to our screens, and our smartphones in particular. The researchers behind a 2015 study in *PLOS One* asked smartphone users to estimate how many times they used their phones over the course of a day. Their best guess? Thirty-seven times. The actual number? Eighty-five times. In most cases, the interruptions were extremely brief, less than thirty seconds. But these types of interruptions can really take a toll over time. In fact, it's been estimated that the cognitive drain associated with smartphone use is roughly equivalent to losing a full night's sleep.

Our smartphones don't just cause our attention to become more fragmented. They can cause us to overlook what's happening right in front of us because our attention is focused elsewhere—a phenomenon that psychologists refer to as "inattentional blindness." A study published in *Applied Cognitive Psychology* in 2010 found, for example, that people walking down the street and talking on a cellphone at the same time are considerably less likely to notice a clown riding a unicycle than people who aren't similarly engaged with their phones. That, of course, kind of begs the question: If your smartphone is captivating enough to make a unicycle-riding clown inattentionally invisible, what else might you fail to notice in your general vicinity? A heavy-duty truck that's barrelling down the street as you step into a pedestrian crosswalk? Baby's first smile?

Smartphones change the way we see ourselves. In fact, they're pretty much becoming extensions of ourselves. We rely on them to store key pieces of data that we used to carry around in our heads, for example, a friend's phone number, a relative's street address, or the hours of a local store. Over time, we become less capable of recalling this type of information—a phenomenon known as "digital amnesia." Instead of trying to remember a particular fact, we simply need to know how to find that information online. Our brains become search engines capable of retrieving data from our ever-present smartphones.

We haven't just turned our brains into search engines; we've also turned them into remote repositories for our memories. Can't quite remember where the family got together to celebrate Grandma's seventy-fifth birthday? No worries. There's bound to be a photo of the banquet hall somewhere in your photo stream or a copy of the event invitation in your email.

Sometimes, we're so busy trying to document our memories—to snap photos at a preschooler's dance recital, for example—that we're too distracted to enjoy the event while it's actually happening. As a result, we end up settling for "a recording of our experience that wasn't directly experienced," as Nancy Colier writes in *The Power of Off.* "Our phones are full, but we feel empty."

Is it any wonder, then, that we feel so attached to our phones, and so anxious when we're separated from them? They feel like a part of us.

Smartphones affect our relationships with other people. For starters, they affect the quality of our conversations. Conversations are lighter and more superficial when a smartphone is present. We're less likely to talk about things that really matter because we understand, consciously or unconsciously, that the resulting conversation could be interrupted at any time.

We don't even have to be actively engaging with a smartphone to have that phone cast a shadow over the quality of our conversations. Its mere presence is distracting, and not just to the phone's owner. As Massachusetts Institute of Technology sociologist Sherry Turkle explains in her book *Reclaiming Conversation*, "If two people are speaking and there's a phone on a nearby desk, each feels less connected to the other than when there is no phone present. *Even a silent phone disconnects us.*"

We have good reason to anticipate that next disconnection. Digital marketers tell us that nine out of ten text messages are read within three minutes of being received, and that Canadians between the ages of eighteen and thirty-four typically send over five thousand such messages each month. And when that text message notification pops up and seizes our attention, we stop tuning into the conversation with the person who is actually in the room. Even if we make an effort to listen, we miss out on most of what the other person is trying to say while our eyes are glued to that screen. Research by psychologist Albert Mehrabian has revealed that just 7 percent of what we're trying to say is actually communicated through words. The rest of our message is expressed through our tone of voice (38 percent) and, most important of all, our body language (55 percent).

Just as an aside, this may help to explain why teens who rely heavily on text messaging as a means of communicating with a boyfriend or girlfriend actually end up being less skilled at navigating tricky relationship issues than teens who communicate with their partners in person or over the phone. The conclusion of a group of researchers led by Jacqueline Nesi of the University of North Carolina who studied the emergence of relationship skills in teens? Teens need opportunities to practise interpreting a partner's tone of voice and body language as well as figuring out how to respond—learning that can only take place during a face-to-face conversation with another person. When they communicate via text message, they miss out on this practice, so they miss out on critically important opportunities to develop these skills.

Up until now, we've been talking about the impact of smartphones on our brains, our sense of self, and in our relationships with other people in general. Now, let's shift the focus to distracted parenting. Because here's the thing: smartphones aren't merely addictive; they're uniquely addictive to us as parents. They offer us a way to escape momentarily from the freewheeling anxiety, guilt, and feeling of being overwhelmed that have become the backdrop to our lives as parents. They offer instant connection—a powerful antidote to the isolation and loneliness that many of us experience. They provide instant validation and in-the-moment feedback, as compared to the far less tangible and considerably delayed feedback that comes from parenting.

Like a high-tech frenemy, our smartphones promise far more than they deliver. They make us more anxious and more irritable, and less able to engage deeply and meaningfully with our children. That's because a distracted brain is a hungry brain—a brain that's constantly craving more distraction but keeps reaching for the mental equivalent of junk food. A smartphone attention fix is anything but satisfying, and actually leaves us hungry for more. And as we burn through our cognitive resources by constantly diverting our attention to our phones, we're left with fewer cognitive and emotional resources to manage our moods, making it harder—*so much harder*—to be the parents we want to be.

What Every Parent Needs to Know About Distracted Parenting

If—like most of us—you've found yourself dividing your attention between your child and your smartphone, you know how awful it can feel. You either feel annoyed with your child because she's trying to pull you away from your smartphone, or you feel annoyed with yourself for pulling away from your child. It can feel like a game of emotional tug-of-war—and you're the one caught in the middle.

What you're experiencing, of course, is "technoference," a term first coined by family life researchers Brandon T. McDaniel and Sarah M. Coyne in a 2016 article in the *Psychology of Popular Media Culture* to describe technology's "everyday intrusions and interruptions" in family life. In many ways, it's similar to role conflict, which we talked about a lot in the previous chapter—that anxiety-and-guilt-inducing feeling of being torn in two directions at once when your working life collides with your family life or vice versa—but in this case, it's technology that's doing the intruding. It can play out in subtle or not-so-subtle ways:

- You find yourself scrolling through your smartphone or otherwise fixated on a different type of digital device while you're breastfeeding your baby—something that happens in roughly one in four feedings these days, according to a recent study published in the *Journal of Nutrition Education and Behavior*. You welcome the distraction and the company, even if it's electronic company, but you feel a little guilty each time you catch your baby staring at you while you stare at your device.

- A text message interrupts a conversation with your child. Your preschooler has been through this enough times to know that you're going to be busy for the next little while, so he decides to occupy himself for the next little while by giving the family dog a bonus meal.

- Your preschooler has returned and he's determined to win back your attention. He's oblivious to the fact that you're trying to resolve an online payment snafu that is demanding your entire focus and even more of your patience. Why should he care? He's just a little kid—an impatient and grumpy little kid who's about to start swinging from the chandelier.

Yep. The impact of technoference (a.k.a. distracted parenting) can be pretty significant, not to mention guilt-inducing when you realize that you've allowed yourself to get swept up in your smartphone again. At least you can take solace in the fact that you're not the only parent grappling with these issues—not by a long shot. As Eric Andrew-Gee noted in a recent article in *The Globe and Mail*, "In the first five years of the smartphone era, the proportion of Americans who said internet use interfered with their family time nearly tripled, from 11 percent to 28 percent." Odds are those numbers would be pretty similar for Canadian parents too. We're pretty similar when it comes to rates of smartphone use. So, if misery loves company, you've got plenty of company, at least.

Before we start talking about what to do about distracted parenting—how to make things better for your family—I want to run through some of the evidence about the fallout of distracted parenting, specifically the ways that it affects both kids and their parents. Because the fallout isn't just limited to kids. This isn't an attempt to make you feel guilty (or guiltier, as the case may be). Rather, it's simply an attempt to get some basic facts out in the open so that you can make more conscious decisions about your use of technology and zero in on strategies that support your goals.

Here's what you need to know.

DISTRACTED PARENTING CAN INTERFERE WITH THE
DEVELOPMENT OF A HEALTHY PARENT-CHILD RELATIONSHIP
AS WELL AS OVERALL CHILD DEVELOPMENT.

Distracted parenting can prevent a parent from being sufficiently tuned in and responsive to the needs of the child. Not only does this interfere with the development of a healthy parent-child relationship (with the parent-child relationship providing a "template" on which all future relationships will be based), but it can also interfere with the child's ability to learn how to focus and direct her attention.

Serve-and-return interactions between parent and child are key to social learning and the building block for all other types of learning. What I'm talking about here are the kinds of interactions that occur when a parent is really tuned in and responsive to a child's cues—the relationship equivalent of two people playing a game of tennis. As Andrew Sullivan explained in a 2016 essay for *New York* magazine, "Truly being with another person means being experientially with them, picking up on countless signals from the eyes and voice and body language and context, and reacting, often unconsciously, to every nuance . . . Those are our deepest social skills, which have been honed through the aeons. They are what makes us distinctly human."

These types of interactions help children learn how to make sense of another person's intentions, how to coordinate actions toward a shared goal, and the fact that you can turn to another person for help and that you can count on that person to be there when you need them—some really key lessons in empathy and trust. As Nicholas Carr noted in his book *The Shallows*, "It's not only deep thinking that requires a calm, attentive mind. It's also empathy and compassion."

But that's not all these serve-and-return interactions do. They also teach children how to focus their attention. Because here's the thing: a child can't learn how to focus his attention until he's had the opportunity to be on the receiving end of this kind of focused attention from another person, repeatedly, over time. As Adam Alter explains in *Irresistible: The Rise of Addictive Technology and the Business of Keeping Us Hooked*, "Distracted parents cultivate distracted children because parents who can't focus teach their children the same attentional patterns."

Distracted parenting gives your child the message that you're simply not available—a worrisome message to a child.

You might think that scrolling through your smartphone when your child is happily occupied in the sandbox is harmless, but you're actually sending your child a powerful message, like it or not. As psychologist Kostadin Kushlev explains it, an averted eye gaze sends strong signals of social exclusion, so the message your child receives when your eyes are glued to your smartphone is, "I am not available to you." That's an upsetting message for a child. Children are constantly checking in to see if their parents are paying attention, even if they don't need them right now. Not only are they checking to ensure that you're still available—hey, they might need you in a couple of minutes!—but they're also watching you monitor the world on their behalf. If your attention is captured by something, they look at it too, taking in the object of your attention (a chipmunk!) and your reaction ("How cute!") all at the same time. That's how children learn where and how to direct their attention, incidentally, via this process that child development experts call "shared gaze." If your gaze isn't available, those opportunities for learning aren't available either—to say nothing of the quiet reassurance that comes from knowing that mom or dad is on the case.

So, don't underestimate the power of your attention, and not just at times when your child explicitly needs you. A recent study found that 28 percent of parents and caregivers feel that it's okay to pull out your smartphone if your child is "safe and occupied"—an assumption that fails to acknowledge the impact of parental sensitivity and responsiveness even when a child appears to be busy playing, and that reflects a widespread undervaluing of the importance of parent-child interaction during less structured times like playtime. Family life researchers Brandon T. McDaniel and Sarah M. Coyne have, in fact, flagged this as an area worthy of future investigation: "whether play is perceived as less important than more task-oriented domains and therefore more permissible for technology use and interference." It appears that the answer is yes.

Giving your child the gift of your undivided attention helps that child feel valued. This is something I was talking to my friend Danielle about recently. She's been trying to be a little less connected to her smartphone when her two school-aged daughters are in the room. It all started when she unplugged for a few days over the holidays and then noticed the resulting impact on both herself and her kids. "It was freeing. I was calmer. I was able to just be," she recalls. She realized that she was giving her kids an important message when she made a conscious decision to ignore the beeps coming from her smartphone. The message was that her kids were more important than that other person who was trying to reach her. She was giving her kids the message that they were "the VIPs in the room."

Distracted parenting can lead to increased incidents of misbehaviour in children. You can't blame a kid for trying—and *trying hard*—to regain a parent's attention when it has wandered back to a smartphone screen. It's hardly surprising, then, that distracted parenting is also associated with an increase in child misbehaviour.

A 2017 study published in *Child Development* noted, in fact, "Even minor interruptions in parent-child interactions—even in fairly highly functioning families—are intricately linked with child behavior." It could be that parents of children who tend to act out are more likely to seek refuge in their phones, or it could be that the kids are acting out in an effort to divert their parents' attention from these attention-sucking devices. Or maybe it's a bit of both, because parents and kids affect one another's reactions in intricate and interconnected ways. But once things start spiralling downward, someone needs to break the cycle, and because you're the grown-up, that someone is you.

DISTRACTED PARENTING INCREASES THE LIKELIHOOD OF CHILD INJURY.

When parents aren't paying attention, kids are more likely to get injured, and increasingly, it's distracted parenting that's to blame. In fact, a 2014 study by Yale University economist Craig Palsson attributed "almost the entire [10 percent] increase in child injuries" in US children under the age of five between 2005 and 2012 to increased parental inattention related to increased smartphone use.

At the root of the problem is the fact that children are more likely to push the limits when mom or dad is distracted, as roughly three-quarters of parents *were* when a team of Long Island, New York, researchers observed them with their kids at local parks. To be fair, parents have always been distracted. Legend has it that Abraham Lincoln was notorious for pulling his young sons in a wagon while he was reading a book. Apparently, he continued to read and pull the wagon even after one of his kids tumbled out—at least that's the word from pediatrician Perri Klass, who chronicled the episode in a recent column for *The New York Times*. But even the most compelling and brilliantly written book is going to have a hard time competing with even a run-of-the-mill smartphone, at least when it comes to the ability to seize attention. Think about it: if books were this addictive, there would be countless public health education campaigns urging parents to "shut that book" and re-engage with their kids, and to date, I have yet to encounter that kind of campaign. My point here is that we're venturing into whole new territory with this smartphone thing, when it comes to both the allure and the impact of these devices.

As McDaniel noted in a recent article for the Institute for Family Studies blog, "Distraction with a device could potentially influence every aspect of parenting quality, leading you to be less in sync with your child's cues, to misinterpret your child's needs, to respond more harshly than necessary, and to respond much too long after the need arose." In other words, it doesn't make for great parenting.

And that's not even the entire picture.

DISTRACTED PARENTING MAKES PARENTING LESS ENJOYABLE.

This last piece of the distracted parenting puzzle isn't talked about as much as the other three pieces, but I think it's just as important to talk about. Because parenting is hard enough; we don't need to make it any harder.

Social psychologist Kostadin Kushlev first proposed this idea back in 2015, when he was a doctoral student at the University of British Columbia. In his doctoral thesis, he pointed out that distracted parenting could also mean being distracted from the very things that make parenting so enjoyable: the moments of connection with your child. "Parents who frequently take advantage of the digital activities provided by the powerful gadgets in their pockets may often be foregoing opportunities to harvest the fruits of joyful times with their children," he explained.

This makes perfect sense to me. After all, if your smartphone can cause you to become inattentionally blind to a unicycle-riding clown, couldn't it also cause you to miss out on much less obvious happenings, like that unspeakably cute thing your kid just did? Those are the moments that buoy our spirits, reminding us that parenting really *is* quite great. If we miss out on those times, we're missing out on the best stuff of parenting. (We'll be talking about how to get more of the good stuff, by the way, when we get to Chapter 6.)

How to Become a Less Distracted Parent

Looking for ways to sidestep all the guilt that can result from distracted parenting? Here are some strategies that are working for other parents and that could very well work for you too.

Be mindful in your use of technology. Have a purpose in mind each time you reach for your phone. Know why you're picking up your phone and what you intend to do with it as opposed to just mindlessly hopping from app to app. And be aware of your triggers. Understand when you're most vulnerable to succumbing to the temptation to zone out in front of that device, and have a plan for managing the underlying situation or emotion.

Pay attention to how you feel when you're using your phone. Make a note of which types of apps make you feel better and which ones leave you feeling worse, and then adjust your app usage accordingly.

Apply friction. One of the most effective strategies for cutting back on your tech usage is to simply make it harder and less convenient for you to use your devices—to apply friction to those habits, in other words.

Start by making your tech less appealing and less accessible. "My personal cure for being on the phone all the time is to have a really old phone that doesn't work particularly well," says Brian, the father of two school-aged boys. "Why would I want to stare at this thing? It doesn't do anything. And that's the whole point. When I'm sitting in front of my desktop computer, I'm constantly being dragged down Facebook wormholes and that's terrible enough. I don't need to take that with me anywhere beyond the basement, where my computer lives. I have a cheap old phone and it saves me."

Optimize your smartphone to make it work for—not against—you. The tech non-profit Time Well Spent recommends the following tips for reducing your smartphone use.

- Tweak your notifications to "allow notifications from people, not machines."

- Organize your apps so that only tools and apps for quick in-and-out tasks appear on the home screen of your device. They also suggest that you bury more time-sucking social media apps deep inside your device and that you force yourself to manually search for these apps using the search function on your device to retrieve them—an annoying and effective additional layer of friction.

- Invest in a stand-alone alarm clock so that there's no reason for your smartphone to ever find its way to your bedroom.

- Take advantage of apps and settings that can help you to get more sleep (by reducing blue light emissions at the wrong time of the day), improve your focus (by blocking access to certain apps and websites for certain periods of time or until you restart your device), and monitor your device use (so that you can learn about your use of technology and make smarter decisions on that basis).

At first, it may feel really uncomfortable to make these kinds of changes. After all, you're pushing yourself out of your tech comfort zone in order to try something new. You can ease some of that discomfort by committing to a temporary trial initially. Tell yourself that you're not necessarily going to make these changes forever; you're just trying them out for now (an hour, an afternoon, or an entire day). This will give you the opportunity to figure out what is—and isn't—going to work for you over the longer term and to tweak some of this advice to better meet your needs. You might decide, for example, that you still want to allow text notifications and phone calls from your nearest and dearest at times when you've unplugged from the rest of the world. Or you might decide to permanently remove certain apps from your phone. And then you might change your mind again. That's okay. That's how this process works.

Shake up other people's expectations. Change other people's expectations about being able to reach you instantly at any time of day or night. If you can reduce their expectations, you won't feel the same compulsion to be completely plugged in all the time.

My friend Lori found a creative way to ease the pressure she had been feeling to respond to emails the moment they arrived. She added a line to her email signature—and set up a corresponding auto-responder message—alerting her email contacts to her new rules of technological engagement: "Can we pretend we're living in a Jane Austen novel? I will read and appreciate your email, savor it, and think of you in the days to come, and respond to you when I have time to do so thoughtfully." I don't know about you, but I feel calmer just reading that message.

Focus on what you stand to gain as opposed to what you're giving up. You'll find it easier to stick with your goal to use your smartphone less often if you focus on what you hope to gain from working toward this goal as opposed to fixating on what you're giving up. "Our goals are usually framed in one of two ways," explains Caroline Webb in her book *How to Have a Good Day.* "Either they're about doing more of something good, or they're about doing less of something bad. A wide variety of research suggests that the first type (known as 'approach' goals) are better than the second ('avoidance' goals) at encouraging high performance." The idea here is to ditch the deprivation mindset. When you tell yourself that you're depriving yourself of your phone, you're likely to want your smartphone all the more. So, turn that thinking on its head by focusing on what you're *getting* by cutting back on smartphone use: a less distracted, more relaxed, and just plain happier you.

Talk to your partner and kids about this too. Make sure you and your partner are on the same page. Tech is a frequent cause of conflict in couple relationships and it can interfere with your ability to parent effectively as a team. So, you'll want to hammer out some ground rules together, perhaps starting with keeping mealtimes and bedtimes completely tech-free. While you're at it, commit to putting the smartphones away when you are enjoying one-on-one time as a couple. (According to a 2013 Harris Interactive survey, 9 percent of American adults admit to checking their smartphones during sex.)

Help your kids figure out how to make wise choices about the use of technology too. That means understanding what is and isn't effective in terms of controlling screen time in kids of various ages. Technology researcher Alexandra Samuel's survey of ten thousand North American parents revealed that attempts to deny kids screen time are likely to result in more problematic behaviours online as compared to the approach that she recommends: mentoring and guiding kids through the process of learning how to manage their own screen time. (More about this in Chapter 8.)

Work for change at the community level. Join the rising chorus of voices demanding that technology companies act with greater social responsibility—and that governments step in, if they don't. What we need to do, now that our initial love affair with technology is over, is to insist on our right to control technology, as opposed to allowing technology to control us. "If you use it wisely and you apply it appropriately, it can be an enormous resource," notes Nora Spinks, CEO of The Vanier Institute of the Family. "If it starts to control you and it causes you to disconnect or disengage—to become distant, unfocussed, or anxious—it can be a huge negative."

We need to steer clear of extreme black and white thinking when it comes to tech—the idea that tech is inherently bad or inherently good. It's obviously much more nuanced than that. As technology writer David Sax put it in a recent article for *The New York Times*, "We do not face a simple choice of digital or analog. That is the false logic of the binary code that computers are programmed with, which ignores the complexity of life in the real world. Instead, we are faced with a decision of how to strike the right balance between the two." And how to help our families to find that tech sweet spot too.

CHAPTER 4

The Truth about Parenting

Parenting has ended up being everything that I could have expected—and so much more. I expected it to be a full-time commitment, but I don't think I anticipated the full physical and emotional side of things.

—Jillian, mother of two teenagers and a preteen

So, is *parenting* just another word for misery?

Is modern parenting a three-ingredient casserole made up of equal parts anxiety, guilt, and feelings of being overwhelmed?

You could certainly be forgiven for reaching that conclusion (and not just because of the first three chapters of this book). If you google the phrase "parents are miserable," you get well over 23 million hits. The top hit? "'Anyone who wants to be a parent is insane': Miserable Dad Describes the Hell of Fatherhood in Viral Rant"—a 2016 article for the UK newspaper *The Telegraph*, reporting on a Reddit post by a father of four who argued that having children is "the worst hobby that anyone would ever think to have" and that he dreamed about emptying the family bank account and "moving thousands of miles away."

The messages we receive about the apparent misery of parenting are anything but subtle. As it turns out, they also happen to be less than accurate. Because here's the thing: despite rumours to the contrary, we parents are actually a reasonably content bunch. That's not to say that some of us don't enjoy parenting more than others, or that some of us don't derive greater meaning from it, or that some stages of parenting aren't more difficult than others. (We'll be getting into all that in a moment.) But there's simply not enough evidence to make the case that parents are universally miserable, not when you really start scrutinizing the evidence—which is what we're about to do.

Show Me the Misery . . .

Think back to that time in your life when you first announced your intention to become a parent. Odds are at least one person (and perhaps an entire roomful of people) felt compelled to point out that you were kind of actually ruining your life. "You'll never sleep again!" "Your sex life is over!" "You're going to be broke!" Then, perhaps in response to the inevitable shell-shocked look on your face, they immediately began to backtrack, wrapping their initial dire warnings in a blanket of euphemisms designed to reassure you that it was, of course, going to be so worth it. Sure, you might end up being an exhausted, sex-deprived, broke shadow of your former self, but at least you'll get to experience one of life's greatest blessings: having kids.

As it turns out, those friends (trust me, I'm using the term loosely) weren't just a bit mean-spirited in serving up all of those dire warnings. They also were more than a little misinformed. Yes, your life satisfaction tends to nosedive a little when you first become a parent, but it's generally little more than a temporary blip—a small yet jarring pothole in the first leg of the marathon road trip that is parenting. As a group of researchers noted in a 2013 article published in the *Journal of Family Psychology*,

"Only a small subset of parents experienced sustained declines in happiness in the four years following the arrival of their first child." Another small group actually expressed increased life satisfaction. And the vast majority of parents? Once they had a chance to regain their bearings after that initial road bump, life pretty much coasted along as per usual. They were just as satisfied with their lives post-parenthood as they'd been back in their pre-kid days.

So, if misery is, at most, the experience of a "small subset" of parents, why is there such a tendency to treat it as the defining experience of parenthood? And why is the "parents are miserable" narrative the dominant one in the mainstream media?

As it turns out, many of the earliest studies proclaiming the supposed misery of parents suffered from a fundamental methodological flaw. Instead of comparing apples to apples, they had compared apples to oranges—parents to non-parents. Instead of specifically drilling down to consider, for example, what types of daily events were most meaningful for specific groups of people like parents, they considered happiness levels across a broad group of people made up of both parents and non-parents. This means that they overlooked a lot of the joy and meaning to be found in the lives of parents. It was only when a subsequent wave of studies began to drill down to this additional layer—to focus on that specific subgroup of people called parents and to consider how their lives were impacted, for better and for worse, by the experience of becoming a parent—that some of the truly noteworthy findings began to emerge.

One of those findings ended up being a complete game-changer for anyone who had swallowed the idea of parental misery. There's now a large and growing body of evidence to show that what actually makes parents happiest is spending time with their kids. As psychologist S. Katherine Nelson and her co-authors put it in a groundbreaking article titled "In Defense of Parenthood: Children Are Associated with More Joy than Misery," published in *Psychological Science* in 2013: "Taking care of children provides parents with more happiness, on average, than their other day-to-day activities." Far from being the source of misery, the time spent with our kids is actually the good stuff in our lives. Part of that "good stuff" appears to stem from the increased sense of meaning that becoming someone's parent can provide. "Contrary to previous reports, parents (and especially fathers) report relatively higher levels of happiness, positive emotion, and meaning in life than do nonparents," the authors noted.

Here's another finding that challenges a lot of the current media hysteria about the supposed hell that is child-centric parenting: the parents who are most invested in their kids also happen to derive the greatest benefits from being a parent. Another groundbreaking study, titled "Parents Reap What They Sow: Child-Centrism and Parental Well-Being," published the same year in *Social Psychological & Personality Science*, made the case that maximizing your child's well-being is, in fact, a highly effective way of maximizing your own well-being. "Contrary to popular belief, more child-centric parents reported deriving more happiness and meaning from parenthood," the researchers noted. "Greater child-centrism was associated with the experience of greater positive affect, less negative affect, and greater meaning in life when engaged in child-care activities. This link between child-centrism and well-being stands in contrast to recent arguments about the pitfalls of overinvestment in children, while dovetailing with a growing body of evidence that personal well-being is associated with investing in others rather than oneself."

The authors made a point of distinguishing between true child-centrism (parenting with your child's best interests in mind) and other much-talked about and much-debated parenting styles, like helicopter parenting (which implies being overprotective and overly involved), being a Tiger Mom (which refers to Amy Chua's bestselling book *Battle Hymn of the Tiger Mother* and implies a strong emphasis on child achievement) or the parenting style that sociologist Annette Lareau dubbed "concerted cultivation" (which involves treating your child like a self-improvement project and doing everything you can to give that child the edge over his or her peers).

The idea that investing heavily in your child could actually be *mental-health enhancing* (as opposed to *mental-health depleting*) was echoed by Florida State University researchers Justine Gunderson and Anne E. Barrett in an equally noteworthy 2015 study published in *The Journal of Family Issues*: "Higher investments of thought and effort into children are associated with better self-rated mental health. This finding may suggest that some of the activities requiring substantial energy give mothers a feeling of satisfaction with their efforts to ensure their children's proper development. . . . Putting increased thought and effort into children may be tied to better parent-child relationships and parental satisfaction, known predictors of increased psychological well-being among parents."

Another factor at play in determining the relative happiness or unhappiness of parents is the issue of choice—whether you made a conscious decision to become a parent and whether that decision was made based on a careful weighing of the pros and cons. That, in a nutshell, is what a 2014 study published in the *Proceedings of the National Academy of Sciences* contributed to the parental-misery conversation. That particular group of researchers reported that parents who make a conscious decision to become parents tend to weigh the pros and cons of going this route and then conclude that they'll be better off with children than without, and that their experiences tend to bear this out. That's not to say that everything is perfect, mind you. As the researchers noted, parents experience "more daily joy and more daily stress" than non-parents. But because they made a conscious decision to sign up for this particular adventure—and they did so with at least a reasonable understanding of what it was they were signing themselves up for—they were willing to accept *both* flavours of "more."

Isn't that pretty much the defining characteristic of parenting, the fact that it's about so much "more"? It's more stressful and exhausting than we might have bargained for on the really bad days, but also so much more joyful than we could have ever imagined possible.

There's No Such Thing as a One-Size-Fits-All Parenting Experience

Now let's drill down a little further by looking at who is most—and least—likely to be reaping the rewards of parenting and why. Because, despite rumours to the contrary, parenting is anything but a one-size-fits-all experience. Some parents enjoy parenting more than others, or derive greater meaning from it, or both. Here's what you need to know.

DADS ENJOY PARENTHOOD MORE.
You know those happy parents we've been talking about? It turns out that a lot of those happy (or at least happier) parents happen to be dads.

This next part of the chapter is going to make for somewhat annoying reading, particularly if you happen to be a non-dad. But I hope you'll slog through it regardless. There's some important stuff here about stubborn gender norms that make life harder for moms and dads alike—which, I should add, means any person of any gender who happens to step into either of those prepackaged roles.

If you've always had a nagging suspicion that being a dad tends to be more fun than being a mom, well, it turns out that science is on your side. There's a solid body of evidence to make the case that mothers report "less happiness, more stress, and greater fatigue" during the time they spend with children than fathers do, as Cornell University's Kelly Musick reported in a 2016 study published in the *American Sociological Review.* She then identified a few key factors that help to explain why this is the case.

For starters, the job description for "father" is a whole lot more manageable than the job description for "mother." There are more flexible and more realistic models of what it means to be "a good dad" as compared to "a good mom." As Musick and her co-authors explain, "Multiple models of good fathering have emerged emphasizing to varying degrees fathers' contributions as breadwinners and caretakers. The existence of multiple acceptable models may make fathers less susceptible to role strain and difficult-to-meet social expectations and leave more room for enjoyment. With one acceptable good mother model—committed, ever-available, deeply involved—mothers may more consistently derive meaning from parenting than fathers, but they may also experience more stress." As Helen Hayward noted in a recent essay for *Aeon*, "It's caring about the daily necessities—the circus of childhood—that is, for so many mothers, both fantastically demanding and weirdly rewarding."

Then there's the fact that mothers tend to spend more of their time with their kids taking care of the hands-on, hard work of parenting, freeing dads up to enjoy more of the fun stuff. Musick and her co-authors note, "Women do more of the day-to-day, time-inflexible basic care and management tasks related to childcare, and they spend a smaller share of their overall minutes with children in play." Every time I read that, I can't help but think of a classic Nancy White song lyric—the one about mommies being "for maintenance" and daddies "for fun."

Feeling discouraged by the state of the world when it comes to parental gender equality? I hate to break it to you, but there's still more bad news to come. There are at least a couple of other noteworthy factors at play. Like the fact that mothers have less leisure time than fathers do—roughly half an hour less per day on average. To make matters worse, they *get less* out of that leisure time. Yes, it's a double whammy. Women get less of it *and* it's less restorative. Not only are women less likely to benefit from reduced feelings of time stress—that ever-present feeling of being rushed—but they're also more likely to spend their leisure time in the company of children or to have family-related tasks "contaminate" (hey, that's the researchers' term, not mine) their supposed leisure time. You know how it goes: you're enjoying a rare lunch out with a friend when one of your kids texts you in a panic to say that she needs you to pick up such-and-such for her science fair project, and she needs it *right now.*

But wait, it gets worse! Mothers also tend to fall short on the sleep front. While mothers and fathers tend to clock comparable numbers of total hours of sleep, moms are less likely to enjoy high-quality, uninterrupted sleep as compared to dads. It could be a by-product of hormones: prenatal, postpartum, perimenopausal—take your pick! It could be because they're more likely to be woken in the night by a child requiring care. Or it could be that they're more likely to wake up in the middle of the night and have a hard time getting back to sleep, perhaps because their brain is hard at work planning and organizing the family's activities for the next day—for example, remembering that stray field-trip permission slip that needs to be tracked down (is it in a backpack or under a bed?), signed and returned the next day. Is there any mother on the planet who hasn't experienced that kind of middle-of-the-night epiphany with the accompanying waves of where-the-hell-is-that-thing-anyway panic?

All mothers feel this pressure to hold it all together and to keep everything on track. It's not just those mothers who buy into the concept of "concerted cultivation," the term that sociologist Annette Lareau used to describe an intensive mothering style in which some middle- and upper-income mothers treat their children as projects to be perfected. As Angie Henderson, Sandra Harmon, and Harmony Newman, three sociologists from the University of Northern Colorado, noted in a 2016 article for the journal *Sex Roles,* sky-high standards are pretty much the backdrop of modern motherhood. As Henderson explained in a related blog post, "It's not any one choice that women make that compounds the pressure to be perfect; instead, it is all around us. It is part of the modern physique of motherhood." And that, in turn, helps to explain why motherhood has become increasingly labour-intensive in recent decades. According to statistics cited by Suniya S. Luthar and Lucia Ciciolla in a 2015 article for *Developmental Psychology*, between 1993 and 2008, college-educated mothers went from spending 12 hours to spending 20.5 hours a week on parenting-related tasks, while less-educated mothers went from spending 10.5 hours a week to spending 16 hours a week. To be fair, dads also began to invest more time and energy into parenting over this same period of time, more than doubling their parental invest-ment from 4.2 hours per week to 9.7 hours per week.

There's a bit more good news on the whole maternal versus paternal well-being front. First of all, according to Musick and her co-authors, the overall differences are relatively small—it's a gap as opposed to a gulf. Second, these differences "can be accounted for by differences in the activities that mothers and fathers engage in with children, whether other adults are pres-ent, and the quality of their sleep and leisure"—aspects that we actually have some hope of being able to change. (There will be more on this in upcoming chapters.)

SOME STAGES OF PARENTING ARE EASIER AND MORE
ENJOYABLE THAN OTHERS.

It turns out that your gut instincts were right: certain stages of parenting *are* tougher than others. Of course, the mere fact that kids are constantly changing is part of what makes parenting such a challenge. It's the ultimate personal-growth opportunity, one that requires you to constantly switch strategies to adapt to your child's ever-changing needs.

Becoming a parent is something that happens in an instant, while parenting is a skill that you practise and develop over time. And it's a lot harder than it looks—much more complicated than you might have anticipated back in your pre-kid days. Children are constantly leapfrogging from one developmental stage to the next, and the lessons that you learned while parenting your first-born might not apply to your next child at all.

Your child is always changing, which means that the parenting challenge that you're dealing with is always changing too. Just when you start to feel like you finally understand the rules of the game, your child decides it's time to rewrite all the rules. This is something Margaret, the mother of three school-aged children, thinks about a lot. She often reflects back upon a conversation she had when she was a brand-new parent. She was chatting with the father of a slightly older child when that father said something that struck her as particularly wise. He said, "The thing is, kids are constantly changing. As soon as you figure out where they are at and what they need from you, everything changes. You have to rewrite the parenting script again. And I feel like that's going to be the journey forever."

That journey begins when you're a brand-new parent. Your life changes dramatically overnight. Rebecca still recalls the intensity of the experience a full decade after her son's arrival. "It's both amazing and also like you've been hit by a truck," she explains. "On the one hand, you're like, 'I made a human being.' And then, on the other hand, you're like, 'This human being needs me twenty-four hours a day for everything.'" Any illusions that you might have had about not allowing parenthood to change your life end up being shattered fairly quickly, adds Brian, the father of two school-aged boys: "It's like there's a war on and the baby is your commanding officer. You might have ten minutes or you might have an hour to do something. You just don't know."

As the baby stage rolls into the toddler and preschool years, we find ourselves stumbling upon a parenting sweet spot. We're no longer feeling flattened by the round-the-clock demands of caring for a young baby. Instead, we're focused on falling head over heels in love with the impossibly cute and endlessly curious tot who has replaced that baby. This is the most enjoyable stage of parenthood, the stage at which we're most likely to feel happy, capable, and confident in our own parenting abilities. As a group of researchers led by sociologist Kei M. Nomaguchi of

Bowling Green State University in Ohio back in 2012 concluded, "Contrary to the common image that parents are drained by the intense daily routines of caring for young children, this study shows that parents are not worse off, or even better in some measures of psychological well-being, than parents with school-age or adolescent children, because of higher satisfaction they experience with the relationships with little ones."

That's not to say that the early years are without their challenges, of course. Not only do younger children require a lot more hands-on help than older and more self-sufficient kids, but parents of younger kids tend to experience fairly high levels of work-life conflict. It's a parenting life-stage issue—something that we talked about at length in Chapter 2. After you weather that particular batch of challenges, different ones await you in the land of school-aged children—increased behavioural issues plus the need to somehow reconcile the differing lengths of a typical school day and workday—and adolescents—a renewed drive for independence plus a brain that's increasingly primed for social comparison and risk-taking.

This has certainly been Margaret's experience. The physical care work definitely eases up over time, she notes, and "life is more civilized and you're more rested." But the emotional care work ramps up considerably. "It's easier for me as a human being to have older kids, but it's getting harder from a parenting perspective," she explains. Elaine, the mother of two teenage girls, echoes those sentiments. "It doesn't actually get easier as the kids get older. Yes, it's less physical, but there's a lot more worry when they go out on their own and learn to drive and start to have their own successes and failures separate from the family. We brought these girls into the world and we want them to be happy and healthy," she explains.

The best way to deal with the ever-shifting sands of parenting is to try to understand what's going on with your child at any given time. Know what's happening with him developmentally and what that means in terms of your own development as a parent (something we'll be talking more about in Chapter 10). "You're raising these small people into adults," says Katie, the mother of three school-aged boys. "But you're learning so much about yourself at the same time."

SOME KIDS ARE EASIER TO PARENT THAN OTHERS.
Just as there's no such thing as a one-size-fits-all parenting experience, there's no such thing as a one-size-fits-all kid. Every child is unique, which means that every parent-child relationship is unique too. "I think at the outset, I really did expect parenting to be a lot more cookie cutter than it was. I remember thinking, 'I'll read all these books and they'll tell me everything I need to know,'" says Alexa, the mother of a teen and a preteen. "And then the reality sunk in: every child is unique, so there isn't a manual you can just read and follow."

It's also a simple (yet frequently ignored) parenting fact of life that some kids are a bit more challenging to parent than others. Rebecca, the mother of a preteen with mental illness, thinks it's important to acknowledge that and talk about that: "I always joke about this by saying, 'They didn't talk about this in prenatal class' when I'm laying bare about my kid's struggles. Because no one expects to have a kid who struggles." Melissa, the mother of a teenager and a young adult who have each experienced mental-health struggles, agrees: "Not all children who struggle have parents who didn't read the right parenting books. Some kids are just more complicated. Period."

It's also important to acknowledge that children play an important role in their own development. Different kids elicit different parenting responses. Instead of talking about the supposedly all-important role that parents play in shaping their children— something that brings to mind an image of a child as a blob of clay on a potter's wheel, with parenting being the force that is moulding and shaping that child—scientists have shifted to emphasizing the fact that parents and children shape one another in intricate and interrelated ways. It's a bidirectional effect. Julia has already picked up on this, just eighteen months into parenting: "What I've learned is that, as parents, we have a ton of influence and a big responsibility to try to shape our kids into great human beings, but a lot of who they are is there from a really early age."

It's not a matter of nature versus nurture; it's actually nature *and* nurture. And there's growing evidence that environment— the so-called nurture piece of the puzzle—may have a greater impact on some children than others. Michael Pluess of Queen Mary University of London has created a tool to classify children on the basis of how much or how little they are affected by parenting. According to Pluess:

- Thirty percent of kids are "orchids"—which means that they're highly sensitive to their environment (both positive and negative parenting). Plant them and they'll thrive under just the right growing conditions.

- Thirty percent of kids are "dandelions"—which means they're highly adaptable and resilient and relatively unaffected by the parenting environment. Plant them and they'll thrive pretty much anywhere.

- Forty percent of kids are "tulips"—which means they fall somewhere in the middle. They're neither as sensitive as orchids nor as hardy and adaptable as dandelions. Plant them and they'll thrive under some but not all conditions.

The metaphor is a bit clunky, I know, and the tool still needs to be evaluated further, but I shared it with you for a reason: it's useful in illustrating a related fact—that fact being that siblings growing up in the very same household can be affected in very different ways by pretty much the same parenting. You'll notice that I said "pretty much the same parenting" as opposed to "identical parenting." That's because every child is unique and so every parent-child relationship is unique. Not even siblings share the same experience of how they are parented.

Understanding this simple yet important fact can help you to take parenting a little less personally. It isn't all about you; it's also about your child. Yep, we're talking bidirectionality again. We'll be returning to this idea in Chapter 10, when we talk parenting strategies, but for now, you might just want to note it and acknowledge the fact that some kids do make parenting a little more challenging. When Johanna, the mother of two school-aged kids, has been pushed to the limit by one of her kids, she's been known to say to them, "You truly made me parent tonight. I really had to parent a lot!"

SOMETIMES LIFE KEEPS LOBBING THE CURVEBALLS.
Just as you can end up with a kid who is a bit more of a challenge than you bargained for, you can find yourself dealing with circumstances that aren't at all like what you'd imagined your life would be. "Life does not present us with ideal circumstances, and most of our decisions aren't decisions at all. They're compromises," says Loren, a mother of two young adults and the grandmother of two young children, who has dealt with her fair share of curveballs along the way, including becoming a single parent and dealing with a child's mental-health crisis.

Sometimes, it's not a matter of dealing with a single curveball—or even a couple of curveballs. At times, it can feel like they're being lobbed at you relentlessly and that they're coming from every possible direction at once. That's how Lynn, the mother of a twenty-three-month-old toddler, feels when she looks back on the past few years of her life—like she's been dodging a constant barrage of curveballs. "Parenting has been very hard on us," she explains. "My pregnancy was healthy but gruelling, miserable, and exhausting. Jonathan was slow to figure out how to be a supportive partner to a pregnant woman and an active participant in preparing for parenthood. Complications following the birth resulted in a series of confusing and worrisome visits to an out-of-town children's hospital. When our daughter was three months old, my mother-in-law fell into a state of chronic illness that required an extremely high level of ongoing care, often provided in our home. I have a complex relationship with my parents, which means that we have limited support from family." Add to that the fact that the couple also faced significant financial pressures, as well as his and her bouts of anxiety and depression, and you can see why she's feeling so depleted: "It feels like I've been in survival mode for nearly three years, getting by day by day."

Katie can relate to those feelings. There have been times when she's felt like she was hitting the emotional wall: "I expected it to be hard, but I don't think I expected it to be so emotionally draining. You know you're going to be tired. You know you're going to be broke. You know you're not going to have as much time with your partner. But you kind of just know those things intellectually, which is different from feeling how much it actually drains you. . . . Before I became a parent, I don't think I even understood the meaning of 'emotionally depleted.'"

What makes it harder, according to Katie, is the fact that no one really talks about just how hard it is. A lot of conversations about the hard work of parenting just skate across the surface of things. "It's trendy on social media to talk about how hard it is. But simply sharing memes that talk about surviving on wine and chocolate is about the extent of the conversation. The serious hard stuff isn't there. It's really superficial. It's not authentic. Even worse, it's not authentic and it's supposed to feel authentic, which makes it doubly inauthentic," she says, clearly frustrated. We're not talking about the things that really matter: "Like how hard it is to find the time to maintain your relationship as a couple during the really hands-on parenting years." (We'll be having that conversation in Chapter 9.)

Most of us are okay with the fact that parenting is hard work because we recognize that it's good work. It's important work.

It's the kind of work that gives life meaning. There's a solid body of research to back that up—research that we've been touching upon throughout this chapter. It's pretty clear that what we enjoy most about parenting is actually spending time with our kids. It's more meaningful than anything else we do, even though it also happens to be incredibly hard work. "Parents find caring for their children to be much more exhausting than the work they do for pay. At the same time, parents find much more meaning in the time they spend with their children than in the time they spend at work," concluded a 2013 Pew Research study.

So, it's not our kids who drag us down. It's the other stuff happening in our lives that robs us of our joy, as the authors of a 2014 *Psychological Bulletin* study noted: "We propose that parents are unhappy to the extent that they encounter greater negative emotions, magnified financial problems, more sleep disturbances, and troubled marriages. By contrast, when parents experience greater meaning in life, satisfaction of their basic needs, greater positive emotions, and enhanced social roles, they are met with happiness and joy."

In the next part of the chapter, we're going to talk about what happens when you get too little of the good stuff and too much of the bad stuff. It's called parent burnout.

Parent Burnout

In recent years, a group of researchers in Belgium have been researching parent burnout as a phenomenon separate and distinct from other types of burnout, like work-related burnout. Sure, it has some things in common with other types of burnout, like the fact you're feeling fried. But, they argued, it's a phenomenon that's worthy of study in its own right because of the far-reaching implications for the parent-child relationship.

The researchers started out by explaining what they were talking about when they said "parent burnout." In a 2017 article for the *Journal of Child and Family Studies*, they defined "parent burnout" as "a specific syndrome resulting from enduring exposure to chronic parenting stress. It encompasses three dimensions: an overwhelming exhaustion related to one's parental role, an emotional distancing with one's children, and a sense of ineffectiveness in one's parental role." In a related study, they pointed out that it's a problem for roughly one in eight parents.

Wondering what parent burnout actually looks like? The impact can be devastating. You feel tired and emotionally drained, you're less involved with your kids—sure, you feed them and make sure they have clean clothes to wear, but you simply don't have anything left to give them emotionally—and because you're so depleted, you're unable to deal with parenting challenges calmly and effectively. You overreact or underreact or both.

Amanda knows what it feels like to struggle with parent burnout. She struggled with it for a very long time. These days, she's the single parent of three children. She's pretty much on her own when it comes to family support. Her ex-husband lives across the country. Even when they were together, he was away a lot—he's in the military—so long before she officially became a single parent, she was already playing the part.

Carrying a heavy load for a prolonged period of time eventually took its toll. "The first time I really experienced it was when my ex-husband was in Afghanistan and I had two young children, one of whom was really high needs. It would get to be bedtime and I just couldn't deal with them anymore. I would have to close their door and just walk away because I knew that otherwise, somebody was going to get hurt. I couldn't control my emotions. I was just so incredibly angry. And so incredibly sad. I would cry for like an hour. And I couldn't focus on anything—not even the things I liked to do, like knitting or sewing or watching a show. I would just stare into space. I felt like I had ceased to exist as a person."

Looking back, she can now see why things started to go wrong. Her entire identity had become wrapped up in the task of caring for her two young children. "I was putting so much pressure on myself—pressure to have every day be full—making sure that we made it to play group and that the kids were taking all these different kinds of classes. And, on top of that, I was trying to keep my house clean, and make food from scratch, and shop at the farmer's market." These were all noble endeavours, to be sure, but it was a pretty big load to be carrying on her own.

She recognized the signs of burnout and tried to do the right thing in terms of reaching out for support. But the people whom she turned to for help repeatedly let her down: "I asked for family to come and help, and nobody came. I went to the social work team at the base and I tried to get some extra emergency child-care, and that request was turned down." In the end, what allowed her to weather that initial crisis was the support she received from another mom—a mom who was struggling with postpartum depression and having an equally tough time. The two of them became a powerful support system for one another. They would get together with their kids twice a week, every Wednesday and Friday: "We just let the kids play and we'd order pizza or takeout, taking turns paying for it. That's how I dealt with the burnout at that time."

The next time burnout struck, it was a few years later. By that time, her marriage had ended and she had moved across the country with three young children, but her old enemy burnout managed to track her down. She was becoming physically depleted, she wasn't eating, and she was feeling completely overwhelmed: "It felt like a huge problem that would never go away. I remember thinking to myself that this was just the way it was going to be. Every day, I would wake up with the very same goal: to somehow make it through to bedtime." Over time, she began to realize that the situation was becoming untenable. What jolted her into taking action was the creeping realization that, as a single parent, she simply couldn't afford to become completely depleted. If something were to happen to her, who would take care of the kids?

She decided that she needed to spend money—money that she really couldn't afford to spend—to pay someone to help her get through the dinner hour with her kids. That person made dinner for the family and ran interference during mealtime so that Amanda could actually sit down and eat a meal from start to finish, something she hadn't been able to do for a very long time. "That really helped," Amanda recalls. In fact, it was a turning point for her. Within a couple of months, she started to feel better physically, which, in turn, shifted things mentally. "I was able to start making decisions that were good for me. I began to see that choosing to prioritize myself—to do something that brought me joy—was actually making things better for me and the kids." It didn't have to be something big. In fact, more often than not, it was something little, she recalls: "Buying the nice three-dollar chocolate bar and having some of that after the kids were in bed. Holding off on washing the dishes so I had time to watch a show on Netflix or call a friend or do something that was just for me." Her best advice to other parents who are struggling with parent burnout? Look for opportunities to join forces with other parents who are facing similar struggles—"We've created a community that feels very much like family"—and ditch the self-blame: "You're not doing it wrong. You're just massively overloaded."

Wondering if you're at risk of parent burnout? The group of Belgian researchers that I referred to earlier has identified a number of factors that increase the risk of parental burnout. Basically, those risk factors amount to two things:

- *Inadequate resources.* You're dealing with a greater demand on your time, energy, or budget than what you're capable of meeting with the resources you have access to right now. That could mean any number of things. Maybe you're a single parent. Maybe you have a child with special needs or a chronic health condition or disability. Maybe you're dealing with all kinds of additional stresses: work-related worries, financial difficulties, or relationship problems, for example, or maybe all of the above.

- *Sky-high expectations.* "Very high parental standards" is how the researchers phrased it, which are likely the result of personality (some of us are more prone to perfectionism than others) or some sort of high-achievement pattern carried over from childhood (more about this in Chapter 5). "It is the most deeply invested and most perfectionistic parents who run the greatest risk of developing burnout, as they inevitably come to realize just how unattainable their goals are and how many obstacles lie in their path."

Minimizing your risk of burnout (or dealing with existing burnout) means either increasing your resources or reducing the load that you're carrying. It might mean looking for other people who are willing to share the load, or it might mean letting some things go, at least for now. And it might mean learning how to steer clear of perfectionist thinking and embrace much healthier and more realistic ideas about what it means to be a good parent. (You'll find that discussion in Chapters 6 and 7.)

By now, my answer to the question "Does parenting actually have to be this hard?", which I first posed in the introduction to this book, should be pretty clear. Parenting will always be hard work, but it doesn't have to be this hard. And this, in a nutshell, is what the rest of the book is about: how to get more of the good stuff of parenting and less of the stuff that drags you down.

In Chapters 6 through 8, we'll be talking about what you can do to increase your enjoyment of parenting; decrease anxiety, guilt, and feelings of being overwhelmed; and become the happiest, healthiest possible you. In Chapters 9 and 10, we'll be zeroing in on parenting strategies that work for you and your kids. Then finally, in Chapter 11, we'll be talking about one of the most powerful ways to lighten your load as a parent—by tapping into support from your "parenting village."

CHAPTER 5

The Thinking Part
of Parenting

Imagine your life as a piece of string. Along the string are a series of knots, with each knot representing a decade of your life. The time you have for parenting a child is this tiny space between two knots.

—Janette, mother of three young children

It's easy to lose sight of the fact that parenting is an extremely limited engagement—just a couple of knots on a string. There are times when the clock appears to be moving impossibly slowly or even spinning backwards some days. Margaret remembers experiencing this slowing down of time back when she was a brand-new mother: "People kept talking about how 'the days go slow but the years go fast,' but it all felt long to me." And yet, while it feels long, the most hands-on years of parenting aren't very long: less than two decades, or roughly a quarter of your life.

This chapter is all about making the most of this time and looking forward to what comes next. It's about allowing yourself to be guided by your hopes and dreams for yourself and your child, both now and in decades to come. Because parenting is forever, and how you respond to the challenges today will help to determine what forever looks like for you and your kids. It's also about the thinking part of parenting: learning how to make more conscious and deliberate parenting choices as opposed to parenting on autopilot, and regularly visiting the place of calm that makes this kind of deep thinking possible.

Parenting with Your Hopes and Dreams in Mind

Zen Buddhist monk Shunryu Suzuki Roshi once said, "The most important thing is to find out what is the most important thing." A powerful way to drill down and discover what exactly the "most important thing" might be for you is to imagine yourself in conversation with your "future self"—you at some point in the future. You might, for example, imagine your future self hosting a family reunion, surrounded by your future kids and your future grandchildren. This is the kind of scene that always comes to mind for me when I engage in this kind of mental time travel (which I do on a fairly regular basis, by the way). I'm pretty sure this particular scene was inspired by the final scene in the cult classic movie *Raising Arizona*, where we see an older couple surrounded by their children and their grandchildren in a place "where all parents are strong and wise and capable, and all children are happy and beloved." Hey, it works for me . . .

So, what are the advantages of connecting with your future self, or more specifically, your future parenting self? Connecting with your hopes and dreams for the future encourages you to make more conscious and deliberate parenting decisions in the here and now. This not only increases the likelihood that you'll actually arrive at that desired destination—that destination being "future happy you"—but it also encourages parenting choices that can significantly improve your quality of life, starting right now. As happiness researchers Kristin Layous, S. Katherine Nelson, and Sonja Lyubomirsky reported back in 2012, the mere act of writing about your "ideal future selves" boosts your mood, increases your sense of optimism, and improves your overall life-satisfaction and well-being. "Many people express a desire to be happy, but often do not pause their busy lives to contemplate what they truly want out of life or to engage in activities and experiences that bring them joy or contentment," they wrote.

Connecting with your future self encourages you to do this deeper thinking and to reap the corresponding dividends, both now and in the future. It's an approach that seems to be working well for Katie, the mother of three school-aged boys. She took a slightly different tack in connecting with her future self. Rather than writing to or about her future self, she created a collage of images—a vision board—to express that vision. She explains, "So much of what makes me happy and fulfilled is my family. So, at the centre of my vision board is a family photo, along with words that capture what I want for my family—words like 'connected' and 'laughs a lot.' Then there are other things that are just about me—things I'd like to try or to learn how to do. There's a picture of a stand-up paddleboard. And there's a picture of a woman doing a pull-up."

Creating this vision board hasn't merely proven to be a source of motivation for herself personally. It has also sparked important conversations within the family about the importance of having hopes and dreams and about setting and pursuing goals. Katie says these conversations have clearly had an impact on her kids: "When I finally did get a paddleboard, which was a while after I made the vision board, my one son remembered. He said, 'Now you can take that off your vision board!'" She hopes that her sons are picking up other important messages from the vision board too: "There's a picture of our family right in the middle of it. I hope they understand what that means"—that they are at the heart of her hopes and dreams for the future.

Visualization can be a powerful way to connect with your future self whether you create a physical vision board, like Katie did, or you simply choose to create those kinds of pictures inside your own head. As positive psychology researcher Barbara L. Fredrickson explains in her book *Positivity*, "Visualization has been shown to activate the same brain areas as actually carrying out those visualization actions." It also helps to connect the dots between present and future: "Visualization . . . gives you insight into how your everyday goals and motives fit into your dreams about your future." What you're creating is a road map to that future.

As you begin to create that road map, you might want to think about the kind of parent you want to be, the kind of family you want to be, and the kind of child you want to give to the future. That way, you can parent with that big picture in mind.

THE KIND OF PARENT YOU WANT TO BE

This is something that Kerri thinks about a lot—something that she's been mulling over for most of the past three decades, in fact. Not only is Kerri the mother of seven biological children who range in age from fourteen through twenty-seven, but she's also fostered an additional sixteen children along the way. So, parenting has been very much top of mind for her for a very long time.

Keeping her big-picture parenting goals in mind has been a key strategy for her over the years. It's what allows her to stay calm—or at least calmer—in the heat of the moment. Reminding herself what she's working toward over the longer term allows her to resist the temptation to resort to an easier but less effective parenting quick-fix. Sometimes, it's simply a matter of asking herself one simple yet all-important question that instantly transports her to the future: "Am I going to regret this ten or twenty years from now when we're all talking about it around the kitchen table?"

It's all about pausing long enough to consider what you want your children to take from their childhood, and how you want them to remember you in particular. When they describe you to friends and colleagues in years to come, what do you hope they'll say about you? What do you want them to say about you (gulp) at your funeral? Will they give you credit for having any of the so-called "eulogy virtues"? David Brooks coined this term in a 2015 column for *The New York Times*, noting that while "the résumé virtues are the skills you bring to the marketplace . . . the eulogy virtues are the ones that are talked about at your funeral—whether you were kind, brave, honest or faithful. Were you capable of deep love?"

The Kind of Family You Want to Be

No one manages to make it through childhood completely unscathed; life happens, and you need a safe place to land. For many of the parents I interviewed for this book, family means being that safe place.

Mireille, the mother of three boys (two teens and a preteen) explains, "You're going to fall and it's going to hurt. You're going to lose or break your toys. You're going to have a fight with your friends. You might not pass all of your classes. A lot of things are going to suck. But it's easier if you have a good support system: parents who are there for you when these things happen." Katie, the mother of three school-aged boys, echoes those sentiments: "I want them to be happy, whatever that means to them. And I want them to feel confident enough to do whatever it is that makes them happy. I want them to know that they will always have a safe place here, with our family, but that they are also free to go wherever they want to go. Isn't that what all parents want for their kids?"

Your Hopes and Dreams for Your Child

Parenting also involves thinking about your hopes and dreams for your child—the kind of person you hope she'll grow up to be and what she'll bring to the world—because the future is waiting for your kid. It also means being mindful of where your hopes and dreams end and your child's own hopes and dreams begin, and finding ways to honour that simple yet all-important fact.

For Johanna, the past few years have been all about figuring out how to support a child on that journey of self-determination. She is the mother of two school-aged children, including a daughter, now seven, who recently made the social transition to live as a girl, a decision which, according to Johanna, "surprised absolutely no one."

"I never thought I'd be dealing with a transgender child. And then all of a sudden it was, 'What do you mean you want to wear that pink shirt?' 'What do you mean you want sparkles?' And this was starting at the age of two or three." Johanna quickly realized that, given what could ultimately be at stake, the best way to proceed was to simply love and support her daughter. That hasn't magically erased all the worry. "I worry about Rosalina and her struggles in the years ahead. I'm not looking forward to her coming to the realization that things will maybe be a whole lot easier and less complicated for her brother," she explains. But her hopes for her two children are the same: "I pray that they are both embraced by the world for who they are and what they have to contribute." She also hopes that they will, in turn, be accepting of others: "I want them to be kind and compassionate—to grow up being tolerant and embracing all the things that make people different and special."

Wrapping her head around the idea of difference has also been key for Laurie, who is now the mother of two grown children. She had to figure out a way to be both realistic and encouraging in helping her daughter, Holly, who was born with an underdeveloped left leg and was fitted with a series of prosthetic legs starting just before her first birthday, to envision a life for herself. She says, "There is a balance between telling a child with a disability that they can do and be anything and educating them about the rights and supports they have as a disabled person. It feels like contradictory advice." Ultimately, she came to the realization that we all have limitations. Just as Holly may not be able to excel at ballet—although she gave it a try—Laurie can't do ballet either, and Holly's able-bodied brother, Andrew, wasn't particularly adept at hockey. For Laurie, it was all about normalizing the idea of limitations—because, hey, we all have them—and shifting the focus to areas of strength. That's where her hopes and dreams for her children live: in the land of possibility, not *impossibility*.

Of course, parenting inevitably involves straddling the gap between the present and the future: seeing your child both as the child he is today and the adult he will ultimately become. Claire, the mother of two young children, believes it's possible to be looking to the future and savouring the present. Or at least, that's what she tries to do. "Yes, I am raising little people and teaching them how to grow up to be great citizens, but I am also just loving them as much as I can right now," she explains. Christina, the mother of an eleven-year-old, is also resisting the temptation to fast-forward through her son's childhood. "I'm trying to be present as much as I'm able because time is scarce and also fleeting," she says. "I see the man inside the child, so I try to hang on to the moment before he is all grown up."

Some parents find themselves struggling to come to terms with a future that's much less certain and less knowable. It's the not knowing that makes things hard. Shannon and Mike are the parents of two preteens, including twelve-year-old Abby, who lives with a rare genetic disorder. Because her disorder is so rare—she's the only person with her particular variation of this disorder in the entire world—there simply isn't a lot known about how her life will play out over the longer term. One thing is clear, however: she will always require a lot of hands-on help with basic daily tasks. Shannon says, "Mike and I struggle with our vision for the future. Knowing that Abby will likely never live on her own or have an independent job is a tough pill for any parent to swallow. We plan and think about our future with Abby in it. We know that she will live with us forever. That can be a bit daunting in a world where most people know that their children will move out one day and start their own lives. I worry about how we will care for her as we get older. And it's sad to think that Abby will miss out on that part of life." They also worry about the impact on their son, Jack—how his life will play out once Shannon and Mike are no longer able to care for Abby. "I pray that Shannon and I will have done enough to ensure that there is no burden ever placed on Jack," says Mike. "He deserves to have the life he dreams of and the ability to pursue any opportunities that come his way without hesitation or regret."

Mike and Shannon have chosen to respond to their worry about the future by fiercely enjoying the present. "I don't think long-term," Mike explains. "I consider it to be a waste of time and, frankly, quite depressing. With the uncertainties we face, I would much rather live now and have short-term goals. My focus right now is to ensure that this year, each child is given the opportunity to learn something new, experience something for the first time, gain life lessons, and just have fun."

Anne is also a firm believer in making the most of the present. She is the mother of three school-aged daughters. She also happens to be living with stage-four breast cancer. This makes her painfully aware that the time she has left with her daughters is limited. "The mean is three years post-diagnosis and I've just come up to two years," she explains. "But, the thing is, I'm actually quite healthy—*other than having terminal cancer.*" The sense that the clock is ticking can leave her scrambling to stockpile happy memories with her daughters. But then she finds herself worrying that trying so hard makes everything impossibly high-stakes, both for them and for her. "Sometimes, I feel like I'm forcing them through milestones because I want to be there for that first day of kindergarten. Or I want them to learn certain things while I'm still around. It's hard to imagine my family without me, but sometimes I do imagine them without me. Sometimes, I'll stop in the middle of what they're doing and think to myself, 'I hope this is a really good memory for when I'm not here anymore, that they'll look back on this day and remember how much fun we had playing Pokémon GO together.'

"I have to curb my expectations of them, to remind myself that all I really want for them is that they grow up happy, resilient, and stable—to figure out what they want to do without the added pressure of my expectations. I don't want to leave this world and have them thinking, 'I have to stick with this particular activity because my mom really wanted me to do this.'" She has also had to ease up on the pressure on herself to expect every moment of parenthood to be filled with Technicolor starbursts of joy. Yes, she wants to enjoy the good times with her daughters, but not every single moment is going to be a good time: "It's like when you have a toddler who's having a meltdown in the grocery store and people are like, 'Enjoy every moment!' And you're like, 'I'm actually not enjoying this moment *at all*.'" She's also had to learn to accept the fact that she may not be able to get everything done that she'd like to do, that at some point in the not-so-far-distant future, she's simply going to run out of time. "The fact that I could experience another health crisis and be suddenly gone scares me," she says. "It scares me because I'm not writing the journals for my daughters that I want to be writing, or making up special boxes for them for when they're older, filled with keepsakes and other precious things. Or even just printing their baby pictures! I'm a prolific photographer and I have nothing printed."

While none of us has endless time with our kids (we just trick ourselves into believing that's the case), living in the shadow of a terminal diagnosis means grappling with that ever-present reality. Even on a bad day—a day when she's not feeling particularly well and she really needs to rest—Anne looks for opportunities to connect with her kids. "They know that, no matter how awful I am feeling, they can always bring a book and lay in bed with me and ask me to read them a story." She has learned to let go of the small, insignificant stuff, to hit the reset button and move on if she says or does something she might otherwise regret. "That's how I choose to live my life. We don't have time to hold grudges."

Making Peace with the Past

Parenting isn't just about looking to the future. It can also be about making peace with the past. Ginette, the mother of two young children, has been shocked to discover how often the past bubbles through to the present: "The most mind-blowing part of being a parent is how much it draws out your own inner issues and baggage. I certainly wasn't expecting that." Marie, the mother of three school-aged boys, has had a similar experience. Her childhood was fairly ordinary, all things considered, but she's still found herself struggling to work through some residual issues nonetheless. "There isn't enough recognition that parenting is an emotional project and that every time we have a problem with our children, it is triggering all the good and bad memories of similar things that happened to you when you were a child, whether you are consciously aware of them or not. And, in order to parent the best you can, you need to find a way to make peace with some of that," she says.

For Karen, the mother of two preteen girls, that has meant confronting and dealing with one of her biggest fears: "I've always had a fear that at some point, my relationship with my children is going to crumble. I think it comes from not having a good relationship with my own mother—something I still don't have. So, my number one goal has always been to have a better relationship with my daughters than I had with my mother. I hope that I have kept the lines of communication open enough. I hope I have kept the place for them to fall soft enough that they can always maintain a strong relationship with me, and I with them, through the teenage years and beyond."

Recognizing that the past is intruding on the present and then taking steps to confront that reality is key to being able to parent in healthy ways, particularly in the wake of trauma. If, for example, you had a harsh and critical parent, you may have a tendency to be highly critical of your own parenting abilities and to resort to harsh yet familiar parenting techniques when dealing with your own child. If you were required to function like an adult back when you were a kid, perhaps because a parent was unavailable or ill, you may find it difficult to give your own child permission to "be a kid," because no one ever gave you that permission.

"If your own needs aren't being met or haven't been met in the past, it can be hard to allow your child to meet his or her own needs," explains Hugh MacMillan, a social worker with extensive experience in providing trauma-informed therapy to individuals and families. It's not that you do this consciously; it's simply that meeting your own needs feels wrong to you. Trauma can play out in other ways as well, according to MacMillan. "Sometimes, we notice ourselves replicating an undesirable trait or action of our parents. Or we spot a pattern of repeated difficulty in managing certain behaviours in our children, or of overreacting to certain traits in our child." That's how things played out for Melanie, the mother of two young children and the survivor of a stressful and chaotic childhood. "I remember one day I was home with my daughter Julia, who was about nine months old at the time. I became frustrated, yelled at her, and then started to cry. Her response was to scream and cry. The tone of her scream and the frightened look on my little girl's face changed everything. I immediately picked up the phone and made an appointment with a therapist. It was the best decision I've ever made as a parent."

Getting help is key. Trauma isn't something you can work through on your own. You're going to need some added support. But getting that support can be a game-changer for you and your child, says MacMillan. "Having a difficult childhood doesn't have to mean that you're going to be a bad parent. You may have struggles and you may have to work at things, but you have the potential to be a good parent. It starts with addressing your past experiences, even if you haven't fully resolved them, understanding that what happened when you were a child wasn't within your control."

Now that you are an adult, you have that control. You have the power to choose to be the kind of parent you want to be. It's not about denying the past; it's about no longer allowing the past to define the future. It's about parenting with your eyes focused forward as opposed to having your gaze fixated on the rear-view mirror. Understanding your reactions—connecting the dots between what you're feeling now and what you experienced when you were a child—can present you with the opportunity to do things differently. As MacMillan puts it, "You not only have the potential to break free of the cycle of abuse; you can be an amazing parent." As for what it takes to get to and stay in a healthier place? Here's what Hugh MacMillan suggests.

Prioritize self-care. "We know that our defenses are weakened by stress, fatigue, hunger, and other compromised states, so we have to look after ourselves really well. Keeping oneself healthy is the first line of defense."

Learn to recognize the warning signs that you're running into trouble and have a plan for dealing with the situation. "It's good to know your triggers, so that you'll know when it's time to step away, and to ask others to step in," says MacMillan. So how do you respond in the moment, when you're being flooded with emotions? The best way to respond is to hit the pause button and give yourself two seconds to think about what you want to do. "Ask yourself, 'How do I want to react here?' and 'What is this related to?'" Then give yourself time to think. Move to a different location or shake things up in other ways by changing your position or modifying your activity level. "If you're stopped, you should walk; if you're walking, you should stop. If you're sitting, you should stand. That mixes up the neural activity. Or take a breath and draw upon a mantra that you've prepared ahead of time, something like 'I can do this,' 'I'm a calm person,' 'I'm a good parent,' or 'One day at a time.'"

Expect setbacks and relapses, and don't be overly discouraged when they happen. "It may feel like you're back to zero, but you're not back to zero at all." One way to keep track of your progress is to do a mental check-in with yourself at different points of the day, perhaps every time you pour yourself a cup of coffee or hit the washroom. "Take a mental snapshot by ranking yourself from one to ten in terms of how you're doing or feeling at that time." Then do something with that information. Figure out how to take better care of yourself on a day when you feel yourself struggling.

Learn how to manage your resources. Get in the habit of saying to yourself, "The kids are going to be walking through the door shortly. I should take it easy for a moment and get ready for that." In other words, give yourself a chance to mentally regroup. And if you happen to say or do something you don't feel proud of, simply hit the reset button and try again.

Celebrate the fact that you're changing the parenting script. You're doing the hard work of making things so much better for yourself and your kids. "My husband and I realized after we had our first child how very much love, attention, and care we ourselves did not receive as children," says Maureen, the mother of two young children. The two of them made a conscious decision to do things differently, to parent their kids in very different ways. All the hard work has been totally worth it: "I spend a lot of time listening to my kids and hearing their stories. I know I am a trusted parent and a source of strength during difficult times," she says. "It's marvellous."

Why Calm Is the Ultimate Parenting Superpower

Up until now, we've been talking about the thinking part of parenting—how to do the mental gymnastics required to make sense of the past and map out a path to the future as you guide your children through the present. Now, we're going to talk about what it actually takes to get yourself into the state of mind that encourages this kind of big-picture thinking, about the how and why of getting to a state of calm.

If you find yourself rolling your eyes and resisting the whole idea of becoming calmer, it's okay; I get it. For many years, I considered calm to be some ideal yet ultimately unreachable place—a Narnia, Oz, or Utopia. I couldn't see how becoming calmer was in any way relevant to my life as a parent, or even the least bit realistic. After all, if my life was all about mainlining caffeine in order to have the energy to get through my day, wasn't it kind of counterproductive, even foolhardy, to flirt with the idea of slowing down?

It turns out I'm not the only one who undervalues calm. Apparently, we have a cultural blind spot in so far as this particular emotional state is concerned. When we need more energy, we go for the adrenalin rush that is stress (at one time, my preferred blend was stress infused with caffeine). This is because Western cultures tend to value what psychologists call "high-intensity" emotions like excitement and stress, which deliver that familiar high-energy jolt. Sure, they may leave us feeling a bit jittery and wired, but that's the price we have to pay for tapping into all that energy, right?

Wrong. There's a price to pay for being constantly keyed up. And we don't have to rely on stress to get things done. Let's tackle the excitement piece of the puzzle first, because a high-intensity emotion like that sounds pretty, well, *positive*, after all. It can feel pretty great, in moderation. But here's the thing: high-intensity positive emotions like excitement take the same kind of physiological toll as high-intensity negative emotions, like anxiety or anger. Heck, they even *feel* the same: your heart starts pounding, you start to sweat, and you tend to startle easily. Just as being in a chronic state of stress is hard on your body, so is being in a constant state of excitement. Keep it up long enough and you'll start to feel exhausted.

So that's excitement. Now, let's talk about every parent's go-to fuel: the adrenalin boost provided by stress. Yes, it can be an invaluable source of energy at times, like when you need to react instantly and grab your toddler's hand when she's about to wander off in a parking lot. But if you rely on this particular fuel source on an ongoing basis—as a means of getting through your impossibly jam-packed days—that's when you can really start to wear yourself down. Even when you're benefiting from this particular energy source—because it's allowing you to power through your day—you feel *too energized*, and you may have a tough time weaning yourself off this energy source at the end of the day when it's time to wind down and go to sleep.

There is a better and more sustainable source of energy: calm. We too often overlook the power of calm because we fail to recognize that there is energy bundled in with that deliciously laid-back, relaxed feeling. As Emma Seppälä explains in her book *The Happiness Track*, "In our overcommitted, overstressed culture we don't usually associate high energy with calm. And that misunderstanding explains why we feel we need stress to get things done."

It's important to recognize that you *can* get to that calmer, happier place, even if your default setting is "highly stressed." It won't happen easily and it won't happen overnight, but you can make it happen. And it's definitely worth the work.

The calmer you are, the easier you find it to focus your attention. You're less anxious and distracted. Your brain no longer feels like a puppy on a leash, tearing off in every direction all at once. And you don't have to work nearly as hard to hold on to that leash to try to control your puppy brain. You end up saving yourself a lot of energy—energy that you can then invest in other areas of your life, like parenting. Suddenly, you have the focus and the patience to make more conscious and deliberate parenting decisions. You're no longer parenting on autopilot. You're actually taking time to think things through and to consider how you actually want things to play out for yourself and your child, both today and into the future, which means you're less likely to act in ways that leave you stuck in a swamp of guilt and regret. That's why calm is the ultimate parenting superpower: it leads to better thinking.

WHEN YOU'RE CALMER, YOU'RE ABLE TO THINK MORE CREATIVELY ABOUT EVERYTHING, INCLUDING PARENTING. Getting to a state of calm encourages broader, more expansive thinking. While stress tends to focus your attention much more narrowly—you have a tendency to zero in on the one thing that you absolutely have to accomplish in the next thirty seconds and what it's going to take to carry yourself and your child over that immediate hurdle—a calm brain is more likely to drink in more of your immediate surroundings and to connect the dots between past, present, and future. That's why you find it easier to come up with more creative solutions at times of the day when you're naturally inclined to be at least a little calmer, for example, first thing in the morning before you've had a chance to fully upload today's to-do list into your brain. According to a 2011 study published in the research journal *Thinking & Reasoning*, your brain will be more inclined to wander in ways that boost your creative thinking abilities during these calmer, less revved-up times of the day. As your mind heads out on a meandering stroll while you're floating around in this relaxing state of calm, you find it easier to see the bigger picture and put everything in perspective. This is why you're likely to have a flash of insight in the middle of a walk with your dog or while you're standing in the shower, waiting for the conditioner to work its magic on your hair. Your brain isn't being asked to focus on any specific task. You're giving it licence to wander.

That wandering can do good things for your parenting. As Ferris Jabr noted in a 2013 essay in *Scientific American*, "A wandering mind unsticks us from time so that we can learn from the past and plan for the future." Instead of being narrowly fixated on the present—the fact that your toddler just bit her brother again—you're able to remind yourself that she's not intentionally being evil; she simply hasn't learned how to manage her frustration in other ways yet. That, in turn, can give you time to breathe and to choose how you want to respond, as opposed to reacting in the moment with your attention hyper-focused on those bite marks on your son's arm.

It can feel like you're zooming in and out with a camera lens, but in this case, the camera lens that you're fiddling with is your attention. You're managing your attention in a conscious and deliberate way that supports your intentions in a particular situation. You can gently nudge your brain in the right direction, by the way, by asking it to zoom in on what matters most in the present situation: "What does my child need from me right now?" Or you can nudge it to zoom out a little by asking yourself a question that's more likely to tap into your big-picture parenting goals: "How can I handle this situation in a way that I can feel good about at the end of the day or a decade from now?"

The superpower that makes all this shifting possible? You guessed it: the power of calm. Your challenge, of course, is to both find the time *and* give yourself the permission to mentally escape to the land of calm, both when you're by yourself and when you're in the presence of other people. A crucial first step is to resist the temptation to jam-pack every moment of every day with endless activity and distraction—something that's admittedly easier said than done during the most hands-on stages of parenting. As we discussed back in Chapter 3 in the context of distracted parenting, a distracted brain is an anything-but-calm brain. That's not to say that you can't get to a state of calm while you're busy doing something else. It just has to be the right kind of "something else." You can have moments of tremendous insight—life's so-called eureka moments—while you're peeling carrots, provided that your mind has the opportunity to go AWOL. If you're simultaneously helping a child with his homework and on hold with your credit card company while you peel those carrots, your most inspired thinking is more likely to be about the hell that is a call centre or the pros and cons of hiring a math tutor, as opposed to, say, the meaning of life.

So, it's about seizing the moment in the midst of the hurricane of daily living, trying to experience the emotion the Japanese refer to as *seijaku*, which basically means serenity in the midst of activity or chaos. If you still find yourself struggling to make sense of what I'm talking about when I speak of calm—a concept that took me a very long time to master—perhaps the next example might help.

A few years back, Norway's public broadcaster began to experiment with a deliberately calming kind of broadcast, something they referred to as "slow TV." Slow TV was designed to calm and relax viewers and allow their minds to wander over an extended period of time. Depending on when you tuned in, you might be treated to a seven-hour view from the front of a train travelling across the countryside, eight hours of a fire burning in a fireplace, nine hours of people knitting, eighteen hours of salmon fishing, sixty hours of hymn singing, or a five-and-a-half-day-long boat cruise. The broadcasts proved to be an immediate hit with viewers, who, like the rest of us, were clearly craving a fix of calm. (If you want to get your fix of slow TV, you can find it on YouTube, by the way.)

A CALMER BRAIN IS A LESS DISTRACTED BRAIN,
WHICH ENCOURAGES BETTER THINKING.

Another reason to tap into the power of calm is that a calmer brain is capable of better, or deeper, thinking. I'm building on the concept of "deep work" that Cal Newport proposed in his book *Deep Work: Rules for Focused Success in a Distracted World*. He defined deep work as "Professional activities performed in a state of distraction-free concentration that push your cognitive capabilities to your limit. These efforts create new value, improve your skills, and are hard to replicate." He also noted that deep work is satisfying *because* it's challenging: "The best moments usually occur when a person's body or mind is stretched to its limits in a voluntary effort to accomplish something difficult or worthwhile."

Reading his book got me thinking about the cognitive demands of parenting. After all, if there's one experience that pushes your cognitive capabilities to the limit, it's the experience of raising another human being. As for creating new value, improving your skills, and being hard to replicate, parenting definitely meets those criteria too. The value you create is expressed in the form of a happier, healthier child; you definitely improve your skills along the way (we talked about this in Chapter 4); and the unique contributions that each of us brings to the complex task of parenting are extremely hard to replicate—which explains why AI-powered parenting apps still fall far short of PI-powered human beings ("PI" meaning parenting intelligence).

Parenting definitely demands the kind of deep work that Newport describes. In fact, it's such a complex task that I would argue that it actually demands two separate yet interconnected kinds of deep work: the highly focused periods of deep thinking that tend to happen behind the scenes, when you're alone and you have time to reflect on what's going on with your child; and highly focused periods of deep connection with your child, when you're both highly sensitive to and highly responsive to her needs. Deep thinking supports deep connection and vice versa, and over time, you become a more confident and competent parent.

Creating room for this kind of "deep parenting" means learning to manage your attention and steering clear of the fire hose of distraction, including self-distraction. It means daring to commit to a relationship that demands so much of you and being willing to invest the time required to form that kind of a connection. And it means slowing down and giving yourself the time and space needed to do the thinking work of parenting—to actually absorb what you've learned and are learning.

As Michael Grabowski, a professor of communication at New York's Manhattan College, noted in a 2017 interview with the culture blog *The Cut*, "Consuming information is just the beginning—our minds need time to absorb and synthesize that information, to critically examine it. That's something we do in silence, by actively disengaging from the digital technology and focusing on the world around us." It's about improving the quality of your thinking so that you can improve the quality of your parenting. And that's where solitude fits in.

The Power of Solitude

If calm is your parenting superpower, solitude is your ticket to that place of calm. The problem is that solitude often feels like a luxury, a frivolous indulgence, at a stage in our lives when so many people need so much of us. And yet it's important to find—even steal—that time. As Courtney E. Martin noted in a 2017 article for the blog *On Being*, "Mothers must guard their own solitude" even if doing so feels like "a radical act." Yes, it's that important, and not just for moms, by the way. Dads need and deserve time alone too.

For Katie, the mother of three school-aged boys, the "radical act" that makes time alone possible is getting up extra early. "I am becoming more self-aware," she explains. "I am starting to understand that because I am an introvert, I need some time to myself. So, I've started getting up early—before everyone else—so that I can have some time to myself while the house is still quiet." Kate, the mother of two preteens, can relate to Katie's cravings for solitude. But she continues to struggle to seize those moments in her own life. In fact, when she starts talking about the hardest things about being a parent, she immediately zeroes in on this very issue: the absence of solitude. "It's my lack of alone time . . . a lack of time to imagine, to be creative, to dream. I have realized that although I'm a social person and I enjoy other people, I need a certain amount of solitude to be in balance. And that is just not part of my life right now. I try to remind myself that now is not forever, and that I can find those moments of solitude if I look for them, but it can feel pretty overwhelming at times." The "radical act" for Kate meant recognizing the importance of being honest and forthright with her partner about her need for this time, not only for her own sake, but for the sake of their relationship too. "I went through a period of feeling very resentful about my lack of alone time, which was poisonous to my relationship. Resentment really is toxic. So, we have learned to talk about this before resentment builds up and gets ugly," she explains.

It can be anything but easy to find or even take alone time. But as it turns out, solitude matters a lot.

SOLITUDE IS CALMING.

For starters, time spent alone is calming. In fact, it's a tool we can use to regulate our emotions in the wake of experiences that leave us feeling anything but calm. As the authors of a 2017 article published in the *Personality and Social Psychology Bulletin* wrote, "People can use solitude . . . to regulate their affective states, becoming quiet after excitement, calm after an angry episode, or centered and peaceful when desired." Solitude is the gift that keeps on giving. That same group of researchers reported that spending time alone each day for a week has a spillover effect that actually carries over into the following week, with the resulting wave of calm continuing to buoy and sustain you. Doesn't that sound *good*?

SOLITUDE ENCOURAGES SELF-DISCOVERY AND PROMOTES SELF-AWARENESS.

Spending time alone provides you with the opportunity to work on a very important relationship: your relationship with yourself.

"I was a person before I became a parent, and it's important to me that 'me as a person' isn't erased by 'me as a parent,'" says Mireille, the mother of two teens and a preteen. Taking time to be alone can feel like an act of self-care and self-preservation. It can give you a chance to figure out who you are and to consider who you intend to become. As Nancy Colier notes in *The Power of Off*, "Introducing silence into our lives is a profound gesture of self-care, an invitation and an opportunity to spend time with ourselves, to remember ourselves as we truly are." Lisa, a mother of three, agrees: "Staying true to yourself really is self-care in the best sense of the word. Being unapologetic for who you are."

Solitude is about shifting the focus of your attention from the external world to the internal you—a simple shift that changes everything. As Sherry Turkle notes in her book *Reclaiming Conversation: The Power of Talk in a Digital Age*, "It is only when we are alone with our thoughts—not reacting to external stimuli—that we engage that part of the brain's basic infrastructure devoted to building up a sense of our stable autobiographical past. . . . So, without solitude, we can't construct a stable sense of self." Being comfortable with solitude is an important thing to model and share with your kids. Turkle explains, "Children develop the capacity for solitude in the presence of an attentive other. . . . We teach the capacity for solitude by being quiet alongside children who have our attention." It's a powerful way to pass along our calmness superpower to members of the next generation.

SOLITUDE PROVIDES A GATEWAY TO OUR INTUITION.
Solitude provides us with opportunities for much-needed mental housekeeping—the kind of mental reorganizing and decluttering that can spark moments of insight. As Nancy Colier explains in *The Power of Off*, "Something is actually happening in that downtime. The subconscious is putting things together, making associations, and doing a different kind of work, which happens outside our awareness. For many people, it is in these gaps that they have their best flashes of insight, as if we need to take our minds *off* of something in order to gain access to our intuition—and, really, to our deepest wisdom."

Parenting is a massively complicated cognitive challenge, so it's a task that benefits from slower, more reflective thinking—the kind of thinking that leads to more accurate intuition, which, in turn, makes parenting easier over time. As we gain experience with certain types of tasks, we're able to automate some of the thinking associated with those tasks, freeing up more cognitive resources for tasks that demand more conscious thinking. "I'm trying to trust my gut more. I'm trying to spend more time in the silence and the stillness. I feel like I need more of that in my life," says Katie, the mother of three school-aged boys.

It can also be helpful to think of parenting as a practice that you engage with on a regular basis, as opposed to treating it like something you absorb unthinkingly on the fly. As Mary, the mother of a seven-year-old son, explains, "I try to be a conscious, peaceful, respectful parent. I see parenting as a spiritual practice and an opportunity to walk my walk."

Of course, no one expects you to think this deeply about parenting all the time. That would be exhausting and unhealthy. That kind of intense focus would pretty much crowd out everything else in your life. It's more a matter of creating room in your life for this kind of thinking on a regular basis, even if it's just for a few stolen minutes at a time. This is the best kind of time investment—the kind where you actually end up having *more* time. The more you commit to doing the deep thinking that parenting requires, the easier and less stressful parenting will be. You'll spend less time and energy spinning your wheels, trying to free yourself from the emotional muck of guilt and regret.

Can you imagine how different our world would be if every parent committed to making this shift? How it would feel to raise your kids in a world where every parent sported a T-shirt proclaiming, "Calm is my parenting superpower!" and every kid wore one announcing, "Powered by calm"? You have the power to shift the entire culture of parenting, both within your own family and the wider world. It's all about unplugging from stress as a fuel source and tapping into the power of calm.

Up until now, we've been talking about why you might want to embrace calm and how solitude can help you find your way to that place. In the next two chapters, we're going to delve deeper into the how. I'll outline specific strategies you can use to reduce anxiety, increase calm, and enjoy more of the really good stuff that can come from parenting.

CHAPTER 6

How to Boost Your Enjoyment of Parenting

Give your kids and yourself time to rest and be together. Build a life with them that you don't need to escape from.

—Glenda, mother of a teenager, and stepmother
to two twenty-somethings

Remember the movie that used to play in your head back when you first started imagining yourself as a parent? You'd picture all the fabulous things you'd get to do with your hypothetical kids, like baking cookies and snuggling up together for bedtime stories, and how much fun you would have teaching them how to ride a bike, paddle a canoe, or build a snowman. It was *such* a great movie. And then the reality of parenting set in, and you got so busy dealing with the day-to-day hard work of raising kids that you kind of misplaced the movie. This chapter is all about reconnecting with all the good stuff in that movie so that you can enjoy parenting more. We're going to start out by talking about what that good stuff actually is—what *actually* makes us happier as opposed to what we *think* will make us happier—and how to get more of it in your life. Then we're going to talk about why happiness doesn't just happen and what it takes to make it happen. In the following chapter, we'll be talking about how to deal with all the other stuff—the guilt, the anxiety, and the feeling of being overwhelmed—that can otherwise interfere with your enjoyment of parenting.

Getting More of the Good Stuff

Of course, the best way to get more of the good stuff of parenting is to be clear about what that good stuff actually is and then to consider how much of it you're actually getting in your day-to-day life. Think of it this way: If you were to invite a documentary film crew to follow you around for an entire day, what would the footage they captured have to say about your life? What conclusions might a viewer of that documentary reach about you based on what they see on the screen? Would the on-screen reality match up with the hopes and dreams for yourself and your family that you're carrying around in your head?

Odds are the answer is no. At least for me, it's always a giant, flashing neon no. There's always a gap between how I am actually spending my time—doing laundry and planning meals—and how I wish I could be spending my time—having heart-to-heart conversations with my nearest and dearest while we're enjoying a lakeside picnic. But by being willing to watch this particular movie in my head, I at least give myself the chance to consider how I would like future scenes to play out and the types of edits I'd like to make to the script. Now, that's not to say that it's realistic to expect every single second of parenthood to be filled with meaning and bliss. Not only would that be exhausting, but you'd end up with a giant mountain of laundry and a very hungry family. But you can make a conscious effort not to waste too much time chasing after the stuff that isn't going to matter all that much a week, a month, or a year from now and to focus your sights instead on the stuff that will: the moments of connection.

MAKING ROOM FOR MOMENTS OF CONNECTION

Lynn knows what she wants more of in her life as a parent: more unhurried times as a family. "The moments when the three of us are just hanging out together without the pressure to be at a certain place at a certain time or to get something done—those are the most joyful experiences for us," the mother of a toddler explains. Those kinds of moments are also when you're likely to feel most positive about your parenting—when you're left feeling that you've just done it right. As Courtney E. Martin wrote in an essay for *On Being*, "The things I am most proud of have nothing to do with my productivity and everything to do with my presence."

Giving your child the gift of your presence can help the world to feel a little less frantic and out of control for both you *and* your child. When you slow down, your child slows down, and you both feel calmer. You are more in sync with one another as opposed to merely rushing past one another in pursuit of potentially conflicting agendas. And that, in turn, gives your child an important message about the nature of relationships: relationships require time and attention, and there are people who love you enough to be willing to take that time.

Parenting is endlessly inefficient—and that's okay. *It's supposed to work this way.* As Henry David Thoreau once said, "The more slowly trees grow at first, the sounder they are at the core, and I think the same is true of human beings." It takes time to nurture a little seedling—or tiny human—along. So, one of the most powerful things you can do to boost your enjoyment of parenthood is simply to allow space in your life for these moments of connection to occur. How do you find this time? By saying no so that you can say yes. Just as you need some "white space" in your home to avoid visual and clutter overload, you need some white space in your schedule in order to avoid life overload. You have to be willing to say no to some things in order to make room for other things—even if you aren't yet sure what those other things might actually be.

It's during these unscripted moments that the magic happens—"when things aren't planned, when everyone's standing in the kitchen laughing at one another's jokes and appreciating one another's quirks and idiosyncrasies," says Jillian, the mother of two teens and a preteen. It's that feeling of being seen and being accepted for who you are and knowing that you are part of something bigger and better than just you. These shared family times function as relationship glue. Not only does sharing positive experiences with the people we care about increase our connection to these people; the experiences themselves become more enjoyable and more memorable, simply by virtue of the fact that we're sharing them with people we love. It's no wonder that we crave these types of experiences. They serve up so many layers of good!

You'll find it easier to create room in your life for these types of experiences if you tell yourself that (a) you have a limited "yes budget," meaning you can't say yes to every single thing you or your kids would like to do, and (b) you're not saying no to a particular thing forever—you're just saying no to it right now. This is an important point to keep in mind when your child wants to sign up for a whole bunch of different extracurricular activities simultaneously. You're not saying that your child can never sign up for gymnastics. You're just saying that she can't do it at the same time that she's signed up for soccer and swimming lessons. At least some of these activities have to be put on hold until the next sign-up period rolls around.

Sometimes, you might want to hit the pause button on everything to give yourself and your kids a bit more of a break. It's a strategy that's working for Noreen, the mother of two preschoolers: "Right now, we're still in charge of the social calendar for the family, so my husband and I have said no to external things so that we can say yes to relaxed family time."

Resisting the Allure of "Goal Culture"

Don't be surprised if you feel a little guilty when you deliberately set aside time in your schedule to be *un*-busy. That's because our culture tells us that we should be trying to shoehorn as much activity into our lives as possible—and often considerably more than what is possible. According to social psychologist Adam Alter, we're living in "an unprecedented age of goal culture"—a time of "addictive perfectionism, self-assessment, more time at work, and less time to play." And, increasingly, we're carrying this mindset into our lives as parents. It's a concern that sociologist Kerry Daly flagged back in 2004, in a paper for The Vanier Institute of the Family, when he described parenting as "a modified work culture that emphasizes the effective and efficient performance of parents." As he explained, "the time that parents and children spend together has become more goal-oriented, structured and saturated with activity" as "parents seek to cultivate in their children the skills and qualities that will position them for success." It's all about viewing the child as a future worker, in other words.

It's not hard to connect the dots between the appeal of goal culture and the anxiety that many parents feel as they try to prepare their children for an uncertain future (we talked about this at length back in Chapter 1). But there's more to our embrace of goal culture than just that. There are certain fundamental aspects of the experience of parenting that make goal culture uniquely appealing, like the fact that the job description for the position of parent is ambiguous and ever-changing, and the fact that real-time validation and positive feedback tend to be in chronically short supply. Because it's so hard to measure the impact you're having on your child right now and to feel confident that you are, in fact, doing this parenting thing right, it can be tempting to look to things you *can* measure, like the number of items you managed to scratch off your to-do list over the course of a day or the progress you made toward any number of parenting goals.

That's not to say that you shouldn't have parenting goals. I've been working at being a more patient parent since the day I became a parent, and I'm still working on achieving that particular goal. But there can be a downside to being too goal-focused when it comes to parenting. It's worth pausing to consider what it is that you're not noticing or not experiencing while you're in single-minded pursuit of a parenting goal. Sometimes, it's important to hit the pause button on even the noblest and most worthwhile goal—say for example, inviting underappreciated vegetables to the family dinner table a little more often—to focus on what your child really needs from you at this moment—perhaps a gigantic serving of attention and reassurance to help him make sense of a really bad day.

Here's something else to think about: As parents, we need to give ourselves permission to challenge the thinking that says "busy is good" and that the only things that are worth doing are things that are immediately quantifiable—something that makes it easy for us to fall into the all too common trap of applying workplace metrics to the hard to measure and even harder to quantify world of parenting. Just because you can't measure something, or at least measure it easily, doesn't mean that it doesn't matter in the life of a parent or child. And even if you *can* measure it, it doesn't mean that you *should* measure it. Does the world really need a parenting app that would allow you to document each and every hug?

Other Ways to Take Back Control of Your Time

Do you feel like there are never enough hours in a day to do everything that needs to be done? Join the club. Time-use studies consistently reveal that we parents are among the most time-stressed people on the planet. We're always scrambling to find ways to get more done—to jam forty-eight hours' worth of living into a twenty-four-hour day. The problem, of course, is that it simply isn't possible to pull off that kind of temporal sleight of hand. It doesn't matter how many time management books you've read or what a pro you are at multi-tasking; you still have to work within the confines of a twenty-four-hour day. That said, there are a few things you can do to make better use of your time—and by that, I mean using your time in a way that leaves room for more of the good stuff of parenting as opposed to trying to shoehorn more of everything into your day. Here are a few ideas.

Think multi-purposing, not multi-tasking. Instead of trying to tackle multiple tasks at the same time—a strategy that leaves you feeling anxious and distracted—look for ways to make a single task achieve multiple purposes. You might decide to treat fitness time as social time, for example. This is a strategy that works well for Elaine, the mother of two teenagers: "My running buddy is my best friend, so I actually look forward to 5:30 a.m. runs with her—even in January."

Think optimizing rather than maximizing. Instead of trying to tackle as many tasks as possible over the course of a particular day, focus instead on the tasks that are most important. "Maximizing is squeezing as many things into the day as possible," explains Nora Spinks, CEO of The Vanier Institute of the Family. "Optimizing is finding those three things that are really, really important and just focusing on those." Maybe one Saturday that means getting a load of laundry done (because everyone is running out of socks and underwear), hitting the grocery store to pick up the essentials (because things can quickly go from bad to worse when you don't have any milk for cereal or tea), and serving breakfast for dinner (because it's an easy, no-stress menu option on a day when you feel like you're running on empty or your child needs a super-sized portion of parental love and attention).

Batch things up. Whether you whip up a single batch of chili or four batches of chili, you're still going to be left with a sink full of pots and pans. The difference, of course, is that you only have to do those dishes one time as opposed to four separate times. Ditto for the trip to the grocery store to round up the ingredients for that batch of chili. You only have to do that once as opposed to four times. But where you really reap the dividends is on those days when you arrive home from work to a delicious homemade dinner that's already made. You simply pop one of those pre-made batches of chili in the oven and, voila, dinner is served. This particular strategy is a favourite of Lynn's, the mother of a toddler. "I spend one day every two weeks prepping batches of food and stocking my freezer with healthy ready-to-go meals, so that I don't have to think about cooking every single day," she explains. Of course, if you're working with a super-tight budget, buying ingredients in bulk may be a luxury you simply can't afford. In that case, you might want to see if you can stretch your dollars a little further and share some of the work involved in meal preparation by joining a food co-op or collective kitchen in your community. (Check with your local health unit to find out if one or both are operating in your neighbourhood.)

Minimize decision fatigue. Ever have days when you feel like you simply don't have it in you to make even one more decision? That's a pretty sure sign that you're dealing with decision fatigue, which results from all the thinking, organizing, and planning that daily living requires. Fortunately, there's a simple way to reduce the amount of decision fatigue you're experiencing. Look for opportunities to minimize the number of decisions you have to make on a daily basis. Lynn has become a pro at working this strategy—she describes it as finding "tiny efficiencies"—in multiple areas of her life. "I cut my hair super short so that I don't ever have to think about styling it or spending any time on it. I wear a 'uniform' [a go-to outfit she doesn't have to waste any time thinking about—like Steve Jobs's trademark black turtle-neck and jeans] to work so that I don't have to spend any time thinking about how to dress. And I scheduled a standing weekly coffee date with a close friend so that I don't go months without social contact," she explains. It's about automating the things that matter so that you don't have to waste any time thinking about them. They just happen.

Separate the thinking from the doing. Instead of asking your brain to come up with optimal solutions when you're feeling stressed and overwhelmed, look for opportunities to do the thinking work ahead of time. If, for example, you know you'd like to go for a walk at least three times this week, spend some time on Sunday evening figuring out when those walks might be able to happen. You can always tweak your plan as the week goes on, but you'll be miles ahead, both literally and figuratively, as a result of having a tentative game-plan. Christine, the mother of a teen and a pre-teen, has learned that even the best of intentions can quickly fly out the window when those intentions aren't anchored by some sort of a plan. "I try to avoid making decisions in the mental clutter of Monday," she says. "Under pressure, I choose what is expedient instead of what meets my needs."

Outsource or eliminate. Nicole finds herself conducting task triage on a regular basis, assessing all the competing demands on her time and attention and deciding what she can reasonably commit to doing: "Obviously, being a single parent with four kids, I have more household chores than time to do them, so I have to decide whether to outsource something or to let it go." Happiness researchers would fully support Nicole's decision to outsource some tasks, by the way, particularly if the tasks she chooses to outsource are ones she doesn't enjoy anyway. Studies have shown that you can actually boost your happiness by buying your way out of unpleasant experiences, for example, purchasing housecleaning or lawn-cutting services. So, that's definitely worth thinking about.

How to Boost Your Enjoyment of Parenting

Aiming to be a happier person and a happier parent can seem like a frivolous aspiration until you stop to consider the far-reaching impact of your happiness on your kids. To put it bluntly, happier parents tend to be better parents. They're more likely to interact with their children in ways that encourage healthy development. They're more loving and less controlling, they're more connected to and engaged with their kids, and they're more "autonomy supportive"—in other words, they see their child's growing independence as a healthy sign, not something to be discouraged, resented, or feared. Happier, healthier parents end up with happier, healthier kids both over the short term and the longer term.

But it's not just about *them*; it's also about *you*. Happy parents are, well, happier! And they enjoy parenting more. So why wouldn't you want to do everything possible to be the happiest possible you? You have the opportunity to create a virtuous cycle for yourself and your family—a cycle in which things just keep getting better and better.

But here's the thing: happiness doesn't just happen. You have to *make* it happen by repeatedly inviting it into your life and then encouraging it to stick around. That's because the default setting in your brain is actually skewed slightly negative. This may have made sense from an evolutionary standpoint—erring on the side of pessimism meant that you were less likely to become some wild animal's dinner—but the brain's tendency to spotlight the negative and overlook the good can make parenting unnecessarily difficult. As psychologist Rick Hanson explained in a 2014 article for *Greater Good Magazine*, "To help our ancestors survive in harsh conditions, the brain evolved a negativity bias that makes it good at learning from bad experiences, but relatively bad at learning from good ones." In fact, we sometimes fail to see the good things at all. The good news is that it is possible to tweak this setting in your brain in much the same way that you might optimize your smartphone settings. Here are some simple yet science-proven strategies for doing just that.

Spend more time doing things that make you happier. This one seems like a no-brainer, but it's actually a powerful strategy for shifting the default setting of your brain from "negative" to "a little more positive." The more time you spend in that desired state of happiness (or at least something resembling happiness), the more your brain will begin to recognize it as its new default setting. Wondering what this means in practical terms? The huge and growing body of research on positive psychology has a lot to tell us about what it takes to create this kind of upward spiral. You'll be happier if:

- You experience a variety of different positive emotions (for example, pride, contentment, satisfaction, excitement, and love) as opposed to putting all of your emotional eggs in a single emotional basket—even if that basket happens to be a really great basket, like love.

- You shake up your happiness routine on a regular basis as opposed to getting stuck in the same happiness rut day after day. Our brains are immediately attracted to anything new, while more routine experiences tend to fade into the background. This explains one of our most remarkable skills as Canadians: our ability to shift from doing cartwheels of joy on the first warm day of spring to complaining about the heat just a few days later. The only way you can counteract your brain's tendency to rapidly "discount" the experience of happiness is by making it hard for it to settle into a happiness rut. That means constantly shaking up your experience by doing new and different things that bring you joy.

- You understand what types of experiences are most likely to bring you joy—and why. The research shows that it's time spent with people, and more specifically, time spent doing kind things for other people, that makes us happier. If you think about it, that's pretty much the dictionary definition of parenting—good news.

- You look for opportunities to increase your sense of mastery. Set a goal for yourself that is just challenging enough to motivate you but not frustrate you, and that will allow you to try something new. Then work at achieving that goal. The resulting sense of mastery—the sense of having achieved something—will boost your overall level of happiness. It doesn't have to have a thing to do with your parenting. Yes, learning how to knit a sweater or fix a bike can, in fact, make you a better parent.

- You resist the temptation to talk yourself out of your own happiness. If your child cleans the kitchen unexpectedly, enjoy the happy surprise. Don't rush in to try to come up with a more cynical explanation for his impromptu act of helpfulness and don't engage in "negative mental time travel" by predicting that the kitchen will soon be a disaster again. Instead, consciously amplify your feelings of happiness by expressing gratitude to your kid and savouring the amazing feeling of being in a sparkling clean kitchen that you didn't have to play any part in cleaning.

Spend less time doing things that make you miserable. A study conducted by Nobel Prize–winning economist Daniel Kahneman revealed that a typical woman (in this case, a woman in Texas who works outside the home) spends about 17.7 percent of her time in "an unpleasant state." That amounts to about three hours a day, assuming you're awake for roughly seventeen hours a day. It would seem that a logical way to boost happiness is to do your best to reclaim at least some of that misery time, perhaps by delegating or outsourcing tasks that you just plain don't love. Maybe you could swap or share some of those tasks with your partner or hire a third party to do them for you. Or maybe you could postpone the ones that don't matter, or that don't have to matter right now.

You might also look for ways to make the hateful but unavoidable tasks a little less hateful, for example, by tuning into your favourite podcast during a painfully slow morning commute. This strategy is known as "temptation bundling," by the way, and it's a proven strategy for motivating yourself to do things you really don't want to do. The idea is to team up something you really don't want to do, say cleaning toilets, with some sort of reward, like tuning into the latest episode of that embarrassingly bad reality TV show that you really can't justify watching at any other time, and then tell yourself that the only time you can access that reward is when you tackle the undesirable task. Your toilets will soon be sparkling! Another related strategy is to promise yourself some sort of reward, say ten minutes curled up on the couch with a cup of your favourite tea, for polishing off some unpleasant task (the toilets, again). And then make a point of keeping that promise to yourself.

Make happiness last longer by savouring the good stuff. Savouring is a powerful happiness booster. Unfortunately, we're often so busy rushing through our lives that we forget to hit the pause button long enough to allow our happiest experiences to really sink in. As Kristin Layous and her co-authors explained in a 2017 study published in *The Journal of Positive Psychology,* "When people take action to savor their surroundings . . . they may feel like they are just where they want to be—making their own choices . . . effectively managing their lives . . . and engaging in meaningful relationships. . . . Alternatively, when people distractedly move through their days— or, worse, repetitively focus on their days' negative aspects—they may feel forced or trapped in their current situation, ineffective in managing daily tasks, and unfulfilled by their relationships."

It's important to know that you can dial up the impact of savouring even further. Don't limit yourself to savouring something wonderful in the moment. Engage in "positive mental time travel" by anticipating happy events ahead of time and remembering them after the fact. We tend to do this when we head out on vacation. We anticipate the trip, enjoy it while we're away, and then recall those happy travel memories after we arrive back home. It's simply a matter of carrying this habit of prolonged savouring into your life as a parent.

Here's another way to come at the whole savouring thing: remind yourself that parenting is a limited time offer. You don't have an endless number of days with your child, and when each of those days is gone, it will be gone forever. A 2017 study published in *The Journal of Positive Psychology* reported that "imagining time as scarce prompted people to seize the moment and extract greater well-being from their lives." I admit that this particular happiness strategy is likely to have you crying at the same time, but at least the tears that you're shedding will be happy tears.

Focus your attention in ways that leave you happier and less stressed. A distracted mind is an unhappy mind. Not paying attention can cause you to miss out on the most enjoyable aspects of being a parent or to fail to soak up the good stuff enough. Not only do you miss out on opportunities to savour, but multi-tasking is exhausting. The more you slice and dice your attention resources, the more you bog down your brain. It's like what happens when you ask your computer to download a large number of files simultaneously: you all but stop making progress downloading any of them. In fact, according to research conducted by neuroscientist René Marois of Vanderbilt University, it takes 30 percent longer to do two tasks at the same time as compared to tackling one and then the other in sequence, and you make roughly twice as many errors. Add additional tasks to the mix—multiple children making multiple demands while you're trying to do your online banking—and what you end up with is a cognitive hot mess.

Part of what makes multi-tasking so exhausting is the fact that some of your attention remains stuck on the previous task, even when you've switched to the next task—a phenomenon that cognitive scientists refer to as "attention residue." Consider what happens to your brain when your child asks you for something when you're right in the middle of responding to an important email. You try to give your child your attention, but that half-written email keeps nagging away at you—the so-called Zeigarnik effect, which is the brain's tendency to fixate on uncompleted tasks. And if your response to that email really is urgent—someone needs to hear back from you right now—you'll be even more distracted.

Fortunately, there's a way to deal with this common problem. What you need to do is have a strategy for switching focus. In other words, you need to find a way to tell your brain to relax about the email. Take a moment to jot down the key points you really need to make in that email so that your brain doesn't have to continue to try to remember them while you're responding to your child. What you're doing is creating a "ready to resume" plan that will allow your brain to hit the pause button on that uncompleted task, freeing up attention to give to your child. The alternative—repeatedly cycling back and forth between your child and the email—doesn't work nearly as well. Not only will you have to keep reading and rereading everything that you've written so far, you'll probably find yourself getting frustrated with your child. Or you'll resort to only half-listening, which dramatically increases the likelihood that you'll agree to a request that you will live to regret in the not-so-distant future. ("But *you said* we could invite all the kids in the neighbourhood to my birthday party.")

It's easy to see how spreading your attention in all directions at once can result in a less happy and more stressed-out you. The solution is to remind yourself that your attention resources aren't infinite and that you do need to budget those resources. It won't always be possible to do so. There will still be times when you will find yourself stuck in multi-tasking mode, despite your best efforts. But at least multi-tasking will no longer be your permanent default setting. That's major progress.

Switch your brain into discovery mode to make parenting more enjoyable. Parenting is sometimes described as boring, even tedious. And I have to admit that it can certainly have its moments—like when your preschooler wants you to play that annoying board game again and again and again. The good news is that you can manage those feelings by managing your attention.

First of all, reduce the boredom of parenting by looking for ways to engage your curiosity. Our brains love to solve puzzles. Switch your brain into discovery mode. Consider what your child might be thinking and feeling and how this might relate to your own experiences as a child.

It's a matter of focusing your attention in a way that works for, not against, you. Yes, there are times when you want your mind to wander (we talked about this at length in the previous chapter in the context of self-reflection and creative thinking), but there are also times when you want to focus your attention on what's happening right now in this moment with your child.

Here's something else to think about: a lot of what we initially perceive as "boring" might, in fact, be more accurately described as "calm." As you may recall from the previous chapter, we have a cultural predisposition toward valuing high-intensity positive emotions like excitement and undervaluing low-intensity positive emotions like calm. Sometimes that causes us to mistake feeling calm for feeling bored. What if instead of thinking of the more repetitive moments of parenting as boring, you embraced them for being "slow"? What if you saw the next game of Candy Land as an opportunity to calm your mind and learn new things about your child? Hey, it's worth at least giving this mindset a whirl.

Don't spend too much time hanging out in the Land of Unrealized Options. Are you in the habit of mentally transporting yourself to a parallel universe—a universe in which you didn't become a parent and your life is playing out in all kinds of fabulous ways? Spending a lot of time in this place—the Land of Unrealized Options—can significantly reduce your enjoyment of parenting. Here's why: When you take one of these mental vacations, you'll inevitably spend your time focusing on all the great stuff that might have happened in the kid-free version of your life as opposed to dwelling on all the stuff that might have gone wrong. That's kind of the point of indulging in this kind of fantasy, after all. But it means that the comparison is hopelessly skewed.

The way to deal with this common problem is, once again, by refocusing your attention. Try looking for the good things in your life or, at a minimum, making peace with the decisions that led you to your present reality. This doesn't need to stop you from looking for ways to make things better, but it does help to put the brakes on all-consuming feelings of regret, which can erode your overall sense of happiness.

Recognize that the hard work of parenting is also the source of much of its joy. Here's another simple mind-shift that can increase your enjoyment of parenting: instead of treating the hard work of parenting like a "bug" in an otherwise joyous experience, recognize that the hard work is an essential ingredient in the recipe for that joy. We're not happy *in spite of* the hard work of parenting; we're happy *because of it*, in other words.

I'm not making this up, by the way. Unselfishly giving to another person results in "greater self-esteem, greater satisfaction and love in [your] relationships, and greater love for humanity in daily life," noted the authors of a 2012 study published in the *Journal of Social and Personal Relationships*. This means that the joy we derive from the hard work of parenting actually has the potential to spill over into the rest of our lives—a rather satisfying return on all that parental investment.

The hard work only becomes a problem when it approaches the point of self-neglect, at which point it can contribute to "negative views of the self, distress, and depression," according to this particular group of researchers. (If you think this might be an area of concern for you, because you're finding parenting far more exhausting than satisfying, you won't want to miss the part of Chapter 7 that talks about self-compassion and the part of Chapter 8 that talks about self-care.)

Increase your feelings of self-efficacy and self-control to boost feelings of happiness. Self-efficacy refers to our capacity to achieve things with our own skills and through our own efforts. It's a force that tends to build on itself over time. As you experience success mastering one task, for example, making scrambled eggs, you feel confident tackling other more challenging tasks, like attempting a soufflé. The next thing you know, you're all set to showcase your soufflé-making skills to an audience of millions via live video stream . . . or something like that.

We don't spend a lot of time talking about self-efficacy. A Google search for the term produces a mere 3.4 million hits as compared to the nearly 90 million hits for "self-esteem." But it actually plays a pretty major role in our overall happiness and well-being, boosting our feelings of confidence and increasing our sense of control. So, maybe we should be talking about it more.

We should definitely be talking about it in the context of parenting. Parenting is, after all, the ultimate exercise in personal development. It's all about mastering a daunting range of ever-changing skills through incredibly hard work. You didn't always know how to soothe a crying baby or calm a raging toddler, but look at you now! The problem is that we sometimes forget to notice and give ourselves credit for all the things we've learned to date because we're pretty much laser-focused on all the things we still have yet to learn. And that can cause our feelings of self-efficacy to lag behind our actual and ever-increasing skill level. So, a simple yet powerful way to boost your feelings of parental self-efficacy, and to reap the resulting happiness boost, is to take stock of all the things you've learned and to give yourself credit for all the hard work that was required.

While you're at it, you might also want to work at boosting your sense of control—the feeling that you're in control of your life as opposed to feeling like your life or your child is controlling you. Researchers at the Johns Hopkins University School of Medicine and the University of Massachusetts Amherst have discovered that parents who feel a greater sense of control are less likely to struggle with anxiety and depression during the early months of parenthood.

So how do you go about increasing your sense of control at a time in your life when you may feel like you've pretty much lost all control? By practising "cognitive reappraisal." Cognitive reappraisal simply means challenging unhelpful thoughts and replacing them with more helpful thoughts. Instead of focusing on all the areas of your life where you've had to surrender some control, like how many times your sleep is interrupted by your newborn, zoom in on the areas where you still do have control, like choosing what you have for breakfast and what you do with your time when your baby is napping, and then work on building upon that sense of control. One powerful way to do this is by validating, as opposed to second-guessing, your own decisions. For example, instead of lamenting the fact that an entire day went by without you making any headway on your family's huge and ever-increasing mountain of laundry, you can remind yourself that it made sense to ignore the laundry so that you could meet the needs of your sick toddler (a toddler who, incidentally, also happened to be contributing to the size of that mountain).

Allow your growing sense of confidence to buoy your enjoyment of parenting. Here's a simple yet all-important fact about parenting: you are the true expert when it comes to your child. No one knows your child better, because no one has spent nearly as much time with him—and no one cares about him more. Understanding this fact changes everything about parenting. You'll be more willing to give yourself credit for everything you've learned and are learning about your child, and you won't be quite so quick to sell yourself short or to defer to some external authority who has never had the privilege of getting to know you and your child.

It's that chorus of external voices that can cause you to second-guess yourself when you're a brand-new parent, notes Karen, the mother of a twenty-two-month-old toddler. "Everybody tells you to trust your instincts—but then your instincts get so confused because there's so much information and advice. Looking back, I can see that my instincts were always spot on. I really just needed to learn how to trust my instincts. That overload of information—that's what was making me doubt myself," she says.

When you rely too heavily on outside experts, you miss out on the opportunity to tap into your growing intuition and to pay attention to the one person who has the most to teach you about parenting: your child. "I've heard people say, 'It's too bad babies don't come with manuals.' But the baby *is* the manual," says Teresa Pitman, the mother of four, grandmother of ten, and author of numerous bestselling books about parenting. "Your baby will show you." Paying attention to your child makes more sense than "putting that expert in between yourself and your child—ignoring your own feelings and what your child is trying to tell you in order to pay attention to that outside expert" and that expert's hard and fast rules. The problem is that these rules are based on the behaviour of a typical child. "And that's really no help at all when what really matters is the child you have in front of you.

"That's not to say that other people don't have good ideas or to overlook the fact that they can give you a fresh perspective on things," Pitman adds. But don't hit the panic button and feel that you need to turn to an outside expert for advice every time you hit a parenting road bump. "It's a bit like sex in some ways," she explains. "You don't rush off to see a sex therapist if the first sexual encounter with a new partner doesn't go perfectly. You focus on getting to know one another. And that's what you and your baby need to do."

Relying on too many outside experts can zap your confidence in your own abilities. Swansea University health researcher Amy Brown has found that mothers who rely heavily on parenting books that emphasize the importance of getting babies to stick to strict sleeping and feeding routines end up being more depressed and less confident in their own parenting abilities, because babies don't always follow all the rules.

Following a prescribed set of parenting rules also makes parenting more boring. According to psychotherapist and author Naomi Stadlen, the more you focus your attention on carrying out the instructions in the parenting world equivalent of an operating manual, the less likely you are to benefit from those exciting and enlightening moments of discovery that come from actually getting to know your own baby—the stuff that makes parenting truly enjoyable, in other words. Then there's all the inevitable second-guessing that happens as you hop from one piece of parenting advice to the next. I mean, why settle for a good-enough solution when you might still be able to stumble upon the perfect solution? It can be exhausting and anxiety-producing, to say the least. Relying too much on outside advice leaves you vulnerable to feeling both guilty and judged. "I think that just as our confidence as parents ebbs and flows, our feeling of being judged ebbs and flows too," notes Karen, the mother of two preteens.

The best way to manage those feelings is to trust yourself to make the best possible decisions for your family. Gordon, the father of two young children, says, "You're going to have people giving you advice from all corners. But, they're not in the boat with you. They don't know what you know. They don't feel what you feel. And so, in the end, you really just have to steer your own boat and do what you think feels right." The good news is that you don't have to parent in the same way that other people do or think you should, says Karen. "Trust yourself as a parent. We don't have to parent by consensus. We can just do what feels right for our family."

Strive to be your real self, not your perfect self. Here's more good news: you don't have to be perfect to be a good parent. In fact, it's probably better if you're not. After all, the best way to equip our children with strategies for thriving in a decidedly imperfect world is by providing them with a gloriously imperfect role model. And that's a role that each and every one of us is eminently qualified to take on. So instead of setting yourself up for failure by striving to be a perfect parent, simply set your sights on being real—being authentic, in other words.

There's a growing body of research to support the advantages of being authentic—of minimizing the gap between your outward behaviour and your inner feelings, values, and beliefs. First of all, it's less stressful. You won't be as drained by the effort of faking an emotion that you aren't actually feeling, which means that you'll have more energy and patience for parenting. Instead of having to constantly switch back and forth from the emotion you're *actually* feeling to the emotion you *wish* you were feeling—emotional multi-tasking at its most exhausting, in other words—you can simply focus on feeling what you're feeling. And that "makes parenting a hundred times easier and more enjoyable," notes Jillian, the mother of two teens and a preteen.

Second, being authentic is healthier for your relationships. When you're being authentic, you find it easier to connect with the people you care about, and they, in turn, find it easier to connect with you. Our kids know us so well that they can't help but pick up on the scrambled signals that we send out when we're pretending to feel something that we're not—like feigning over-the-top excitement at the prospect of yet another game of Candy Land. They end up being confused by those signals: "If Mom's so excited about playing another game of Candy Land, why is she gritting her teeth?" And that, in turn, causes them to pull away, creating distance in the relationship.

So, what's the best way to respond to a frustrating and annoying situation involving your child? You want to be able to respond in a way that you can feel good about but that also feels real. In other words, you don't want to give in to your impulse to toss the board game in the garbage, nor do you want to settle for smiling through gritted teeth. The secret is to find a way to shift your thinking, to find something about the situation that you can actually feel good about—perhaps the fact that playing

Candy Land is giving your child valuable practice in managing her emotions when the game isn't going her way. Making this mental shift allows you to shift from surface acting, which is merely playing the part of the happy parent when you're actually feeling anything but happy inside, to deep acting, which is changing your perspective on the situation so that you're able to experience genuine happiness or a renewed sense of purpose and meaning—another powerful source of parenting fuel.

Feel grateful for the good stuff and express that gratitude on a regular basis. Another simple yet powerful strategy for feeling happier as a parent is to tap into feelings of gratitude on a regular basis, as opposed to taking good things for granted. Positive psychology researchers have identified gratitude as one of the top four predictors of life satisfaction. (The other three are hope, zest, and love, just in case you're keeping track.) People who experience gratitude more often are less anxious and less depressed. They sleep better at night. They have better social and emotional skills and healthier relationships, at least in part because they're more likely to do kind things for other people when they feel grateful for the kind things other people have done for them. They feel an increased sense of meaning and purpose in their lives. And they find it easier to bounce back from life's curveballs. Gratitude acts as a buffer against negative events and stressful experiences by encouraging you to treat difficult experiences as opportunities for growth.

The secret to tapping into this powerful resource is to find ways to steer clear of gratitude guilt. Instead of feeling guilty about the fact that someone just did a nice thing for you—feeling indebted to that person—remind yourself that you don't actually have to settle the friendship debt today. As Barbara L. Fredrickson explains in her book *Positivity*, "Indebtedness pays back begrudgingly, as part of the economy of favors. In contrast, gratitude gives back freely and creatively."

Want to feel more grateful more often? Here are two science-proven strategies for boosting your feelings of gratitude, which will, in turn, boost your overall levels of happiness at the same time.

- Keep a gratitude journal. This isn't a new or fresh idea. It has been over two decades since Sarah Ban Breathnach first published her bestselling gratitude journal, *Simple Abundance.* But it's an idea that continues to stand the test of time. Keeping a gratitude journal doesn't have to take very long; a couple of minutes a day is all that is needed to jot down a sentence or two about the things you're feeling grateful about that day. But the impact can be far-reaching. Not only does keeping a gratitude journal encourage more positive life appraisals at the moment that you're making notes in your journal, but you're also more likely to have more positive expectations of life in the coming week as compared to people who journal about their daily struggles.

- Write a gratitude letter. Want to ramp up the impact of your gratitude journal? Write a gratitude letter to someone who played an important role in your life, expressing gratitude for how they inspired you or otherwise made your life better. If you want to increase the impact of this particular intervention, arrange to deliver the letter and read it in person, or read it via video chat if geography makes a face-to-face delivery impractical. That way, you can really savour the other person's response, amplifying your own feelings of happiness at the same time.

In this chapter, we've been talking about how to be a happier parent, how to get more of the good stuff of parenting, and how to really boost your enjoyment of all that good stuff so that it doesn't fly under your radar unnoticed, robbing you of much of the joy of parenting. In the next chapter, we're going to focus on the flip side of parenting: the stuff that can really drag you down.

CHAPTER 7

How to Tame the Anxiety, Guilt, and Feeling of Being Overwhelmed

Embrace all the emotions that come with parenting—the positive, the negative, the anger, the bliss. It's all part of the experience.

—Casey, father of two young boys

It's easy to fall into the trap of believing that being a good parent means experiencing round-the-clock bliss when, in fact, that's simply not how things play out in real life.

Even the happiest parent isn't happy all the time.

Ditto for the happiest child.

So, a big part of parenting is learning how to manage those less-than-blissed-out emotions—yours as well as your child's. That's what this chapter is all about: helping you to develop the coping strategies that will allow you to thrive as a parent and that will encourage your child to thrive too. We'll be talking about the impact of developing a positive stress mindset, in which stress is viewed as a biological call to action as opposed to something damaging and scary that needs to be feared or avoided at all costs. We'll discuss ways to tame that ever-present guilt and feeling of being overwhelmed. And we'll also talk about how to do battle with unproductive thought patterns that make parenting even harder, and why it's so important and so much more effective to treat yourself with self-compassion instead.

Developing a Positive Stress Mindset

Allow your mind to linger too long on the word *stress* and you're likely to find yourself feeling, well, *stressed*. That's because most of us have come to see stress as a negative to be avoided at all costs. In recent years, researchers from Stanford University have been challenging this idea, arguing that stress itself isn't the problem; it's the unhealthy response to stress that's the problem. Their research has shown that simply reframing your response to stress and seeing it as an opportunity to face up to a challenge can actually decrease the toll it takes on your body. Changing your thinking about stress can actually make stress less stressful, in other words. And it can also increase your ability to cope. A recent study conducted by researchers at the University of Mannheim in Germany found that having a positive stress mindset encourages you to use proactive coping strategies to deal with a challenging situation. If, for example, you know that you have a tough day ahead of you because your child has the stomach flu, you'll take pre-emptive steps to manage the challenge, like drastically cutting back your to-do list to the bare essentials. Here are some strategies for making stress work for, and not against, you.

Understand the biological functions of stress. Stress is designed to boost your energy, heighten your alertness, and narrow your focus so that you can zero in on what matters most: the specific threat that you're facing in this moment. This is good—in moderation. You don't want to flood your body with performance-enhancing hormones like adrenalin and dopamine on an ongoing basis. That would be like revving your car's engine 24/7. For the sake of that engine, you need to figure out how to take your foot off the throttle.

Acknowledge your stress. One of the ways to take your foot off the throttle—to minimize the impact stress is having on you, in other words—is to name it, label it, and describe it: "I am feeling stressed about _____." What you're doing is engaging the problem-solving parts of your brain as opposed to allowing the emotional parts of your brain to spin their wheels indefinitely. This buys you time to choose how you want to respond as opposed to reacting, or overreacting, in the moment. At the same time, it helps you to steer clear of avoidance, which happens to be one of the least effective ways of managing stress, because your brain has to work hard at suppressing that undesired emotion, causing you to feel even more stressed.

Own it. That's what Stanford University psychology researcher Alia Crum suggested in a 2015 article in the *Harvard Business Review*, that you should really lean into the source of your stress. Instead of trying to talk yourself out of the fact that you're feeling stressed about a particular situation, acknowledge that you're feeling stressed about that situation because you truly care about how things turn out. Then allow that increased sense of ownership to motivate you to find effective ways of dealing with the situation. Remind yourself that the feeling of restless energy you're experiencing is your body getting ready to tackle a particular challenge—one you care deeply about. Allow that restlessness to spur you to action.

Have your own personal toolkit of strategies for managing stress. Too much stress can feel overwhelming—picture that poor car engine being revved over and over again—so you want to have a toolkit of strategies for bringing it down to a more manageable level. The strategies that work well for you could be very different than the strategies that work well for other family members, notes Anthony, the father of two preteens: "Video games are a good outlet for me. For my wife, it's different. She reads her stress away." Other tried and true methods for managing stress that you might want to experiment with, and that you may want to teach your kids about as well, include practising relaxation breathing (slow, deep, stomach-level breathing as opposed to the fast, shallow, chest-level breathing we switch to when we're feeling stressed), positive visualization (taking a mini-vacation in your own head by evoking an image of safety and calm), progressive muscle relaxation (tensing and then relaxing each small muscle group in the body in order to encourage relaxation or aid sleep), mindfulness meditation (focusing your attention on the present moment in a way that both fosters feelings of self-compassion and suspends feelings of judgment), and yoga (a mind-body practice that combines relaxation breathing, meditation, and body movement).

Don't wait too long before you hit the brakes on stress. One thing I've learned, after decades of treating myself like a human stress guinea pig, is that it's a whole lot easier to manage symptoms of stress before they shoot sky-high. The secret to tackling symptoms of stress while they're still manageable is to train yourself to spot the early warning signs of rising stress. This means paying attention to how your body is feeling, and stopping to consider what other people might notice if they happened to be observing you right now. How do you look? What are you saying? What is the tone of your voice?

Resist the temptation to run away from the uncomfortable feelings associated with stress. Challenge yourself to consider whether your go-to methods of managing these feelings might actually be making things harder, not better. This is a pattern that Brandi, a mother of four, spotted in herself. "My strategy of dealing with stress was to add something new to my life to take my mind off the stress I was already dealing with," she explains. "However, instead of adding things that benefited me, like reading a book or having coffee with a friend or going for a workout, I only ever added activities that benefited other people. I had to learn to pay attention to where my energy was going and to ask myself whether I was investing that energy wisely."

Help your child to develop a positive stress mindset and proactive coping skills too. Be the kind of family that talks about the fact that a certain degree of challenge and stress can be life-enhancing. Be the type of parent who models healthy strategies for managing stress. "I have made an effort to stay very positive at home and at work to show that some level of challenge and stress in life can actually be a good thing, and that we should welcome it, within reason," says Elaine, the mother of two teenage girls.

Becoming Comfortable with Uncomfortable Emotions

We've talked about the importance of being willing to cozy up to stress as opposed to trying to run away from it. Now, let's talk about the importance of becoming comfortable dealing with other uncomfortable emotions, everything from anger to resentment to guilt. It turns out that one of the best ways to cope with negative emotions is to embrace your darker moods. This may sound counterintuitive, but it actually works because letting go of some of the pressure to be relentlessly upbeat actually results in a happier and less stressed-out you. Instead of fixating on how awful you're feeling, or worse, beating yourself up for not being blissed out 24/7, you simply accept the fact that these emotions are part of the experience of being human. This means that these emotions are going to be part of your life as a parent, and they're going to be part of your kid's life too. Because here's the thing: there is no such thing as a bad or a wrong feeling. It's important that our kids grow up understanding this simple yet all-important fact.

The good news is that, in most cases, uncomfortable emotions tend to run their course and disappear on their own, like dark clouds moving across the sky. Resisting dark emotions only increases their power over you and the likelihood that they'll stick around. Of course, if you find that these emotions are sticking around too long and you feel like the proverbial black cloud has taken up permanent residence right over your head or your child's head, you may want to seek some additional help in chasing that black cloud away. You don't have to handle this on your own, in other words.

Digging Yourself Out of the Emotional Muck

Psychologists tend to distinguish between adaptive self-reflection and non-adaptive self-reflection, which is more often referred to as "rumination." The first type of self-reflection is fuelled by a curiosity about yourself and a desire to learn and grow. It's the kind of self-reflection that we were talking about back in Chapter 5—the kind of self-reflection that supports better thinking.

The second type is more about fixating on everything that's wrong, and by that, I mean everything that's wrong right now, that has already gone wrong in the past, and that is likely to go wrong in the future. It's about endlessly rehashing the negatives and the obstacles as opposed to identifying the positives and the solutions. We're talking about getting stuck in some seriously nasty emotional muck, which only serves to make life and parenting harder.

Rumination doesn't just make parenting harder; it also makes your parenting efforts less effective. When you're narrowly focused on your worries, it's harder to see the big picture. This is a point that happiness researcher Barbara L. Fredrickson makes in her book *Positivity*: "When you ruminate, you see everything through the distorted lens of negativity. And negativity doesn't play fair. It doesn't allow you to think straight or see the big picture." In fact, "There is no big picture, no dots to connect."

The best way to break free of this cycle of rumination is to regain that broader perspective by focusing on something or someone other than yourself. "When you lose focus, your mind tends to fixate on what could be wrong with your life instead of what's right," notes Cal Newport in his book *Deep Work: Rules for Focused Success in a Distracted World.* Your brain tends to go AWOL a lot—something like 47 percent of the time. It's kind of like what happens when your dog spots a squirrel. The squirrel captures his attention and he's gone. Focusing your attention on some sort of activity is a means of controlling those squirrelly thoughts, which can lead you down the path to rumination.

Here are some other strategies to try:

Engage in cognitive reappraisal. If you find yourself stuck in a rut of negative thinking, don't passively accept the thoughts that are making your life miserable. Challenge all the ones that are unhelpful or just plain wrong.

Cut yourself some slack. Ask yourself if you would be this harsh and unforgiving to a friend who was struggling, and then commit to treating yourself with at least as much kindness as you'd extend to that friend. Practise self-compassion, in other words.

Practise "worry triage." Use expressive writing as a tool for managing rumination. Make a list of all the things that are worrying you and then divide those worries into two categories: things you can and can't do something about. For each thing you can control, identify the first step in taking action. For the things you can't control, focus on acceptance ("It is what it is") and processing your emotions ("It makes sense that I'm feeling what I'm feeling"; "Feelings come and go"). It's all about looking for ways to find meaning in difficult experiences and seizing opportunities to learn and grow. (More on this later in the chapter.)

Managing Unrealistic Expectations

If there's one thing that modern parents have in abundance, it's guilt. Despite the fact that we're devoting more time and effort to parenting than ever before, we continue to fall short of our sky-high expectations of ourselves.

"The expectations are just so high," says Katie, the mother of three school-aged boys. "I feel like you should be able to have a good job and a beautiful family, that you should be happy in your family pictures and be able to take your kids to hockey three days a week—to do all those things." Here are some strategies for steering clear of three flawed thinking patterns that tend to fuel those sky-high expectations.

Sidestep the "shoulds." Part of the problem is that we get caught up in what Christine, the mother of a teen and a preteen, describes as "all the shoulds," which are all the things we tell ourselves we should be doing, without ever pausing to consider whether these things even matter to us at all. Her advice? Be clear about whose "should" it is. Do you actually own it or have you borrowed it from someone else without thinking—perhaps some super-critical "friend" on social media? Is this "should" actually working for you? "If you get something out of the standards that society sets, then by all means, participate in them to your heart's content," she says. "But do take time to consider, 'Does this matter to me?' 'Does it serve me and my family well?' and 'What else do I have to give up in order to meet this standard?'"

Look for opportunities to let go of some of the self-imposed shoulds. Figure out whose voice is telling you that you should do something and talk back to those expectations. Get in the habit of asking yourself, "What could I do?" as opposed to "What should I do?" when you find yourself faced with a challenging situation. And do your best to schedule what actress Ellen Burstyn likes to call an occasional "should-free" day—a day free of other people's expectations. (Pro tip: If you can't swing an entire "should-free" day, maybe you could pull off a "should-free" hour instead.)

Of course, the most powerful antidote to all those shoulds is to refuse to define success on anyone else's terms but your own. This particular strategy has proven to be a lifesaver for Germaine, the single parent of an eleven-year-old son. "There is a lot of pressure to be perfect," she explains—with "perfect" being all about having the right stuff and shuttling your kid off to the right activities. "You are alienated if your child isn't part of a particular sport (hockey to name but one), if you don't drive the right vehicle, or if you're not in a certain salary bracket." Her approach to dealing with all that pressure has been to define happiness on her own terms: "Once upon a time, I was ashamed to be a waitress living in a basement apartment. Now, I couldn't care less because I'm happy with where I am in life. Could it be better? Yes, it could always be better. But could I be any happier? Nope."

Don't allow planning fallacy to conspire against you. Ever wonder why your estimates of what you should be able to accomplish over the course of a day are unfailingly optimistic? Blame it on planning fallacy, our all-too-human tendency to treat our most-productive-ever day as the standard for what should be possible each and every day. Remember that one time when you managed to do ten loads of laundry and batch-cook seven casseroles over the course of a day? That becomes your new benchmark for normal. It's a nasty piece of cognitive work, a point Caroline Webb makes in her book *How to Have a Good Day*: "We typically expect tasks to take less time than they actually do, because we base our estimates on one standout memory—our *best* past experience—rather than the average time it's taken us to do similar tasks in the past."

But here's the thing: to-do lists are supposed to be grounded in reality, not treated as aspirational documents. It's not realistic to expect ourselves to be super-productive, super-patient, and super-positive every single day. This isn't how human beings work. We all have our off-days. Asking yourself to measure up to a standard set on that rare near-perfect day means dooming yourself to fall short, and feel guilty, the rest of the time.

Oh yeah, and here's a related point: we forget to take new circumstances into account, like the fact that we're going to be a whole lot more sleep-deprived, and hence a whole lot less productive, when we're caring for a brand-new baby, so maybe it isn't terribly realistic to plan to launch a new business or organize a family reunion at the exact same time.

To prevent planning fallacy from doing a major number on your head, you might want to get in the habit of checking your expectations of yourself. You can do this by asking yourself two key questions: (1) "Is this realistic for me?" and (2) "Is this realistic for me *right now*?" Know your limits and respect those limits rather than treating wishful thinking as a planning tool.

Master the art of chunking. This is all about breaking tasks that feel too overwhelming to tackle all at once into a series of much more manageable, bite-sized chunks. Let's say, for example, that the weather has made a classic Canadian U-turn and your kids have gone from needing snowsuits to needing swimsuits overnight. Instead of telling yourself, "I need to do the entire winter-to-summer wardrobe switchover for every single member of the family right now," you could simply say, "I'm going to dig out an outfit or two for everybody—enough to carry us through the next few days." Then, once you've made progress on that initial task, you'll be motivated to start tackling related tasks, like washing and packing away the snowsuits, sorting through and matching up all the mittens, identifying wardrobe gaps as you pull out your kids' shorts and T-shirts, figuring out what to do about those wardrobe gaps, and so on. The results can be pretty magical, both in terms of what you're able to accomplish (no more snowsuits hogging all the space in the front hall closet) and how much less anxious you feel because you managed to plow through rather than avoid an otherwise overwhelming task.

Don't compare your Google searches to other people's Facebook posts. As it turns out, hell isn't other people; it's comparing yourself to other people. Once again, you can blame your all-too-human brain. Cognitive science tells us that we have a tendency to compare the worst of ourselves with the best of other people—an inclination that inevitably dooms us to failure. (We'll be talking about this more in Chapter 11.)

To make matters worse, we have a tendency to create a hellish hybrid of expectations by combining the most stellar achievements of each of our friends—the friend who just ran a marathon, the friend who just went back to school to earn yet another degree, the friend who was recently celebrated as volunteer of the year in her community, the friend who grows her own heritage vegetables, bakes her own organic bread, and has developed a near-cult following online as a result—and then asking ourselves to measure up to each and every one of those standards all at once, ignoring the fact that we're only one person—and a mere mortal person at that. It's ridiculous and tremendously unhelpful, I know.

Taming the Guilt

Of course, it's one thing to recognize that your expectations of yourself are outrageously unrealistic and quite another to figure out how to tame the resulting tsunami of guilt. Here are some strategies for doing just that.

Celebrate the fact that parents don't have to be perfect. No one gets parenting right all the time. What matters is that you get the right stuff right as often as possible—which means ensuring that most of your child's needs are being met most of the time. Loren used to feel a lot of regret about the way things played out back when her kids were younger. At that point, she was a single parent and "working really hard to take us from a very marginal lifestyle to the kind of lifestyle that I wanted for us." As a result, she wasn't able to spend as much time with her kids as she would have liked, and there were times when she fell short of her own expectations of herself as a parent. "I was reactive sometimes when I should have been more empathetic," she recalls.

Eventually, Loren was able to shift the spotlight from all the things she'd done wrong to all the things she'd done right—and under really challenging circumstances, no less. Once that happened, she was finally able to see that the things she'd managed to do right were actually the things that mattered most of all: "My children have both told me that, no matter what, they felt loved. And, no matter what, they felt seen. And so even though it was far from perfect, we managed to stumble through together."

Master the art of relationship repair. Everyone stumbles and everyone has to figure out how to get back up. That's what parenting is all about. Part of "getting back up" means knowing how to get your relationship with your child back on track and teaching your child how to do the same. "Forgiveness on both parts is key," says Noreen, mother of two preschoolers. "You have to hope your kid will forgive you for being human, and you have to forgive them."

How you approach the actual apology may vary depending on whether you're a mom or a dad. A 2015 study conducted by University of South Dakota doctoral student Eliann R. Carr found that while mothers place a stronger emphasis on "care reasoning" ("I did this because I care about you"), fathers place a stronger emphasis on "justice reasoning" ("I did this because it was the right thing to do") when looking for a reason to explain their actions. She also reached an even more important conclusion regarding the impact of parental apologies, noting that "children equate a parental apology as a display of love."

The takeaway message is clear: a sincere and heartfelt apology can go a long way in making up for the inevitable missteps and stumbles you're destined to make as a parent. This is something that Mary, the mother of a seven-year-old, thinks about a lot. "It helps immensely when I'm able to remember that I'm the adult and I need to be the one to model the skills I want him to learn and use with others. I find that when I allow myself to get curious, ask questions, and really listen with an open mind and heart, it allows us to get to the healing and forgiveness more quickly." This is very different from what she experienced as a child: "I don't remember my parents ever apologizing. I think they were afraid that they would lose their parenting authority if they admitted they were wrong." Needless to say, she sees things very differently: "Rather than undermining my authority, I think it actually promotes mutual respect."

Lynn is already seeing the benefits of prioritizing relationship repair in her relationship with her daughter: "When I lose my cool, make a mistake, or screw up, I try to help her understand what happened, why it was wrong, and what I'm doing to make it right. I try to model a healthy approach to messing up, and in doing so, I'm learning to be kind and forgiving to myself, which my daughter reflects back to me. She is already developing a level of empathy and emotional intelligence that truly astounds me."

Parenting isn't just about what's happening in a particular moment. It's also about all the accumulated past interactions between you and your child. It's a relationship movie, not a relationship snapshot, in other words. What you're doing when you apologize to your child is indicating your desire to delete a botched snapshot and try this thing again, because this relationship matters to you. As Loren puts it, "I've learned to say that my intentions were good, but my execution was really crummy."

Resolve to learn and grow together. Like Loren, Gordon is a big fan of the parental apology. "We haven't tried to be perfect to our kids. That relieves a lot of the stress," he says. "I guess that's the best parenting advice: to find your own way and to keep learning and growing alongside your kids."

It's all about learning and growing for Marie's family too. Her first son, Lawrence, was placed with the family three years ago, back when he was just three. Then, a few months ago, two other boys—a set of brothers—joined the family as well. Daniel is one year older than Lawrence, and Reid is one year younger. The past few months have been a major transition for all of them, including Lawrence, who is trying to figure out "how to be a brother" and "how to share his mom and dad." What's helping Marie and her family to weather the resulting challenges is her recognition that they're all new at being a family, and her commitment to figuring things out together. "Right now, we're just learning. We're all learning. There's a fluidity to all of this and we have to be ready to meet and adapt to each challenge," she explains. It isn't always easy to go with the flow—she and her husband are the type who like to be in control, "so that kind of goes against our grain," she admits—but she knows that it's the only way to deal with the challenges her three sons are facing. She says, "No child who is adopted only has the standard baggage of life. They did not come from a good start, so let's not assume for a second that they did. Their parents might have had the best of intentions, but something clearly fell apart. In order for my family to be created, someone else's had to fall apart. And that's the hard reality."

The good news is that parents and kids can get through the tough stuff together. According to the Center on the Developing Child at Harvard University, the single most important factor contributing to a child's resilience is "at least one stable and committed relationship with a supportive parent, caregiver, or other adult." You can be that person for your child—an anchor in even the stormiest of storms.

Recognize that life doesn't have to be perfect to be pretty great. A 100 percent stress-free childhood is not the goal here—nor is it even remotely possible, of course. Sure, you don't exactly want to rush out to sign your child up for the Terrible Experience of the Month Club, but there's no need to panic or allow yourself to get swept up in a tidal wave of regret if difficult circumstances happen to arise. Working through a difficult situation as a family can actually help to inoculate your child against future episodes of stress, by strengthening his ability to cope. It may also increase his feelings of connectedness to, and compassion for, others, because empathy is the gift you get to carry forward from difficult experiences.

As it turns out, having a completely stress-free childhood can actually leave you at a slight disadvantage. Research has shown that adults who have somehow managed to squeak through life dodging any and all possible curveballs actually score lower on measures of well-being as compared to others who have done a bit of time in the school of hard knocks. "It is people who have been through at least two traumas, and less than six, who score the highest" in terms of well-being, noted science writer Benedict Carey in an article in *The New York Times*.

Part of our job as parents is to help our children understand that struggle and frustration are part of life, and that we can get through these experiences together. It's an important message about resilience and about being real. "There are two ways to deal with non-ideal circumstances," says Loren. "One is to pretend that there's nothing going on, to refuse to talk about it, to treat the kids like they're the problem, like it's their fault that there's chaos in the home. And the other is to acknowledge that the circumstances that you're dealing with are less than ideal and to commit to finding a way through together." That's the path the mother of two young adults chose to take during her years as a single parent—a path that "enlisted the health and agency of my kids while making them feel loved."

Anne has decided to take a similar approach in helping

her three young daughters, who are ages four through nine, to deal with the reality of her stage-four breast cancer diagnosis. For starters, it is about being honest: "I never wanted to lie to them about this. I have a hard-enough time lying about Santa Claus, which is actually a fun thing!" she says. They do talk about the fact that she won't always be here, but she tries to do so in a way that is reassuring rather than scary. She wants them to know that they're going to be okay: "I tell them that in all the great stories, the kids lose their moms and then the kids turn into superheroes," she jokes, trying to inject a bit of levity into a conversation that would otherwise be impossibly dark.

Lindsay's two children (a teen and a preteen) are also learning important lessons about resilience—lessons learned in the wake of a serious car accident four years ago that left her with a traumatic brain injury. "I think if the last four years have taught me anything, it's that I'll probably be able to get through anything. I can't say it will necessarily be pretty, but I know that I'll come out the other side," she says. She is proud of the fact that she's been able to model this kind of resilience for her kids: "This experience has shown the kids that life isn't perfect, and it's allowed them to watch me change while still being strong and determined." They've weathered the storms as a family.

Treating Yourself with Self-Compassion

Learning about self-compassion can be life changing. It certainly was for me. Instead of listening to a harsh, bullying voice in my head that was constantly telling me what I was doing wrong, I was able to tune into a kinder, gentler voice that was focused on what I was at least trying to do right. Self-compassion is basically just compassion directed toward the self. It's about seeing yourself as someone who is loveable and worthy of care—and who is acceptable, flaws and all. It's about shifting to an inner dialogue that's gentle and encouraging as opposed to harsh and belittling. It's about treating yourself with at least the same degree of kindness that you would extend to a friend who was struggling.

Wondering why self-compassion is such a powerful resource in your life as a parent? Here's what the research has to say.

SELF-COMPASSION IS GOOD FOR YOUR MENTAL HEALTH.

Self-compassion helps to silence the voices of self-criticism and self-blame that simply serve to make parenting harder and that can lead to feelings of anxiety and depression over time. Treating yourself with compassion reduces feelings of stress by deactivating your body's threat system and activates its self-soothing system instead. It also lessens the grip of negativity, and in a way, that is all about accepting as opposed to avoiding negative emotions. You begin to treat negative emotions as sources of information and to be curious about what those emotions have to teach you.

SELF-COMPASSION IMPROVES YOUR THINKING.

It reduces your feelings of defensiveness, allowing you to see things more clearly, size up the situation more accurately, and engage in effective problem-solving (as opposed to energy-zapping rumination). It also opens the door to change, because unconditional self-acceptance leaves you less afraid to try new things or to take risks.

SELF-COMPASSION IMPROVES THE QUALITY OF YOUR RELATIONSHIPS.

You're more likely to accept other people's flaws and better able to cope with their feelings of distress. And you feel more connected to and compassionate toward others. You recognize your common humanity—the fact that you, like every other person on the planet, struggles. Instead of feeling imperfect, defective, and separate from others when things go wrong, you feel united by that shared struggle. (This is very different from the feelings that are derived from self-esteem, which is more about feeling like you're in competition with, and hence separate from, others. Self-compassion reminds you that we're all on the same team.)

SELF-COMPASSION CAN HELP YOU TO ROOT OUT UNHELPFUL BELIEFS ABOUT YOURSELF.

Some of these beliefs may be foundational or "bedrock" ideas on which you've constructed your entire conception of yourself as a person. Others may be more fleeting, like the harsh, judgmental voice in your head that constantly narrates your life and is always eager to point out what you're doing wrong. Cognitive reappraisal (something we've talked about a couple of times in this book) is an essential first step in uprooting this unhelpful inner dialogue. Self-compassion takes things a step further by replacing those self-critical messages with other messages that are kinder and much more helpful.

Is self-compassion a cop-out? Actually, it's a call to action. Practising self-compassion encourages you to accept more responsibility for your actions, not less. At the same time, it's action-oriented. It's rooted in concern for your own well-being and a desire to relieve your suffering.

For a time, Lindsay's suffering was pretty extreme in the wake of her traumatic brain injury. "It used to be that when I had a bad day, I would go to bed at seven o'clock at night and lay there dwelling on everything that had gone wrong. I'd be telling myself things like, 'I'm screwing my kids up. I'm ruining my relationship with my husband. I'm doing all these things wrong,'" she says. "That bad thing was maybe five minutes in a day when there are, in fact, twenty-four hours in a day. It's a minor blip in the big picture, but for a while, those minor blips became really big things. I made them into big things because they are all I focused on. I didn't focus on the things that were going well; I only focused on the things that were going wrong."

At some point, she recognized that beating herself up wasn't making things better. It was actually making things worse. And so, she resolved to do things differently and start treating herself with more compassion. That changed everything. Her life stopped feeling like such a struggle and she found herself looking to the future with hope. It all came down to recognizing that things were difficult and acknowledging that she was doing her absolute best: "I started telling myself, 'You know what? I'm doing the best that I can. The day is done. And tomorrow is a new day.'"

Ginette, the mother of two young children, has also recognized the importance of treating herself with compassion. "Every so often, I feel like I'm not being the parent I want to be," she says. "I'm running on fumes. I don't feel empathy for my kids—just annoyance and frustration. And I get very angry at myself for not being better, for not being the picture of parenthood that I remember idealizing as a small child: someone who is patient, cheerful, forgiving, and gentle. Empathy is central to my parenting and, after not bothering to have any for myself for a few years, I realized I was having a harder and harder time mustering it up for anyone else. So, I'm trying to be gentle and nurturing and patient with myself for a change. Progress is slow, but this was a major parenting epiphany for me."

Self-compassion is simple and it's magical, at least according to Loren: "It's all about saying, 'Okay, this is what went wrong. Now I forgive myself. And I'll get up and try again tomorrow.'"

CHAPTER 8

The Guilt-Free Guide to Healthier Living

After many years of not really believing it would make a difference, I have finally learned the value of regular exercise for stress management. I always feel better after moving my body. Why I have to relearn this lesson all the time, I don't know.

—Kate, mother of two preteens

It's not your imagination: becoming a parent *can* take a toll on your health. For starters, your workouts may have gone AWOL. Researchers at the University of Victoria and the University of British Columbia have flagged the experience of becoming a parent as "a critical transition point for physical activity decline." As many as 50 percent of adults who were regularly active before becoming parents cut back on their amount of physical activity after they become parents, and that dip continues for at least the next five years. It's an issue for both moms and dads, but the impact is more pronounced for mothers, who experience a steeper decline in their amount of physical activity. To make matters worse, reduced physical activity isn't just a new-parent thing. The trend continues across the parenting life cycle. As a 2017 report from Statistics Canada noted, "Canadian adults with children are less active than those without children."

Then there's the fact that becoming a parent can also interfere with your ability to eat as well as you'd like. A study of the eating habits of a group of parents in British Columbia revealed that new moms and new dads are both highly motivated to improve their eating habits after they become parents, at least in part because they want to be positive role models for their children, but that the rather daunting challenges of new parenthood can make it difficult for them to translate these intentions into action. They simply don't feel confident that they can make these health changes right now, given the heavy demands of early parenthood. While dads find it easier to tackle these health changes over time, moms actually become less motivated to make changes to their eating habits, particularly once second and subsequent children arrive on the scene. The researchers wrote, "Some mothers may find that focusing time and energy on preparing healthy meals for multiple children leads to subsequent decreases in motivation for their own dietary behaviours."

Then there's the fact that sleep tends to be in chronically short supply when you're a parent—and not merely when you're a first-time parent. A study conducted by the American Academy of Neurology and Georgia Southern University measured the impact of the number of children on the odds of a parent getting adequate sleep. The conclusion? Each additional child increases the likelihood that you're not getting at least six hours of sleep each night by an astounding 50 percent.

So, you're exhausted, you're poorly nourished, and you're slowly but surely slipping into couch potato mode. That's the bad news. The good news is that the situation isn't entirely hopeless— although it can feel that way some days. There are things you can do to improve your physical and mental health, and to help your kids improve theirs at the same time. Becoming a parent doesn't just present a health challenge; it also provides a health opportunity: a chance to switch things up, do things differently, and become the healthiest possible you. That's what this chapter is all about: journeying to that healthier place in a completely guilt-free way. In keeping with the theme of this book, we're going to start that journey by shining the spotlight on you and talking about the importance of self-care. Then we're going to shift the spotlight to your children and talk about how your health impacts theirs (and vice versa), and how you can use that information to your advantage. We'll be zooming in on the four pillars of good health—sleep, physical activity, moderate screen time, and healthy eating—and delving into the science of habit change for strategies to make your new health habits stick.

Why It's Important to Prioritize Self-Care—and What That *Really* Means

When I first started interviewing parents for this book, I started those interviews by launching into a series of questions about self-care. I asked parents what they were doing to try to prioritize their own health and well-being in the midst of the day-to-day challenges of parenting. I quickly discovered that I had to switch tactics. Starting a conversation by talking about self-care was pretty much a sure-fire way of shutting the entire conversation down. The response that I received from Lisa, the mother of a preteen with special needs, was typical: "The fact that I literally just finished eating a pack of Skittles because it's been a horrible week makes me absolutely unqualified to answer that question."

Julia, the mother of an eighteen-month-old toddler, told me that, for her, the term "self-care" had pretty much become synonymous with guilt: "The whole self-care thing can kind of be a double-edged sword, because you can feel like you're not 'self-caring' right. I'm not making the time to go to the spa and work out for an hour every day and to drink a green smoothie every morning, because most mornings, I'm lucky to eat a piece of toast. And then I feel guilty, and that's not helping anybody." Too often, self-care can feel like one more thing to add to an already out-of-control to-do list, added Katie, the mother of three school-aged boys: "If you're not doing it, it's just another thing you're failing at." The guilt can zap you either way, whether you're practising self-care or you're not, she added. "I should be able to take care of myself—and I'm supposed to take care of myself—but at the same time, there's this guilt for taking care of myself."

It can be hard to give yourself permission to take care of yourself when you're feeling maxed out by the demands of parenthood, notes Olivia, the mother of a two-and-a-half-year-old. "My son has become the number one priority, so his needs are met first. My partner has fallen to number two, and sometimes I don't even get to meet his needs. And I'm still trying to figure out where I fall into the mix." Lynn, the mother of a twenty-three-month-old, can relate to those sentiments: "I'm the least well-cared-for person in my household. It's nearly impossible for me to take good care of myself, but I try—and then I feel shitty when I fail."

Janine, the mother of a five-year-old, resents the fact that she has to take the initiative when it comes to caring for herself, because no one else is going to do it for her: "I was expecting my husband to come home and say, 'Oh my gosh, you look exhausted. Go have a bath. I'll take care of dinner and put the baby to bed,' or 'Go for a walk.' But he never did that because his focus is so much on himself. So, I realized that if someone is going to take care of me, that person has to be me."

GETTING REAL ABOUT SELF-CARE
Of course, it isn't easy to prioritize self-care if you feel like it's something frivolous, indulgent, or even selfish. When it's too narrowly defined and seems to be more about pampering yourself with luxury goods or spa treatments than actually replenishing

yourself in any meaningful way, it can sound pretty frivolous. Katie says, "Some people think that self-care is about going and getting a manicure and a pedicure. That might be self-care for some people, but it's expensive and it's not accessible for everyone." Kim, the mother of two teenage girls, also challenges the whole idea that self-care should be all about doing something expensive: "I think that's just more guilt for parents who can't do that—who have no money to do that."

In reality, self-care is about so much more than that. It's about nurturing yourself and your relationships, safeguarding your right to good health, and ensuring that activities that actually involve meeting some of your own needs—as opposed to solely focusing on meeting everyone else's needs—show up on your calendar a little more often. It's a mindset, a way of living, as opposed to a short-lived indulgence that you might feel you have to justify to yourself or anyone else.

"We need to rethink the idea of self-care or adjust our expectations of what it means to practise self-care," says Annabel Fitzsimmons, an author, fitness and meditation instructor, and mother of two. It doesn't have to be something huge and unattainable. It's simply about caring for yourself in the same way that you could care for another person you care about, like your child. Annabel explains, "Think about what it means to care for another person. We spend time reading to our kids. We help them to establish a bedtime routine. We care about what they eat. We make their doctor's appointment. We ensure that they have ample activities that make them happy: time with friends and doing sports that they love or making art. So, what if we simply looked at our own lives and tried to treat ourselves as well as we treat our kids? That's the kind of perspective I've tried to adopt for myself. Am I eating well? Am I doing activities that I enjoy? Am I spending time with friends who make me feel good and make my soul feel full? Am I giving myself enough small moments throughout the day that nourish me?"

That's the kind of self-care that Kim can relate to and that she actually has a hope of making happen in her very busy life. In fact, she's started practising this kind of self-care: "One of the things I do—and I think a lot of parents do this—is to sit in my car for ten to fifteen minutes before I head into the house. I sit there so that I can transition from whatever crappy thing might have happened in my day to the next part of my day. Maybe I go on Facebook. Maybe I text or talk with a friend. But whatever it is, I make a point of giving myself that break before I head into the house. Because once I go in the house, I can't guarantee what's going to happen."

One powerful way to practise self-care is to look for ways to connect with the parts of yourself that most define who you are as a person. You might start out by making a list of the types of situations and activities that help you feel like the best version of yourself, and then look for opportunities to introduce those types of experiences into your life once again. Feeding your essential "me-ness" can be tremendously restorative, and it doesn't have to be hugely time-consuming or expensive. You can make it happen on a budget—and with a baby in your arms!

Speaking of which, you'll find that it's easier to fit in self-care if you look for ways to make it happen while you're with your kids, since that's how you're going to be spending a lot of your time. That's the approach Marie, the mother of three school-aged boys, has chosen to take. She practises self-care in a way that doesn't have to involve getting away from her kids. She explains, "Even when Lawrence was little, we'd go on bike rides together. Or we'd head down to the park so that he could be active and I could run after him a bit. This freed me from the worries of, 'Is he going to break something by being active in the house?' 'Is he going to knock something over?' 'Is he going to hurt himself by jumping off the couch?' If we were having a hard time, it wouldn't be unusual for me to say, 'Let's run to the park.'"

Self-care is less likely to feel like a huge, guilt-inducing monstrosity if you focus on what's realistic and possible right now—while also allowing yourself to dream about what might become more possible over time. Sometimes, you're just plain maxed out, and nothing short of a miracle intervention by some self-care fairy godmother is going to change the situation. Kim wishes she had time to go to yoga class, but she hasn't been able to fit that in recently. "I work full-time and have five jobs and I don't know how to fit it all in," she explains. She looks forward to getting back into her yoga routine once circumstances allow it: "My kids say I was much nicer when I was going to yoga. I loved having the chance to just sit there and mentally regroup." That's simply not possible for her right now, and until something shifts and she finds herself a little less pressed for time and money, she's going to stick with her self-imposed driveway time-outs and her other favourite self-care activity these days: going for "a good drive" to clear her head.

Sarah finds herself in a pretty good place these days, at least when it comes to practising self-care. Having to do without it for an extended period of time when her three children, who are triplets, were really young has made it all the more precious for her at this stage in her life. "I find it's important to have one activity a week that is just for me, with adult conversation and some creativity, and being present in the moment," she says. "I couldn't do that for three years when my kids were small, and I felt like I'd lost an important part of myself. Choir is one of my favourite activities. It involves deep breathing, letting go of control and following somebody's directions, listening carefully, contributing to a whole that is greater than the individual parts, and making something beautiful that only lasts a few minutes. I often leave choir rehearsal feeling much more energized and happy than when I arrived."

Dani also tries to prioritize self-care, in part because she wants to model this all-important skill for her three children: "I try to spend time caring for the parts of me that aren't just about being a mom. When I do these things, I'm teaching my family that it's possible to take care of yourself—and that I'm worthy of being cared for too." She's hoping that modelling these skills will encourage her children to get in the self-care habit early in life—as opposed to trying to figure this stuff out decades from now, like many of us did. It's an approach that Annabel Fitzsimmons supports wholeheartedly: "If we can model for our kids that we do things for ourselves to maintain a quality of life that keeps us happy, energized, and healthy, it leads the way for them to make those choices too."

Of course, you don't have to practise self-care simply because you hope that doing so will make you a better parent, or because you want to be a healthy role model for your child. You can do it to feel better about yourself, to feel stronger, healthier, and more in control, and as an act of kindness toward yourself. "Taking care of yourself for your own sake is perfectly okay," says Christine, the mother of a teen and a preteen. "You don't have to take care of yourself just so that you'll be a better parent. If that's what it takes for you to not feel guilty about it, feel free to go with that. But know that it's okay to take care of yourself for yourself. You are a person who is deserving of care and love. And the fact that you have children does not in any way negate that. In fact, it amplifies it."

GETTING TO A PLACE WHERE YOU CAN PRACTISE SELF-CARE
You're more likely to practise self-care if you're already in a reasonably happy, healthy place. You'll be more motivated and have more energy to devote to developing healthy habits like getting enough sleep, exercising regularly, and enjoying healthy meals. If you haven't quite made it to that happier place yet, you might want to increase your odds of getting there soon by drawing upon some of the happiness-boosting and anxiety-taming strategies we discussed in the previous two chapters. And you might want to review the strategies we discussed back in Chapter 5 about tapping into the power of calm. Each of those chapters was building toward this chapter by providing you with the

mindset and coping strategies needed to become the happiest, healthiest possible you. Now, it's simply a case of applying everything we've talked about so far to ramp up your motivation to practise self-care. Here are some questions you might want to consider as you look for opportunities to make self-care a more regular part of your life:

- How do you feel, both mentally and physically, after you've made an effort to take extra good care of yourself? How long do you feel the benefits? What could you do to prolong the benefits even longer?

- What are some ways you might be able to work self-care into your day?

- Are there ways you could automate that self-care—and by that, I mean are there ways you could build it into your daily routine so that you don't even have to think about it?

- What are the peaks and valleys in your day—the times when you are particularly happy and energetic or extremely anxious and depleted? What are some self-care strategies you could use to level out the valleys or sustain the peaks? What might be the impact on your parenting?

The Truth about Self-care

Still struggling to give yourself permission to take the best possible care of yourself? I know how that feels. I grappled with that feeling for entire decades of my life! But here's what I figured out in the end: Self-care isn't selfish. It's self-preservation. It's an act of kindness toward yourself and your child. By taking the best possible care of yourself, you're giving your child the gift of a happier, healthier you. And it's a gift that just keeps giving:

- You'll be better able to model healthy behaviours for your child.

- You'll have the energy and patience required to help them acquire these habits for themselves.

- You'll be able to parent in a way that you can actually feel good, as opposed to guilty, about.

"What our children want most from us is that we be happy and that we be well," explains Loren, the mother of two young adults. "Because if we're happy and we're well, we're also present. And that presence is what matters most." And it all starts with a healthier, happier, and less stressed-out you.

The Stress Piece of the Puzzle

Managing your own stress level is key to becoming a happier, healthier family. When parents are massively stressed, everything tends to fall apart on the health front. Consider the evidence for yourself:

When parents are stressed, kids are less likely to be physically active. They're also more likely to spend their time in front of screens and to be obese. Researchers from the University of Guelph have come up with two different theories to explain what could be going on here. It could be that a parent's high stress level triggers the child's own physiological response to stress, encouraging a series of unhealthy behaviours that may ultimately lead to obesity. Or it could be that a massively stressed-out parent is simply too exhausted and overwhelmed to create the kind of home environment that encourages healthy behaviours; for example, there's no time to grocery shop, so there aren't any fruits and vegetables available for the kids to snack on, and no one has time to sign the kids up for soccer, let alone commit to taking them to all of their games. Of course, it's possible that both of these theories come into play.

The health impact is even greater when mom is the one who is feeling stressed. A mother's stress level has the greatest impact on the health habits of other family members. When moms are stressed, children are less likely to eat healthy foods and more likely to eat fast food; and they're less likely to benefit from the behind-the-scenes help that encourages children to be involved in physical activity, like registering kids for and transporting them to sports activities and lessons. Everything kind of falls apart . . .

Stress has a spillover effect on partners. When one partner feels stressed, the other partner is less likely to take time for physical activity or other kinds of leisure. That can spark resentment and lead to conflict between the two partners.

The good news is that you can decide to put the brakes on this downward spiral. You can learn strategies for managing stress that will not only benefit you, but will benefit the rest of your family as well. You'll find many of these strategies outlined in previous chapters in this book, but sometimes reading a book isn't enough to help you break deeply entrenched habits. Sometimes, it makes sense to seek professional help as well.

Up until now, we've been talking about the "why" of healthy living. Now we're going to shift our focus to "how" by considering strategies for getting more sleep, becoming more active, managing screen time, and improving our eating habits—and helping our kids to do the same.

Solving the Problem That Is Sleep

It's an inconvenient truth: our bodies need sleep. No matter how hard we try, we can't wish that fact away.

Why Our Bodies Need Sleep

The best way to appreciate the importance of sleep is to consider the far-reaching impact of sleep deprivation. There are many ways that your body, mind, and relationships pay the price when you miss out on sleep:

Your emotions are more volatile. Not only do you have more difficulty managing your emotions when you are sleep-deprived, but those emotions tend to skew negative. A sleep-deprived brain is an anxious or angry brain. When you are sleep-deprived, the parts of the brain that are associated with the processing of fear are 60 percent more reactive, which means that you're more likely to feel anxious or angry. To make matters worse, a sleep-deprived brain does a better job of storing negative memories, resulting in "an overriding dominance of negative memories, and far fewer positive or neutral memories," according to researchers at the University of California, Berkeley. Want to store more happy memories? Give your brain, and mood, the gift of adequate sleep.

You feel like you're running on empty. Less sleep means less energy and less staying power. Athletes who try to get by on anything less than eight hours of sleep each night (and less than six hours of sleep in particular) see their endurance drop off by anywhere from 10 to 30 percent. That crushing feeling of fatigue makes life so much harder. Is it any wonder that so many of us try to compensate for our lack of sleep by boosting our energy in other less helpful ways, like ramping ourselves up with caffeine and diving into a sea of carbs?

You're less productive. While cutting back on sleep may seem like a sensible way to squeeze more hours out of your day, it's a strategy that tends to backfire big time. Brian, a father of two, admits to having to learn and re-learn this lesson on a regular basis: "I'm fifty-four years old and I'm still trying to figure out that if I sleep more, I'll get sick less often, which means I'll actually have more time. I guess I'm still trying to convince myself that sleep is good for me productivity-wise."

You're more distracted. When you're sleep-deprived, it's harder to focus. Not only does your motivation take a hit: you're also less alert, which increases your risk of injury. That risk increases exponentially depending on how much sleep you've missed. You're 4.3 times more likely to have a car accident if you've had five hours of sleep or less, and if you've had four hours or less, that risk factor skyrockets to a mind-blowing 11.5 times.

You're less likely to remember things, and that makes it harder to learn. Daytime alertness and memory take a hit once you've racked up a sleep debt of eight hours, meaning that you've missed out on an hour or two of sleep most nights during the past week. That's a pretty common state of affairs for many parents, and it can impact our ability to both remember things and learn. Sleep is the time when we do our mental housekeeping: processing and storing important memories and discarding data that is no longer relevant, which is essential to keeping our mental hard drives clean. When you miss out on sleep, you miss out on the opportunity to file away everything you've learned. As Caroline Webb puts it in her book *How to Have a Good Day*, "going short on sleep is like forgetting to save a document that you've worked on all day."

Your health takes a hit. Lack of sleep affects your immune system, meaning that you're more likely to get sick and it will take you longer to recover from the virus du jour. Sleep deprivation is also associated with weight gain, because of a decrease in leptin, the hormone that makes you feel full, and an increase in ghrelin, the hormone that makes you feel hungry. Long-term sleep deprivation can actually lead to serious disease, such as cardiovascular problems and diabetes. It can affect everything from sperm count quality, which is 29 percent lower in sleep-deprived men, to how well you respond to your flu shot.

Sleep deprivation is baked into the experience of parenting. You're not just on call from nine to five; you're on call from birth to age eighteen and beyond.

Sleep deprivation tends to be more of a problem for mothers than for fathers. This is not just because mothers still tend to take the lead on middle-of-the-night parenting. Women are more likely to have difficulty getting to sleep and staying asleep. It's a problem for 35 percent of women as compared to 25 percent of men. And there may be an additional factor at play as well, although the jury's still out on this one: UK neuroscientist Jim Horne makes the case that women need more sleep than men, about twenty minutes extra each day, because their brains spend more time multi-tasking, which means their need for recovery time is greater.

It's not just about getting the right amount of sleep. You also need the right mix of different types of sleep—what sleep experts refer to as "sleep architecture." While it's obvious that a night-waking infant is a complete and utter wrecking ball when it comes to sleep architecture, we sometimes overlook the fact that less dramatic sleep interruptions at other stages of parenthood—the toddler with an ear infection, the preschooler who is prone to nightmares, or the teenager who is out socializing with friends long past mom and dad's preferred bedtime—can take a toll as well.

Parenthood is basically a circadian rhythm disorder. It disrupts the rhythms that allow us to function at and feel our best. We function at our best when our sleep schedule is regularly synchronized to our internal circadian rhythms and the external light-dark cycle, which helps us to know when to feel alert and when to feel sleepy. Our circadian rhythms are notoriously intolerant of major disruptions to our sleep-wake schedules, which is pretty much a dictionary definition for early parenthood. The result is the parenting world equivalent of jet lag: a feeling of being out of sync with the world around you. That can express itself in a wide variety of symptoms, everything from poor concentration to slower reflexes to increased moodiness and even feelings of nausea. And that's just the physical fallout of sleep deprivation. There can be relationship fallout too. As researchers from Public Health Ontario noted in a 2017 article in *BMC Public Health*: "Child sleep and family functioning (e.g., marital conflict; parenting stress) are inextricably linked and thus it is imperative to view sleep from a family context." The takeaway message? Treat sleep as a shared resource and make sure that all family members are getting their fair share, which means roughly seven to nine hours a night for an adult.

WHY SLEEP DEPRIVATION IS SUCH A PROBLEM FOR KIDS

Of course, sleep deprivation isn't just a problem for parents. It's also a growing problem for kids. Children and teens are sleeping less than they did a generation ago, roughly thirty to sixty minutes less each day. According to some recent data from Public Health Ontario, 31 percent of school-aged children and 26 percent of teens are chronically sleep-deprived.

Wondering how many hours of sleep children and teens actually need? It varies by age. The *Canadian 24-Hour Movement Guidelines for Children and Youth* recommend fourteen to seventeen hours for infants aged zero to three months, twelve to sixteen hours for infants aged four to eleven months, eleven to fourteen hours for toddlers (ages one and two), ten to thirteen hours for preschoolers (ages three and four), nine to eleven hours for children aged five through thirteen, and eight to ten hours for teens aged fourteen through seventeen. In younger children, those hours of sleep will be made up with a combination of nighttime sleep and daytime naps. When they are older, the sleep should occur in an uninterrupted stretch at night, bookended by consistent bedtimes and wake times.

One factor that seems to be contributing to sleep deprivation in children and teenagers is their increased use of technology—how much time they spend on devices and at what times of the day or night. Here's a quick roundup of the relevant research:

Screen use at bedtime is cause for concern. Children who use mobile devices at bedtime are more than twice as likely as other children to be sleeping for fewer than nine hours per night. This is likely the result of too much visual and mental stimulation at the very time of day when their bodies and brains should be winding down. The blue light emitted by the screens of electronic devices has been proven to suppress melatonin, the hormone that helps us to sleep. It's not just smartphones that are a problem at bedtime. As Penn State College of Medicine researchers reported in a study published in *Global Pediatric Health* in 2017, "Children who reported watching TV or playing video games before bed got an average of thirty minutes less sleep than those who did not, while kids who used their phone or computer before bed averaged an hour less of sleep than those who did not."

Smartphones in the bedroom are a particular problem. Teens who keep their smartphones in their bedrooms are 50 percent more likely to experience poor quality sleep and 200 percent more likely to experience excessive sleepiness during the day. Text messaging after lights out makes a bad situation even worse, with one study published in the *Journal of Child Neurology* reporting that "students who reported longer duration of messaging after lights out were more likely to report a shorter sleep duration, higher rate of daytime sleepiness, and poorer academic performance." The secret to controlling smartphone use in the bedroom is to prevent the devices from finding their way to the bedroom in the first place (as opposed to trying to evict them after the fact). Sensible role-modelling can help too, but apparently we adults have some serious work to do on this front if we want to model healthy smartphone use at bedtime. As social psychologist Adam Alter noted in an interview with *The New York Times*, 60 percent of adults report that they sleep with their smartphones, and roughly 50 percent report checking their emails during the night.

Screen use at bedtime isn't the only problem. Researchers have found that it's the total amount of time spent on a smartphone over the course of a day that matters, and not just whether a smartphone is being used too close to bedtime or interfering with sleep in the middle of the night. While two hours or less of recreational screen time doesn't have a major impact on sleep, once a child or teen starts to use a smartphone for more than five hours a day, sleep time really drops off, likely as the result of too much sedentary behaviour combined with too much stimulation and stress delivered via the screen.

Teens face an additional biological challenge. Teens are also contending with a biological phenomenon known as "phase shift delay," which makes them want to stay up later and then sleep in. While a typical adult will start to feel sleepy at around ten at night, teens don't experience this same sense of sleepiness until roughly an hour or two later. There's a similar lag in the morning. While a typical adult will feel wide awake sometime between six and eight in the morning, teens don't experience the same feeling of alertness until an hour or two later. Because the school day doesn't flex to accommodate these adolescent shifts in sleep patterns, teens end up having to get out of bed while they're still sleepy and, as a result, they end up being sleep-deprived. A study of fifteen- to seventeen-year-olds in Switzerland found that 63 percent of teens this age reported being tired upon awakening.

Clearly, there's work to be done on the sleep front. We need more of it and so do our kids. Here's how to make that happen:

Make sleep a priority. Treat it as a necessity, not a frill. Recognize it for what it is: the glue that holds everything else together. Elizabeth, the mother of two young boys, has learned to treat sleep as a precious resource and to make efforts to stockpile it when she can: "I have learned over the years that sleep is so important to my ability to cope. Some evenings when my husband is away, I will forget about the housework entirely and go to bed right after the kids so that I can catch up on my sleep. This makes it easier for me to be able to keep my cool with them."

Practise good sleep hygiene. This means creating a sleep environment that is sleep-enhancing—think cool, quiet, and dark—and developing bedtime habits that encourage, rather than discourage, sleep, such as avoiding melatonin-suppressing blue light from screens, not eating too close to bedtime, limiting caffeine intake during the day, and avoiding alcohol at bedtime because it results in poorer quality, less restorative sleep. It also means maintaining consistent sleep patterns from day to day: getting out of bed at roughly the same time each morning and resisting the temptation to nap indiscriminately throughout the day—unless, of course, you're the parent of a brand new baby, in which case indiscriminate napping is definitely encouraged.

Maximize your sleep opportunity. If you calculate the amount of sleep you're getting by noting the time you hopped into bed and the time you climbed back out of bed in the morning, you're overestimating the amount of sleep you actually got, which means you're shortchanging yourself when it comes to sleep. You don't actually fall asleep the moment your head hits the pillow and you're likely to wake for brief periods in the night, with or without help from your child. So, one of the ways you can ensure that you actually clock more hours of sleep is by giving yourself a bigger window of opportunity to get that sleep. According to sleep researcher Matthew Walker, most people give themselves a sleep opportunity of five to six-and-a-half hours each night, which, in the end, only translates into four to six hours of actual sleep. Someone who is aiming to get seven hours of sleep—the minimum amount of sleep recommended for a healthy adult—should plan to spend at least eight hours in bed. This gives you time to fall asleep and to wake up for that middle-of-the-night trek to the bathroom and for kicking the covers off or putting them back on all those times.

Help your body to feel sleepy at just the right time. A smart way to maximize your sleep opportunity is to ensure that you actually feel sleepy when you go to bed. Be sure to get exposure to daylight first thing in the morning so that your circadian rhythms stay on track, get adequate physical activity during the day so that your body is physically tired at bedtime, minimize caffeine intake so your body is actually ready to wind down when your head hits the pillow, avoid screens in the hour or two before you go to bed (or use screen settings and apps to limit your exposure to blue light), and skip that sleep-disrupting nightcap. In addition to taking care of these basics, there are a few additional tricks you can try if you find yourself struggling to get or stay asleep. First, take a hot bath an hour or two before you want to head to bed. Taking a hot bath causes your blood vessels to dilate, causing heat to be radiated away from your body core. This, in turn, causes your core body temperature to drop, cueing sensations of sleepiness. Second, dump your worries. Writing a detailed to-do list before you head off to bed isn't just an effective way to clear your brain of worries at bedtime; it's also a proven way to help yourself fall asleep more quickly, according to research conducted at Baylor University. So, get those worries out of your head—and out of your bed—and onto a piece of paper.

Try not to fixate on all the sleep you're not getting. If you wake up at three in the morning and you're having a hard time getting back to sleep, try to resist the temptation to mentally calculate the number of hours remaining until you have to drag yourself out of bed and to start obsessing about that. Replace what sleep scientists refer to as negative sleep thoughts—"I can't believe I'm still awake! I'm going to be exhausted tomorrow!"—with more positive sleep thoughts—"I may not be able to get back to sleep right away, but I can lie here and rest and think calming thoughts, even if I'm not fully asleep." You'll find it easier to do this if you remind yourself that there are things you can do to boost your energy and improve your ability to cope even if you don't manage to get as much sleep as you'd like. Eating a protein-rich breakfast will help you feel more alert. The quick energy blast from a bowl of carbs might be tempting, but it won't deliver the energy staying power that protein can provide. Fitting in some light to moderate physical activity will not only give you energy during the day, it will also contribute to better sleep the next night.

Don't be afraid to establish and enforce some basic family rules around bedtime. Wondering what helps to ensure that children and teens get adequate sleep? Having mom or dad establish and enforce some basic bedtime rules, that's what. At least, that's the word from Public Health Ontario, which recently studied the issue. It's worth noting, however, that bedtime rules only seem to work on weekdays. "On weekends, no parental support behaviours predicted children meeting sleep guidelines," the researchers admitted. Of course, kids will find it easier to buy into the idea of bedtime being a good thing (as opposed to evidence of personal failing), if they see you prioritizing sleep as well. Nicole, the single parent of four school-aged children, tries to be a good role model on this front, for her own sake as much as for her kids: "I place a high priority on sleep for myself. My kids deserve the best version of me. I've learned to power down my devices at 8:00 p.m., no matter what. I structure my day so that I don't have to work in the evenings. That way, I can be enjoying my kids, getting them to bed at a good time, and getting myself off to bed at a good time too."

Overcoming Hurdles to Physical Activity

Exercise boosts your energy. It improves the quality of your sleep. It increases blood flow to the brain, leaving you calmer and better able to cope with stress—27 percent better, according to a group of University of Bristol researchers. It improves your level of alertness as well as your focus and concentration—by 41 percent, according to the same group of researchers. And it makes you feel better about yourself. In other words, it has far-reaching effects on your physical and mental health, which in turn, has far-reaching effects on your parenting.

Most of us have pretty amazing intentions when it comes to physical activity. We understand that being physically active delivers big benefits on both the physical and emotional health fronts, and we're highly motivated to tap into those benefits. Where we run into trouble is when we attempt to translate those intentions into actions. That's when we find ourselves bumping up against some rather daunting roadblocks. That's what this next section of the chapter is all about: understanding why it can be tough to get enough physical activity when you're a parent and how to deal with this reality. We'll also be talking about how your physical activity level affects your child's physical activity level (and vice versa) and the important role you have to play in helping your child acquire the lifelong habit of being physically active.

WHY IT CAN BE TOUGH TO FIT IN A WORKOUT WHEN YOU'RE A PARENT

Most of us parents are highly motivated to get more physical activity in our lives—but something gets in the way of those intentions. More often than not, that something is a tiny someone who requires a lot of our time and attention. This helps to explain why getting enough physical activity is a particular challenge for new mothers. Becoming a mother for the first time typically leads women to become less physically active over the next four years.

But it's not just new moms who are missing out on their workouts. The arrival of a new baby can throw a wrench in dads' workout plans too. A study by a group of Australian researchers found that new dads often feel pressured to cut back on time spent exercising on their own in order to meet the increased demands of parenthood and to avoid triggering feelings of resentment in their partners ("What do you mean you're heading to the gym again?"). And so that solo trip to the gym ends up being replaced with a family trip to the park, or nothing at all.

Speaking of that family trip to the park, being active with your kids is great—when it comes to modelling an active lifestyle. But when it comes to actually getting enough of a workout yourself—to say nothing of actually finding the experience relaxing and rejuvenating—that family walk *to* the park isn't always a walk *in* the park. You know how this plays out. Your baby decides she doesn't want to be in the stroller anymore, your toddler is more interested in dawdling than walking, and your pre-schooler wants to go up and down the slide at the playground, which pretty much leaves you sidelined, watching all the action. And we haven't mentioned your school-aged child, who finds it totally annoying that you want her to go to the park with her younger siblings at all.

There's no point in trying to whitewash the facts: being active with children isn't always a universally positive experience. It's a point that the same group of Australian researchers made in an article published in *Psychology of Sports and Exercise*: when you're physically active as a family, "the activity tends to lack the intensity and amount of which is required for an adult to keep fit and healthy; the activity performed does not keep multiple children happy; the activity is often disrupted from the need to attend to the children; and the activity is not stimulating, challenging, or relaxing enough for an adult." The solution, of course, is to supplement those trips to the park with solo workouts, such as a walk or run around the block or a trip to the gym. But, as most new parents figure out pretty quickly, that's easier said than done. Being the parent who is primarily responsible for caring for a young child makes it tougher to fit in a workout. One study found that an astounding 98.6 percent of mothers reported that time commitments related to child care were a barrier to physical activity, which kind of leaves you wondering how the other 1.4 percent actually managed to pull it off.

Time constraints and the challenges of finding someone to take care of your child aren't the only barriers that you have to contend with in finding ways to be physically active. But they're definitely two of the biggies, showing up in study after study. Other barriers that show up on the radar of researchers looking to explain why parenthood can result in a dip in physical activity include fatigue, a constant battle for many parents; bad weather, an ever-present reality for any Canadian who is planning to be active outdoors; and financial barriers, which are a particular concern for parents living in communities with few appealing free or low-cost exercise options.

Parents who manage to maintain their level of physical activity after having children, or in some cases, to actually boost their physical activity level, are the parents who find ways to troubleshoot these barriers. They tap into social support from partners, family members, and friends; they have a game plan for dealing with bad weather, like doing a video workout at home when it's too icy outdoors; they look for or even create their own free or low-cost workouts; they minimize fatigue by prioritizing sleep and healthy nutrition; and—most important of all—they take time to plan their workouts ahead of time.

It turns out that this last piece is key. Exercise doesn't just happen. You have to have a plan for making it happen. One study found that physical activity rates in parents could be boosted simply by encouraging those parents to take the time to come up with a physical activity game plan at the start of each week, and to reflect on how well their plans did or didn't work out the previous week so that they could then tweak their plans accordingly. The researchers also encouraged the parents to treat physical activity as a family resource and to look for ways that family members could support one another in getting enough physical activity, either separately or together. This is the same strategy we talked about earlier on in this chapter in the context of sleep, and the same underlying principle applies: it's easier to achieve your personal health goals if you feel like the entire family "team" is behind you—if you feel like you're working with one another, as opposed to competing against one another, when it comes to sharing the resources that support good health.

Mindset is also important. Your attitude toward exercise and even simply how you conceive of exercise play a major role in determining whether or not you manage to fit in that workout. To put yourself in the right mindset, stop thinking of exercise as something you *have* to do. Instead, think of it as something you *get* to do. You'll be much more motivated to put on your running shoes and chase yourself out the door if you know you're about to indulge in an activity that you love. For Andrea, that means inviting a friend who has a dog to join her and her toddler for their walks: "It's easy to enjoy breaking a sweat with a speed walk when you're getting some adult conversation," she explains.

When you're shopping around for a fitness activity, keep in mind that exercise needs to be both comfortable and enjoyable in order to produce a boost in mood. It's hard to feel good about an activity that's simply making you feel miserable. But don't expect to feel super-motivated all the time. Remind yourself that we humans are notoriously bad at predicting what's going to make us feel better. According to two Iowa State University researchers who have studied this phenomenon, we allow the "momentarily perceived barriers"—the effort it takes to get off the couch and head out for a walk—to interfere with our ability to enjoy the resulting boost in mood. Having a plan for fitting physical activity in is an effective way of dealing with this common problem, because you remove the decision-making piece of the puzzle. You no longer have to decide whether or not you want to fit in that workout; you simply have to stick to your plan.

The second step to improving your mindset about exercise is to rethink your ideas about where and for how long exercise needs to happen. If you convince yourself that the only thing that qualifies as a workout is an hour of vigorous physical activity at the gym that's sandwiched between a lengthy warm-up and a relaxing cool-down, you're setting the bar pretty high for yourself. I'm not saying that it's an unattainable fitness goal; I'm just saying that it's a tougher-to-achieve fitness goal than, say, defining physical activity as any time when you're moving your body vigorously enough to get your heart pumping at a healthy rate—in which case, running up and down a flight of stairs or taking a brisk power walk around the block or hopping on your bike for your morning commute definitely qualify. Taking a less black-and-white approach makes physical activity a whole lot more attainable. You can nibble away at your thirty-minutes-a-day-of-physical-activity goal in five- or ten-minute chunks, say by getting off the bus a stop or two sooner than you have to, as opposed to waiting for a lengthier fitness window that simply might not be available on a particularly jam-packed day. And you can still feel good about getting some physical activity in as opposed to beating yourself up for not getting all of your physical activity in. It doesn't have to be an all-or-nothing proposition.

Making the effort to be physically active may sound like a lot of work, given everything else that you've got going on in your life as a parent. But it's definitely worth the effort to make physical activity part of your regular routine. It's not about being as active as your super-athletic best friend or about hitting the gym as often as your neighbour who doesn't have any kids. It's simply about aiming for what's possible for you in your life right now. "I aim to do one thing better today than I did yesterday, as opposed to aiming for a wholesale transformation," says Sarah, the mother of seventeen-year-old triplets. Yes, it takes work, but those efforts will be rewarded with increased energy and greater calm. And you'll be increasing the likelihood that your kids will decide to follow in your increasingly active footsteps. Let's talk about that next.

How Parents and Kids Influence One Another's Physical Activity Levels

It's something we've talked about a couple of times already in this book, and that we'll be talking about again: the fact that parents and kids shape one another's behaviour in intricate and interrelated ways, in bidirectional ways, to be specific. Not surprisingly, this effect carries over into the world of fitness. Parents and kids can influence one another's physical activity levels in many ways. Here's what the research shows:

More active parents have more active kids. There's even math to back this up! Every extra thousand steps you accumulate over the course of a day inspires your child to boost their own step count by an extra two to three hundred additional steps.

Active kids become active adults. Not only are your kids more likely to be active during their growing up years, as a result of having physically active parents, but they're also more likely to continue to be active as adults. This is something that Margaret has witnessed first-hand. The efforts that she and her ex-husband made to encourage their two boys to be physically active during their growing up years continue to reap dividends now that the boys are young adults: "Twenty years later, the boys are still benefiting from this active lifestyle. They call me with stories about their mountain biking, climbing, camping, hiking, and surfing pursuits."

It's important to help kids establish the fitness habit early. Parents have the greatest influence on health behaviours like physical activity while children are still young, particularly before the age of eight. After that, your influence starts to wane and the opportunity may be lost. If, for example, a girl isn't physically active by the age of ten, there's only a 10 percent chance that she'll be active at age twenty-five. The good news is that it's easy to inspire children who are young to be active. That's what they're naturally inclined to do. The challenge is in sustaining that interest as they grow older. Most children achieve their peak levels of physical activity at the age of six. After that, things start to decline—and that decline continues through middle school and adolescence. By the time an adolescent reaches the age of nineteen, he's likely to be as sedentary as a typical sixty-year-old.

Having one parent who is physically active is good. Having two parents who are physically active is great. As a group of researchers from Australia and Germany reported in a 2016 study published in *Pediatric Exercise Science*, "Children's sport participation is highest when both parents participate in sport as compared to neither parent, or one parent."

Kids notice which parent is hitting the gym—and this affects their own physical activity decisions. "Maternal sports participation remained significantly associated with higher leisure-time physical activity in girls, but not in boys. In contrast, paternal sports participation was significantly associated with higher leisure-time levels in boys, but not in girls," the same group of researchers noted.

More active kids have more active parents. Having a child who is active in sports doesn't just result in that child being more active; odds are his parent is more active too. That's the word from Statistics Canada anyway. So, it appears that parents don't just inspire kids to be more active; kids can inspire parents to be more active too. Of course, it could be that there are certain families in which everyone is naturally inclined to be more physically active—they all carry a sports-loving gene, perhaps, or the family environment fosters a love of all things sport. But whatever force is at work, it's worth noting the general effect: active living seems to beget more active living in families. In a perfect world, it would be easier for parents to be active alongside their kids. Brian, the father of two school-aged boys, thinks that recreation facilities should come up with creative solutions: "You take your kids to the Y for their swimming lessons and you end up just sitting there. They should have bicycles that the parents can ride while they're watching their kids' swimming lessons."

Active kids benefit from greater parental support and encouragement when it comes to being physically active. Here's another interesting tidbit also via Statistics Canada: parents are more likely to support and encourage physical activity in a child who is already physically active as compared to a more sedentary child. It could be that parents do a cost-benefit analysis and decide that they're likely to get better results from encouraging a sports-loving kid to be physically active as opposed to trying to sell a sports-loathing kid on its merits.

What Actually Encourages Kids to Be More Physically Active

Your kids see you lacing up your running shoes and heading out for a run on a regular basis—your parenting work is pretty much done, at least on the active-living front, right?

Actually, that's wrong. While being a physical-activity role model is important, it isn't enough. Parents need to be health facilitators too. That means actively encouraging children to be physically active by boosting feelings of competency and motivation, and offering hands-on support, which could mean anything from signing kids up for lessons and providing transportation to ensuring that you have the necessary sports equipment on hand to volunteering to coach your child's soccer team. It's when you put the two pieces together—the health role modelling and the health facilitating—that you dramatically increase the likelihood that your child will be physically active over the long term.

It's worth the effort to make that fitness habit stick. Physical activity is linked to all kinds of important outcomes in children: better growth; better physical and mental health, which includes everything from cardiorespiratory fitness to musculoskeletal strength to body composition; better development, which means everything from cognitive development to motor skills development to the development of self-regulation skills; better quality of life; and a reduced risk of injuries. Of course, physical activity doesn't just happen. You have to have a plan for making it happen. And making that plan starts with an understanding of just how much and what type of physical activity children of various ages actually need, according to the *Canadian 24-Hour Movement Guidelines*.

- Babies should get at least thirty minutes a day of "interactive floor-based play."

- Toddlers (one- and two-year-olds) should get at least 180 minutes of "a variety of physical activities at any intensity, including energetic play."

- Preschoolers (three- and four-year-olds) should get "a variety of physical activities . . . of which at least sixty minutes is energetic play."

- Children and youth ages five through seventeen should get sixty minutes or more per day of moderate to vigorous activity, with vigorous activity and muscle and bone-strengthening activities being incorporated at least three days a week.

Wondering how to motivate your children to be more active? Here's what the research suggests:

Be active together. One of the best ways to motivate your child to be physically active is by being active together. Not only do children enjoy working out with their parents, but it can actually strengthen the parent-child bond. As University of Oxford anthropologists Jacob Taylor, Emma Cohen, and Arran Davis noted in an essay for *Aeon*, "Synchronizing movement with others leads to feelings of togetherness or 'oneness'—perhaps because the intentional act of coordinating with another person necessitates sharing mental states."

Head outdoors. The more time children spend outdoors, the more likely they are to be physically active. And, what's more, time spent in nature (as opposed to playing on the sidewalk on a busy street) delivers some added benefits: better body image, improved mood, increased feelings of connectedness to others, and a chance to relax and unwind. As Lisa Miller notes in her book *The Spiritual Child*, "Children and teens need time to watch the bee and sit with the tree, let their minds wander and wonder, and engage what neuroscientists call the 'default mode,' essentially a time of reflective reverie and a mental housekeeping."

Make it fun. Family activities that focus on fun and play are more appealing to children than more regimented activities that are narrowly focused on health outcomes. You don't find jumping jacks or chin-ups particularly inspiring, and neither do your kids. So, keep the spotlight on active play, which involves moderate to vigorous physical activity, and plan to get in the game yourself. According to research conducted by the Canadian Fitness and Lifestyle Research Institute, only 37 percent of parents report that they "often or very often" play active games with their children.

See the section "Turning Health Intentions to Health Actions" at the end of this chapter for more tips based on the science of habit change.

Managing Screen Time

Your ability to manage screen time can make or break your other health goals. Spend too much time in front of a screen during the day and you'll have a harder time fitting in physical activity, finding the energy to make healthy meals, and enjoying truly restorative sleep at night. That's why it's so important that we learn how to manage our screen time effectively, and teach our kids to do the same. We already talked about the impact of distracted parenting back in Chapter 3. Now let's talk about a related issue: the impact of screen time on our kids, and what we, as their parents, can do about it.

MANAGING YOUNGER CHILDREN'S SCREEN TIME

There's no doubt about it: we're raising the most plugged-in generation of children ever. Thanks to the rise in the use of mobile technology, kids are plugging in at an increasingly early age—much earlier than leading health authorities recommend, in fact. A recent study of infants in the United Kingdom found that 51 percent of them use a touch screen daily—this despite the fact that screen time actually isn't recommended for babies at all.

It isn't difficult to figure out why this happens. Parents have always looked for ways to distract and entertain young children so that they can get other things done, and mobile devices like smartphones tend to be both highly distracting *and* highly entertaining. A recent study of 242 Vancouver parents conducted by researchers at the University of British Columbia identified an additional reason why many parents hand their smartphones to their infants and toddlers: they believe that doing so helps to encourage speech and language development.

It turns out that quite the opposite is true. Screen time can interfere with the development of these skills in young children. A study conducted at the Hospital for Sick Children in Toronto found that babies and toddlers who spent more time using handheld devices faced an increased risk of experiencing delays in expressive language as compared to other children the same age who spent less time on those devices. The effect was quite dramatic, with the researchers reporting a 49 percent increase in the risk of such delays for every thirty minutes of daily use.

The problem is that young children have a hard time connecting the dots between what they see on a screen with what they're experiencing in the real world. So, not only are they wasting time on app-based interactions that don't deliver any measurable benefits, but they're actually missing out on the far more beneficial interactive language-learning experiences that happen in real time with a caring and tuned-in parent. As the Canadian Paediatric Society (CPS) noted in its recent position on screen time and young children, "Early learning is easier, more enriching, and developmentally more efficient when experienced live, interactively, in real time and space, and with real people."

This is why the CPS advises against screen use by children under the age of two—"There are no proven benefits of media exposure on infants and toddlers, and some known developmental risks," the organization insists—and recommends minimal screen time for children between the ages of two and five, meaning less than an hour a day. "Minimizing screen time leaves more time for face-to-face interactions, which is how young children learn best," the CPS stresses. Spending too much time in front of a screen can interfere with development in other critical ways as well, reducing the quality of parent-child interactions—interactions that provide young children with opportunities to practise reading and interpreting human emotions, which is critical to the development of empathy—and getting in the way of opportunities for real-world play, which is integral to the experience of childhood.

So, what does this mean in practical terms?

It's a good idea to hold off on introducing screens for as long as you can—ideally, well into the toddler years. Screen use is habit-forming, with early exposure increasing the likelihood that screens will be over-used later in life. Besides, the early years are a time when overall health routines, including the amount of physical activity versus sedentary activity, are being established, and you want those habits to be healthy ones.

When you do decide to introduce your child to screen time, be purposeful and intentional about that use. Instead of allowing screens to provide a permanent backdrop to daily living, have a plan to "watch or play *this* content, at *this* time, for *this* reason," suggests the CPS. Make a point of choosing "educational, age-appropriate, and interactive programming." And avoid screen time for at least one hour before bedtime.

MANAGING OLDER CHILDREN'S AND TEENS' SCREEN TIME

Managing screen time continues to be a challenge as children grow older. In fact, many parents would argue that it actually becomes more of a challenge, with battles over screen time becoming an increasing source of frustration.

Unfortunately, it's a battle that most of us parents are losing. Fewer than one in four Canadian kids between the ages of five and sixteen is managing to meet the recommendations for healthy screen time, which is capped at a maximum of two hours of *recreational* screen time each day. This means that more than three in four Canadian kids are playing on their devices for more than two hours each day—screen time that is above and beyond the time they spend using computers and other devices at school.

There is definitely cause for concern. High levels of screen time are associated with an increased risk of obesity, poorer performance at school, and reduced sleep quality, as well as risky behaviours in older children, and cognitive, learning, and social skills delays in younger children. If that wasn't enough, the Canadian Association of Optometrists and the Canadian Ophthalmological Society recently flagged an additional concern: a growing incidence of eye problems in children. A recent US survey found that 80 percent of kids between the ages of ten and seventeen reported burning, itchy, or tired eyes after screen use. And, what's more, rising rates of myopia (near-sightedness) in children have also been observed. This is likely the result of children spending fewer hours outdoors, thereby reducing their exposure to outdoor light, which plays a key role in eye development.

Wondering what it takes to encourage children and teens to develop a healthier relationship with screens? Here's what the research suggests:

Think moderation, not abstinence. Resist the temptation to turn screen time into "forbidden fruit." A 2017 study by researchers in The Netherlands revealed that parental efforts to rigidly restrict screen time tend to backfire, resulting in "an increase of child BMI and a decrease in child physical activity behavior." The researchers explained in the *International Journal of Behavioral Nutrition and Physical Activity* that just as children who are prevented from eating certain foods tend to increase their desire for and intake of those foods, children who are prevented from having screen time could increase their desire for other sedentary behaviours, like flaking out on the couch, and as a result, they gain weight.

There's an additional reason to steer clear of the abstinence approach: screen time in moderation can actually be good for kids. A University of Essex study of 120,000 fifteen-year-olds concluded that moderate use of digital technology is beneficial for teens' mental health, while no use or too much use is detrimental.

Mentor and guide; don't dictate. In an article for the online publication *JSTOR Daily*, technology writer Alexandra Samuel described the nuanced parenting approach that works best: "Mentoring your kids means letting go of a one-size-fits-all approach to tech use, and thinking instead about which specific online activities are enriching (or impoverishing) for your specific child. Mentoring means talking regularly with your kids about how they can use the Internet responsibly and joyfully, instead of slamming on the brakes." It also means accepting that kids will make mistakes when it comes to the use of technology—and that they can learn from those mistakes. You can help to guide the learning process along by helping your child to understand how smartphone apps work—how they are engineered to attract and keep your attention—and how to tweak your settings so that you're the one calling the shots, not the device. You can also encourage your child to become more mindful of his technology use, for example, to notice how he feels after using a particular app and to think about what it is about that particular app that makes him feel that way. This is an approach that has worked well for Brian, the father of two school-aged boys. He makes an effort to encourage his sons to notice how spending too much time in front of a screen is affecting them: "I'll say something like, 'You're unhappy and fighting with your brother because you've been watching YouTube videos for an hour. Let's go outside.'"

These kinds of conversations can have a significant impact over time, as children and teens begin to figure out how to make technology work for, not against, them. Jillian has witnessed this in her own family. "Back in the spring, our teenage son gave us his phone and asked us to keep it for him for the next three months. He told us, 'I don't want to be online right now. It's just causing me stress and anxiety.'" When her son decided he was ready to head back online once again, he made two significant shifts. He deleted his Instagram account entirely, and he made the decision to switch to a social media–free smartphone, so that he no longer felt tethered to the online world 24/7—two high-impact solutions that were entirely of his own making.

Be conscious of the screen habits you're modelling for your child. I'm not just talking smartphone use here, which is, of course, hugely important. I'm also talking about TV viewing. Here's why: every hour that parents spend watching TV translates into an additional twenty-three minutes of TV-viewing for their kids, according to research conducted by Public Health Ontario. It's important to be conscious of how you're choosing to spend time as a family and whether your downtime is always centred on a screen, which means you're creating a habit of being sedentary together. The researchers aren't suggesting that you should cancel family movie nights entirely, by the way. They're simply suggesting that you balance those fun times on the couch huddled around a bowl of popcorn with more active leisure-time pursuits as well. Speaking of which . . .

Provide appealing alternatives to screen time. The best way to motivate kids to reduce their screen time is to provide them with a convenient and appealing alternative, which could be anything from taking a hike at a local conservation area to planning a family board-game night. This is because most of us, including kids, find it more motivating to focus on an approach goal (something you want to do) as opposed to an avoidance goal (something you're trying to avoid) when it comes to trying to break a habit like screen time. Failing to offer an appealing alternative can cause kids to gravitate from screen time to other types of sedentary behaviour—and that only solves part of the problem. "Reducing the amount of time spent on digital devices will not automatically increase the time spent on physical activities," noted a UNICEF discussion paper on this subject.

Keep screens out of the bedroom and away from the dinner table. Not only do screens interfere with the quality and duration of sleep, which we discussed at length earlier on in this chapter, but they also displace other more valuable activities, like reading. To make matters worse, once a screen finds its way into your child's bedroom, you have much less control over the ways in which that screen is being used. You'll also have fewer opportunities to mentor your child through the process of learning how to conduct himself online. It will be harder to know if your child is being bullied or bullying others, for example. Make a point of parking the devices at mealtimes too. As we noted back in Chapter 3, the mere presence of a device detracts from conversation quality, even when the notifications on that smartphone are turned off.

Resist the temptation to give your child a smartphone before she's ready. Sometimes, kids inherit smartphones automatically when parents upgrade their own devices—and without anyone ever pausing to really consider whether it's actually the right time for the kids to have access to the devices. Here's a simple way to encourage yourself to make that decision a little more consciously and deliberately: Ask yourself if you'd be rushing out to get your kid a smartphone if you had to pay full price for it, as opposed to just handing over a device that might otherwise end up languishing in a drawer. If the answer is no, perhaps your child doesn't really need that phone, or at least not yet.

Join forces with other families. Look for opportunities to work together to make the shift to valuing and enjoying unplugged time. Help kids to understand that you don't have to be connected 24/7. A 2016 survey conducted by Common Sense Media found that 78 percent of teens check their devices at least once an hour, and that 72 percent feel pressured to respond immediately to text messages and other notifications.

Healthier Eating

If we are what we eat, it's no wonder so many of us feel like we're running on empty. We're not exactly giving our bodies optimal fuel. Not only are we relying more heavily on processed foods; we're eating fewer fruits and vegetables than ever before. If you feel like your family would benefit from a bit of a nutritional makeover, this next part of the chapter is for you. I'll be giving you a crash course in the basics of healthy eating—lessons I learned through the school of hard knocks—and then sharing some strategies for getting the entire family on the road to healthier eating.

THE FUEL YOUR BODY CRAVES

The products that show up on the grocery store shelves may be constantly changing (remember when Greek yogurt wasn't even a thing?), but what doesn't change as food trends come and go is the fact that our brains and bodies need a healthy balance of complex carbohydrates, essential fats, proteins, vitamins and minerals, and water to function at their best.

- Complex carbohydrates, which are found in foods like whole grains, vegetables, and beans, provide us with a stable and steady source of fuel and help to relieve feelings of stress— which explains why you're likely to find yourself craving carbs in a major way when you're having a really bad day.

- Essential fatty acids are critical to brain function.

- Protein helps us to feel alert.

- Vitamins and minerals perform vital housekeeping functions in the body, converting carbohydrates into glucose, fatty acids into brain cells, and amino acids into neurotransmitters. Some function as antioxidants, protecting the brain from cell-damaging oxidants from food, smoking, alcohol, and stress.

- Water keeps us hydrated, something that is critical to functioning at our best. Even mild dehydration can lead to restlessness and irritability, loss of concentration, weakness, and feeling unwell.

It's also important to understand that the timing and makeup of meals and snacks affect your mood and energy levels in a major way. Go too long without food and your blood sugar will dip, triggering fatigue and mood swings. Have a protein-heavy meal too close to bedtime and you'll have trouble falling asleep. You'll still have energy left a couple of hours after a meal made up of protein and complex carbohydrates, tuna on whole-grain bread, for example, whereas your blood sugar will spike and crash if you rely on simple carbs alone, like a plain bagel, taking your mood down with it.

It took me decades of my life to figure this stuff out, so I think we really need to make a point of talking about it with our kids, to help them understand how food affects their bodies and how they can use this knowledge to their advantage. Of course, we also need to make a point of having healthy food on hand and doing what we can to make food choices both convenient and appealing. Making raw fruits and vegetables available for snacks makes it five times as likely that children will consume adequate servings of those foods each day.

THE REAL-WORLD GUIDE TO FAMILY DINNERS

Something else you can do to encourage your children to develop a healthy relationship with food, and to support their healthy development in all kinds of other important ways, is to try to eat dinner together as a family as often as you can. The trick is to avoid allowing family dinners to become a massive source of anxiety, guilt, and stress—something that can happen all too easily.

According to sociologist Tracy Bacon, who has studied the physical, mental, and emotional labour involved in serving up a family meal, the family dinner isn't all joy all the time. It's also about hard work and guilt. That hard work is mainly done by mothers, who are still doing most of the heavy lifting when it comes to mealtime preparation and cleanup. According to Bacon, mothers spend anywhere from two to five times as much time on these tasks as fathers. And the guilt? Moms are carrying a lot of that too as a result of all the hard-hitting messages about the benefits of family dinners—messages that can leave us feeling guilty if we fail to serve up ample quantities of mealtime bliss. That's not to say that there aren't far-reaching benefits to eating meals together as a family. There's a solid body of research to show that children of all ages benefit, in fact. Younger children benefit from having more opportunities to work on their language and communication abilities around the dinner table, which provide them with an academic boost once they start school. School-aged children demonstrate stronger social skills, healthier relationships with their parents, and fewer problem behaviours, thanks to family mealtimes. And adolescents who dine with their parents on a regular basis make healthier food choices, develop healthier eating habits, are less likely to be engaging in substance abuse, and demonstrate improved academic outcomes.

The secret to enjoying the benefits while minimizing the guilt is to bring realistic expectations to the dinner table. Take what's best about the family meal—fun and togetherness—and find new and less stressful ways of making that happen. "Feeding is not just about nutrition, it is about relationships," notes a group of researchers from the University of Guelph. It doesn't always have to be dinner, and it doesn't have to be elaborate. Breakfast-for-dinner is a perennial favourite at our house, and sometimes that means teaming up cereal, fruit, and yogurt.

You can also cut down on the work of making family dinner by treating meal preparation like a team sport. Join forces with other families and look for ways to divide and conquer the menu planning, grocery shopping, or food preparation, perhaps by swapping recipes, organizing a formal or informal food-buying co-op, or getting together to batch-cook or share meals. While you're at it, get your children involved in mealtime preparation. Helping your children to acquire cooking habits now leads to better nutrition down the road. A recent study published in the *Journal of Nutrition Education and Behavior* found that adolescents who feel confident about their cooking skills are more likely to include vegetables in their meals most days when they become adults. They're also less likely to consume fast food.

Caffeine and Alcohol

Of course, no conversation about healthy eating would be complete without a quick word about caffeine and alcohol. Let's start with the unfortunate truth about caffeine: while it can feel like every exhausted parent's best friend, it's actually more like a frenemy. Sure, it delivers the quick energy fix that you're craving, but it can also leave you feeling jittery and dehydrated. And it can prevent you from getting a good night's sleep, which leaves you exhausted again the next day.

As for alcohol, it promises all kinds of good times, but then it kind of leaves you in the lurch. Not only is it a depressant that actually brings down your mood; it also robs your body of important nutrients that your brain needs in order to ward off feelings of depression. If you consume alcohol too close to bedtime, it interferes with your ability to get a good night's sleep. While you won't have any trouble getting to sleep, you'll have trouble staying asleep. And it prevents you from enjoying the most restorative type of sleep, increasing the likelihood that you'll start your day feeling groggy and distracted.

How do I know all this stuff? Because I've lived it. For the better part of a decade, I relied on a glass or two of wine at bedtime to wind down. It was my desperate attempt to counter the effects of a day spent fuelling my body with too much caffeine and too many simple carbs. The net result was weight gain—I gained over a hundred pounds, which I then had to work really hard to lose—as well as physical and emotional depletion. To put it bluntly, I was pretty much the poster child for self-neglect.

I've since figured out that there are much healthier ways to get the daytime energy boost I need: teaming up protein with complex carbs, getting adequate sleep at night, and making physical activity a regular part of my day. I've also discovered that there are much more effective ways to wind down at night than to pour myself a glass or two of wine—like enjoying a relaxing cup of caffeine-free tea and curling up with a good book. The good news is that, over the past five years, these healthier lifestyle habits have become my new normal, providing me with more sustainable forms of energy and a sense of lasting calm—which, as it turns out, was what I was actually craving all along.

Turning Health Intentions to Health Actions

Ready to make some health changes? Here are some strategies drawn from the science of habit change that can help you turn your health intentions into health actions, including how to stay motivated and inspired—and how to motivate and inspire your kids too.

Feel confident in your ability to make a change. Think of other times in your life when you were successful at making significant changes. Then identify the specific strategies you used and personal strengths you tapped into while you were making those changes. Figure out how you can make use of those same resources again. Then set yourself up for success by setting small, highly achievable goals. "I limit myself to two cups of half-caf coffee a day, and I make a point of including protein at every meal," notes Sarah, the mother of seventeen-year-old triplets.

Make an identity shift. Instead of merely vowing to exercise more often as a family, start seeing yourself as an active family: "We're the kind of family that is physically active every weekend." It may seem like a minor distinction, but the impact can be monumental. You'll be motivated to want to live up to the new image of yourself. For Dani, the mother of three boys, this means seeing herself as a person who takes good care of herself—someone who "goes to power yoga, hits the gym regularly, and tries hard to get ten thousand steps a day."

Dare to venture outside your comfort zone. That's exactly where Rob found himself—outside of his comfort zone—after signing up to run his first 5K. In fact, he felt so uncomfortable that he actually considered dropping out of the race the day before. "I kept telling myself, 'I can't run 5K. I'm going to embarrass myself and I'll be stranded on the other side of town'—because the race took a pretty big loop around town." After much inner debating, he decided to go through with the race after all: "A friend pushed me to do it and I ended up running the entire 5K," he explains. "That was a huge game-changer for me. It really cemented my commitment to taking much better care of myself."

Take advantage of the fresh-start effect. Researchers at the Wharton School of the University of Pennsylvania have identified a "fresh-start effect" that motivates people to try to achieve health goals. They noticed that people have a tendency to associate past imperfections with their past selves whenever they switch to a new "mental accounting period" in their lives, with that new accounting period creating a distinction between "now" and "then." It's the very same phenomenon that fuels all those New Year's resolutions: the desire to become a new person this year, as opposed to the version of yourself that you happened to be last year. The transition to parenthood can provide a powerful impetus to engage in this kind of self-reinvention, because becoming a parent typically affects our daily lives and routines in countless ways. Significant life events also encourage us to take a step back and "take a big picture view of [our] lives and thus focus more on achieving [our] goals," the researchers noted. Of course, the early months of parenthood could also feel like the worst possible time in your life to consider embarking on anything even remotely resembling self-improvement. So, don't beat yourself up if you somehow failed to join the gym the week your baby arrived. You simply need to look for a new excuse to make a fresh start, which could be anything from finding a new walking buddy to embarking on the start of a new school year to moving to a new neighbourhood. It's never too late for a new fresh start.

Have a plan for dealing with obstacles. New York University psychologist Gabriele Oettingen has devised a goal-setting strategy that she calls WOOP (which stands for wish, outcome, obstacle, plan). Here's how it works: you figure out what you want to achieve (the wish), you become clear about why you want to do it (the outcome), you identify potential obstacles, and then you come up with a plan for dealing with each of those obstacles. Doing this added thinking massively increases your odds of success in achieving your goals. While the success rate for people who are relying on more standard goal-setting strategies is roughly 30 percent, those odds of success jump to an incredible 80 percent when you rely on WOOP.

Tap into the wisdom of your future self. Psychotherapist Bill O'Hanlon pioneered this technique, suggesting that if you're struggling with a problem or trying to achieve a particular goal, you should turn to your future self for advice. Specifically, he recommends writing a letter to your current self from your future self, explaining what it took you to solve this problem or achieve this goal. "Tell yourself the crucial things you realized or the critical steps you took to get there. Give yourself some sage and compassionate advice from a better future," he suggests.

Treat yourself with self-compassion. People who treat themselves with self-compassion when they're trying to make a health change tend to set more realistic goals. As two Duke University researchers noted in a study published in *Self and Identity*, "Self-compassionate people . . . recognize they can improve over time and thus [don't] feel pressured to engage in extreme . . . health goals." They also find it easier to get back on track when (not if) they get temporarily sidetracked by one of life's curveballs. Instead of throwing in the towel altogether, they simply pick up where they left off—a process known as "goal re-engagement." A separate study conducted at the University of Saskatchewan and the University of Alberta highlighted the importance of self-compassion for women who are trying to become more physically active. The researchers noted that a typical motivation for becoming physically fit—the desire to measure up to societal ideas about what the perfect female body is supposed to look like—can actually be extremely de-motivating because that pressure is external and fuelled by a fear of not measuring up, as opposed to internal and fuelled by your own personal desire to be healthier and more fit. When women learn to treat themselves with self-compassion, they're able to silence that critical voice and tap into a more sustainable source of motivation: a feeling of self-acceptance that is not contingent on how you look in a swimsuit or how well you perform at the gym. You're exercising because you want to treat your body with kindness so that you can keep it healthy and strong; you're not trying to punish it or to force it to measure up to someone else's ideals. You're doing this just for you.

CHAPTER 9

Parenting as a Team Sport

I don't know how to deal with the level of resentment I have—resentment of the fact that my life did a 180 turn after the birth of our son and my husband's life shifted maybe 45 degrees. I made so many compromises in my career because we were moving all the time—and now all of a sudden, I'm a single parent every other week for as long as a week while he's away travelling for work. We made the decision to have a child together, but I didn't realize what a huge impact it would have on my life. And that's a huge thing.
—Evie, mother of nineteen-month-old Rowan

Evie isn't the only parent to feel like her marriage has been rocked by the experience of becoming a parent. Most couples find the experience pretty jarring, either temporarily or over the longer term. As relationship researchers Philip A. Cowan and Carolyn P. Cowan have noted, 92 percent of couples report an increase in conflict after the birth of a baby, and by the time those babies have reached age eighteen months, one in four couples are experiencing marital distress. What's more, according to research led by psychologist Erika Lawrence of the University of Iowa, the couples who were happiest prior to the birth of a baby are the ones who are most likely to find the experience of becoming parents particularly jarring. "Parents who were more satisfied before pregnancy experienced steeper declines in satisfaction across the transition to parenthood compared to parents with lower levels of pre-pregnancy satisfaction," she and her co-authors noted.

That's not to say that couples without children are guaranteed to find themselves living in the Land of Perpetual Relationship Bliss. Brian D. Doss of Texas A&M University followed two hundred couples over the first eight years of their marriage and noted that a deterioration in relationship functioning was a fact of life for both parents and non-parents alike. What was different for the couples who had children was the suddenness of the decline, with the falling-off-the-cliff effect happening after the birth of a baby. "Parents and non-parents generally show similar *amounts* of decline in overall relationship functioning over the first eight years of marriage, but that these changes tend to occur suddenly following the birth of the baby for parents and more gradually over time for non-parents," he and his co-authors wrote.

What these new parents ended up experiencing, according to the researchers, were "clear increases in negativity, conflict, and problem intensity following the birth of a child." Not surprisingly, the resulting hit on couple relationship quality ended up being greater for some parents than for others. For mothers, the key factor in determining the extent of the dip in relationship satisfaction was a childhood experience of witnessing parental divorce or relationship conflict—in other words, growing up in a family where the parents were either divorced or embroiled in relationship conflict. For fathers, it was the speed at which the baby arrived on the scene—in other words, having a baby more quickly following marriage as opposed to waiting longer to have that baby. "It may be that couples that have been married longer have more time to develop a shared understanding of relationship responsibilities and goals that help to buffer them from the stressors of increased childcare and general disorganization after birth," Doss and his co-authors explained.

The period around baby's first birthday tends to represent a relationship low for most new parents, with marital satisfaction rates rebounding slightly during the second year of parenthood. It's possible that this temporary dip represents a shift in focus from the couple relationship to the intense demands of early parenthood, with the relationship finding its way back to happier ground once the new parents have had a chance to adjust. Knowing ahead of time that the early years of parenthood may be a tough time for you and your partner can be oddly reassuring. It's not just your relationship that's stumbled onto rockier ground—it's a pretty common thing—and there are ways to navigate these challenges as a couple.

That, in a nutshell, is what this chapter is all about: guiding your relationship to that healthier, happier ground. We'll be talking about the kinds of things couples fight about after they have kids and what you can do to try to keep your relationship with your partner on track after you become parents, to the extent that this is possible—and how this is good for the kids. We'll also be talking about what it takes to continue to function well as a parenting team, even if you and your child's other parent are no longer a couple, and about the important lessons the two of you can teach your child about working through relationship rough spots, whether you're together or not—because every relationship has them.

What Couples Fight About after They Have Kids

Feel like you've been arguing more often with your partner since the two of you became parents? It's not your imagination. Most couples report an increase in marital conflict after their first child arrives on the scene. In fact, one UK study of three thousand parents cited a 40 percent increase in the number of conflicts. Here's what parents end up fighting about:

Resentment over Unshared Workloads

The issue that couples argue about most after becoming parents is how to share the increased workload that goes along with having a child, which can be everything from who gets up in the middle of the night to who gets dinner on the table. If one partner feels like they're shouldering a disproportionate load and that they've been doing so for a very long time, the resentment can be huge.

It's not hard to figure out what's fuelling these feelings of resentment, or why resentment continues to provide the backdrop to so many couple relationships after partners become parents. Women continue to shoulder a heavier load. *Making Women Count*, a 2016 report published by Oxfam Canada and the Canadian Centre for Policy Alternatives, noted that Canadian women perform nearly twice as many hours of unpaid work each day as compared to men—61 percent of housework and 65 percent of hours spent caring for children, according to Statistics Canada data for 2015.

What fuels the resentment for Lola, the mother of a toddler and two school-aged children, is frustration about how much her life has changed and how little her husband's has changed in comparison. While her entire life is premised on the assumption that she needs to be available to take care of the kids, her husband is pretty much able to operate like a free (or at least *freer*) agent. "When we had a newborn, my husband decided he wanted to do yoga-teacher training. So, he worked every day, and then every Saturday, he would do this yoga training. And then there were two weekends away. And then he thought nothing of saying that he wanted to go and do a yoga retreat for four days. I never said no to any of this stuff because I knew that he needed this time," she explains. But what positively infuriated her was the fact her husband seemed oblivious to the fact that she desperately needed time off too: "It's not like he ever said no when I asked for time off, but it was obvious and clear that it was not going to be easy for him to look after the children. But somehow the expectation was that I'm somehow magical, so it was going to be easy for me. And it's not. It's really not. It's hard." Lola is not optimistic that things are going to get any better anytime soon: "My husband wants to be more helpful, but I don't think he'll ever get to the point where I feel like it's equal. I'm married to this man who is driving me crazy in increments by the lack of things he does."

Like Lola, Janine has been profoundly disappointed by the way that parenting has affected her relationship with her partner in the five years since they became parents. "I thought I married a feminist. It turns out I married a man. That was the biggest disappointment for me," she says. "I love my husband, but *the way* I love him and *the way* I feel about him have changed, because I feel so let down by the type of husband he's been since we had a child. It's coming to terms with the fact that he will never be the equal co-parent that I expected and that, at some point, he promised to be. We're five years in, and I've tried many different things to bring equity to our marriage. And I've come to accept that it's impossible—that the social forces are stronger than us. He will never be the kind of man who just comes out to the car and helps me with the groceries. I have to text him to say, 'I'm coming home. Please come outside and help me with the groceries.' That I have to become the stereotype of the nagging wife was profoundly disappointing because I thought it would be different for us. I thought my marriage would stay romantic through everything. That we would not be like every other couple that experiences a bump in the road. What happened instead is that he prioritizes himself first, and then whatever's left over, he'll give to our family.

"Sometimes, I wonder if equity—if a shared system—is even possible, because there is a mental load that I don't think can be shared," she adds, referring to the so-called emotional labour of parenting—the thinking, planning, and organizing work that is both invisible and demanding. "Things could get messy and complicated if both people were trying to plan the same things.

Besides, I have the skills for the organizing, so I've taken that on. But a little support—a little recognition of just how much work that is—would go a long way."

Lynn agrees that something needs to shift, both within our individual relationships as couples and at the broader, societal level. "We need new ways of thinking about parenting and, in particular, gender roles for (hetero) couples," the mother of a twenty-three-month-old toddler explains. "Dads have come a long way, but there's more to do. My partner and I are both committed to sharing parenting responsibilities equitably, and we've made some great progress over the past two years, but it's still not equal. And it's exhausting for me to be the one who has to keep pushing things in that direction. Women still carry so much of the load, and in general, we just tend to accept it. It's a structural issue that's really hard to make progress on."

Once those norms start to shift, it can be tough for individual parents to make sense of the rules in a radically rewritten playbook, says Simon, who was a full-time stay-at-home parent for an extended period of time, starting when his son was a toddler. He notes that his wife, Julianne, struggles with the fact that Francis typically turns to Simon for comfort. After all, Simon was the one who established Francis's daily routines and was the go-to parent for middle-of-the-night soothing. "Nobody ever talks about how difficult it can be if a child ends up being more attached to the dad," he notes. While it has been great in terms of Simon's relationship with his son, it's been a source of pain for Julianne to work through: "Sometimes, Francis just wants to be with me and that hurts her feelings." Julianne is also embarrassed when Francis shows a preference for Simon when other people, like her parents, are around: "She feels judged by that." Simon has responded by encouraging Julianne to focus on her strengths, like the fact that she's really good at coming up with fun activities to do with Francis. "Don't try to be me," he tells her. "Don't try to compete with the daddy thing—whatever it is he's looking to me for."

Casey, the father of two young boys, agrees that these are confusing times to be a dad. There's a lot of talk, for example, about aiming for a fifty-fifty split on all things parenting, but what if your baby refuses to respect the math? Casey remembers how this felt when he first became a parent: "I felt like a secondary character in my child's life and I stayed in that place for a good five to six months or so." He has also encountered some rather patronizing attitudes toward fatherhood in this supposed era of increased gender equality: "Overall, the bar is still set really low for dads. When I started taking my oldest son to school this year, there was practically applause for the fact that I was consistently getting him there every day on time." Would a mother have faced the same enthusiastic reaction? Hardly, he says.

CONFLICTS ABOUT PARENTING
Over time, conflicts about how to share the workload equitably tend to shift to more generalized conflicts about parenting. A study led by Lauren M. Papp of the University of Wisconsin-Madison found, for example, that parents of preteens and teens are more likely to argue about parenting issues than anything else. Johanna, the mother of two school-aged children, can certainly relate to the challenges posed by differences in parenting styles. "My husband and I parent very differently. We come from very different upbringings and that's a significant challenge for us and, I think, also for our kids." The two of them continue to work hard at finding common ground and learning how to function more effectively as a parenting team—"how to get on the same page so that I'm not always the go-between, the mediator, the calmer-down of all things stressful," is how she puts it.

CONFLICTS ABOUT SEX (OR THE LACK OF SEX)
When partners don't see eye to eye about how much sex is desirable or even possible, conflict can arise. Not surprisingly, the early months of parenthood tend to represent a bit of a parenting drought, with frequency declining to once or twice a month

and sexual dissatisfaction increasing. By six months postpartum, roughly one-third of mothers and one-half of fathers are unhappy with their sex lives, according to one Swedish study. The problems can continue over the longer term if partners feel emotionally distant or are experiencing high levels of relationship conflict, like resentment over unequal workloads. "Of course, when you don't feel supported and appreciated, you don't really want to get naked with your partner," explains Janine, whose youngest child is now five. "But I'm not sure that's all that's going on. I feel like there's been some profound biological shift—that I'm actually just not interested in very much sex anymore." She wishes that there was wider acknowledgement that this can happen, because without that acknowledgement and conversation, "it's just one more layer of guilt that moms feel." She'd also like to see more strategies for dealing with different sexual needs in a relationship, including how not to feel guilty when you're the one who isn't interested.

Sometimes, the best way to work through differences about sex is by going for couple's therapy. As Lauren M. Papp of the University of Wisconsin-Madison and her co-authors noted in a study published in *Couple and Family Psychology*, conflicts about sex can be tough for a couple to resolve on their own: "It is one of the issues that cannot be settled by partners agreeing to disagree, and the difficult work of reaching a solution can negatively affect the desire of one or both partners," something that can make a bad situation even worse. At the root of the problem is the fact that conflicts about sex sometimes function as the proverbial canary in the coal mine, alerting you to other, bigger problems in the relationship—perhaps perennial resentments or a corrosive breakdown in trust. As parenthood transports you to new territory in your relationship, you may find yourself questioning how—or whether—to journey on together. A therapist can help you work through some of these complex, intertwined issues.

Conflicts about Money

Starting a family can certainly do a number on your budget. Not only do your expenses go up, but your income tends to take a major hit at the same time. And that, in turn, can lead to increased conflicts about money. That's certainly how things played out for Simon and his wife following the birth of their son three and a half years ago. "We went into a fair amount of debt, both because of the cost of daycare and the fact that we no longer had two people earning 100 percent of their salaries," he recalls. (She was in school and he was working as a freelance writer.) The resulting shift in their financial circumstances alarmed Simon—"It really scared me at first. I did not want to be in debt"—leading to conflict between him and his wife about how they should, or shouldn't, spend their limited funds: "She would want to spend money on something that would make our lives easier, such as paying for housecleaning services. But I fought against it because I didn't think that we could afford it. And, objectively speaking, we couldn't afford it."

Looking back, he has some regret about the way he chose to handle the situation. "I now realize that we were destined to end up in debt—that there was no way we were going to get through those first few years without accumulating some debt." If he had the chance to do it all again, he'd spring for that housecleaner. "In the big picture of things, an extra two thousand dollars in debt isn't going to make that much difference. And, if we'd had that housecleaner during that first year, my wife's mental health would have been a lot better. It definitely would have been worth it," both to have had the extra help and to have had fewer fights about money. "Many of our fights were financially related," he explains. "And had we been a little bit less strong as a couple, we might not have survived that."

As Simon and his wife discovered, conflicts about money can be particularly intense. In fact, a study led by psychologist Lauren M. Papp of the University of Wisconsin-Madison found that spouses rated conflicts over money as being "more intense and significant" than conflicts over other issues. Even worse, financial conflicts were likely to "be mishandled and remain unresolved" without professional help. "To the extent that enduring money struggles represent concerns over broader relationship processes, such as power, decision making, self-esteem, or self-worth, [couples] are likely to require additional relationship assistance." (More on the benefits of seeking professional help in the section "How to Keep Your Relationship on Track" in this chapter.)

Spillover from Work-Life Conflict
When the stress of work spills over into family life, the couple relationship takes a hit, either because the partner who is feeling stressed is irritable or just plain unavailable. As the researchers involved in a recent study of over two thousand Australian parents reported in the journal *Child: Care, Health and Development*, "Negative experiences in the workplace adversely affect the quality of emotional exchanges within the intimate partner relationship."

Trying to juggle the needs of two small businesses and two small children became a chronic source of stress in Angie and Gordon's relationship. "We were fighting about him not having enough time and me not making enough money. So, nobody had enough time or was making enough money," she says. The solution was to start operating as a team. They figured out how the two of them could work together to generate enough income while still meeting the needs of their family. That has really helped to relieve the stress and to bring the joy back into their relationship, they both report.

How Nurturing Your Relationship with Your Partner Is Good for Your Kids

I can think of at least three key reasons for nurturing your relationship with your partner (to the extent that this is possible, of course, because some relationships can't and *shouldn't* be saved): (1) for your own sake, (2) for your partner's sake, and (3) for the sake of your kids. Because this is a parenting book, I'm going to skip over reasons one and two and zero in on reason three by talking about why a healthy relationship between you and your partner is beneficial for your kids. There's a solid body of research to show that whatever is happening in the couple relationship spills over into family relationships, for better and for worse. High levels of conflict in a couple relationship have far-reaching effects.

- *It affects your ability to function as a parent.* High levels of conflict between partners can cause both parents to be harsh and overly controlling, or inattentive, and it can cause fathers to disengage.

- *It affects your ability to function as a parenting team.* High levels of conflict in the couple relationship can make it harder for partners to be in sync on parenting issues.

- *It affects your child.* If you and your partner are feeling stressed, your child will be affected by that stress, which means that your child may experience sleep disruptions, emotional and behavioural problems, difficulty concentrating at school, and increased relationship conflicts with siblings and with peers. A social worker friend of mine likes to point out that children often function as barometers—finely calibrated instruments that measure and display "family barometric pressure."

Now that we've considered why the couple relationship matters, let's talk about what it takes to keep your relationship healthy and strong during the years when you're busy raising your kids (again, to the extent that it's possible). Note: This next section of the chapter is more likely to be of interest if you and your child's other parent are still part of a couple relationship. If you're not, you might prefer to flip ahead to the end of the chapter for a discussion on what it takes to thrive as a single parent.

How to Keep Your Relationship on Track

Relationships take work, lots of work. And there may be times when you feel like you simply don't have anything left in you to give to your partner. Olivia, the mother of a two-and-a-half-year-old, is upfront and honest about the fact that there simply isn't enough of her to go around these days: "I give the best of myself to my son, and my spouse, unfortunately, gets the leftovers." While most of us can get by on what's left over in the refrigerator for short periods of time when we're too busy to hit the grocery store, we can't survive on leftovers indefinitely. And this is true of relationship leftovers too. The good news is that there are practical ways to shift out of leftover mode and start nourishing your relationship again. What follows are some strategies for doing just that.

Give your relationship the time and attention it deserves. "Keep that relationship healthy and keep it fed," says Brian, the father of two school-aged boys. This could mean making a commitment to connect for a couple of minutes at the start or the end of each day. On days when it simply isn't possible because life or kids get in the way, you can reaffirm that commitment by saying to your partner, "We didn't get a chance to talk at all today, and I really missed it."

While you're working at staying connected, remember to make time for fun. According to psychologists Amy Claxton and Maureen Perry-Jenkins, joint leisure time is the first thing that gets sacrificed when parents find themselves in overload mode. As a result, parents end up with very little shared time for communication and connection, which causes them to miss out on a powerful source of relationship glue.

Sometimes, you have to get creative in order to find this time. "We don't have a village to rely on for dates or nights away," says Danielle, the mother of two school-aged girls, one of whom has autism. "As our kids are in school now, we carve out the moments to have a meal in peace in the middle of the day."

Sometimes, you have to find a way to reconcile your needs as a couple with your children's needs. For Marie, the mother of three school-aged boys, that means being flexible about what might happen at bedtime when someone other than she and her partner are at home to put the boys to bed. "Worst-case scenario: the kids don't get to bed until we get home. Maybe this isn't the end of the world."

Remind yourself that you're on the same team. This is an approach that Anthony and Gwen, the parents of two preteens, have brought to their entire relationship as partners and that they have carried over into the parenting arena as well. He explains, "It's a bit funny because neither of us were into team sports and we were, perhaps, labelled 'independent' as kids growing up. But we have been operating with this 'all for one and one for all' kind of mentality for many years." Keep telling yourself that it's not you *versus* your partner; it's you *and* your partner—an important point to keep in mind if you're still trying to figure out a way to share household duties and child-care responsibilities more equitably. Speaking of which, you'll find it easier to find common ground on that front if you remind yourself that "equality" doesn't have to mean "sameness." As Brock University sociologist Andrea Doucet explains, "Difference is not always a problem. It's when difference becomes a disadvantage that it becomes a problem."

Have a career plan as a couple. Talk through your career plans together so that you're clear about your shared goals, which might include having enough money to support the family and enough time to enjoy the family while also pursuing satisfying work.

Recognize that you'll need to tweak and adapt these plans to take into account shifting circumstances. "Right now, Cynthia's career is really taking off, so we decided that I would cancel some work that I had coming up so that I could focus on things on the home front: fixing things, getting the kids fed and dressed, and getting them to and from school," says Brian, the father of two school-aged boys. "It feels so much better now that everyone's getting their needs met because one of us isn't working quite so hard at other things."

Have the kind of relationship where it's okay to lean on one another. "There's a traditional teaching where men are supposed to be like a willow tree because the roots are very deep and the trunks are very strong and immovable," says Stephanie, an Indigenous midwife and lactation consultant who is raising six children in a blended family. In her community, fathers are taught to be a source of strength to a new mother, and pregnancy is treated as an experience that is shared by both expectant parents—"Mom and dad are both pregnant," she says. "When a woman is pregnant or has a new baby, when her emotions are all over the place, she is supposed to be able to turn to him for emotional support. He is able to move with her, to support her, and to be with her so that she's not alone. To know that somebody else will be with us to keep us safe—that's a pretty powerful feeling." And it's a pretty magical relationship possibility to model for your kids.

Notice and appreciate the contributions your partner is making. According to behavioural economist Dan Ariely, we have a tendency to over-estimate how much effort our own contributions require, and to underestimate the amount of effort our partner's contributions require. This is because we're intimately familiar with everything that's involved in completing our own tasks (say, getting a meal on the table), but we might not understand or fully appreciate all the steps involved in a task our partner is responsible for (say, changing the snow tires). In that case, we simply notice the outcome: "Hey, the tires got changed!" The solution is simple: either switch jobs or, at a minimum, get the lowdown on what's actually involved. While you're at it, consider whether the current chore split is still working for the two of you. Does the split seem fair? Have you been able to divvy up the chores according to each person's strengths and on the basis of who hates a particular chore a little less? If your partner happens to agree to take on a chore that both of you loathe equally, be sure to express gratitude for that. Research has shown that expressing gratitude for a partner's genuinely unselfish act—an act done out of kindness for you as opposed to any direct benefit to the partner—reaps tremendous relationship dividends. You'll both feel happier and more connected.

Practise "active constructive response"—and encourage your partner to do the same. This is a simple yet highly effective strategy for boosting happiness and couple connectedness. Here's how it works: When your partner shares exciting news, don't just say, "That's great, honey," and go back to staring at your smartphone. Express genuine excitement. Encourage your partner to elaborate on what happened in order to amplify and prolong the joy. Schedule a celebration for later on, so that the two of you will have that to look forward to. In other words, turn a great moment into an outstanding moment by being your partner's number one cheerleader and fan. And if this tip sounds impossibly utopian, know that you can dial it down a little and still get seriously great results. If you don't feel like you're up to reaching for the pompoms, simply remind yourself to keep asking your partner questions: "And then what happened?" "How did that make you feel?" Not only will this encourage your partner to continue talking; it's a powerful way to telegraph the fact that you're actually interested in what he or she has to say, as opposed to merely going through the motions of pretending to listen.

Don't expect your partner to be perfect. "You have to recognize that your partner has strengths and weaknesses and that you have strengths and weaknesses," says Simon, the father of preschooler. "I am improving as far as noticing the mess around the house goes, but cleanliness is never going to be a natural skill of mine. And she's never going to be as patient as I am. So how do we use our strengths to our advantage and forgive one another for having those weaknesses? I think that's where I'm at right now. Every time I get frustrated by her lack of patience, I remember that it comes bundled together with the strengths she has a parent and as a partner."

Give your partner the benefit of the doubt when things go wrong. Assume the best of intentions unless proven otherwise. Many people in unhappy relationships tend to attribute their partner's frustrating behaviours, like forgetting to pay an important bill, to character flaws ("He's scatterbrained") as opposed to external circumstances ("He must have had an exceptionally busy day if he forgot to pay that bill"). If you're struggling to find a way to reframe the situation in a way that is sufficiently kind to your partner, ask yourself how a neutral third party "who wants the best for all involved" might view the situation. This strategy was pioneered by a group of researchers in Chicago and has proved to be effective in maintaining marital satisfaction. It's like tapping into the wisdom of your wisest friend, except in this case, you're having the conversation inside your own head. You'll also want to heed the wisdom of that ever-wise "inner friend" if that friend keeps pointing out that your partner may no longer deserve the benefit of the doubt, because every day is a bad day for him. Erring on the side of kindness doesn't mean issuing your partner a relationship blank cheque every single day, because doing so would be an act of unkindness toward yourself.

Remind yourself that you don't have to have a lot of sex to have a great relationship. "For couples with busy lives, work responsibilities, and children to care for, feeling the pressure to engage in sex as frequently as possible may be daunting and even stressful," noted a group of University of Toronto researchers in a 2015 study. Their reassuring takeaway message? "More is not always better. . . . Sex may be like money—only too little is bad." Besides, intimacy doesn't always have to be about sex. Holding hands while you go for a walk or cuddling on the couch with a baby on your lap can help you stay connected while you wait to find your way back to your sexy place again.

Don't be afraid to seek professional help if you keep slamming into the same relationship roadblock. "Gordon and I had been pretty much having the same fight for over a decade," says Angie, the mother of two young girls. Going for counselling allowed them to find a way to work through that conflict and come up with a game plan for dealing with it in future. "Now, we can say to one another, 'Hey, we're going down that road again. We know where this is going.' And we know how to back out of it, to say, 'What's really going on here?'" Going for counselling was a total game-changer for the couple. She insists, "I would pay our counsellor double! There has been a great return on investment."

Don't expect your relationship to meet each and every one of your needs. Those kinds of expectations can strain a relationship to the breaking point. Instead, invest in other relationships that can help to sustain you and take some of the pressure off your relationship with your partner. Get by with a little help from your friends, in other words. As Arizona State University psychologists Suniya S. Luthar and Lucia Ciciolla noted in a 2015 study, "Having close relationships may help to sustain the marital relationship by reducing the burden on the relationship to meet all of one's emotional needs." Therefore, "in the interests of their own psychological well-being . . . women should prioritize fostering close relationships as much as they value maintaining good marriages." Ditto for men.

Keep your eyes on the prize. Remind yourself that the most time-consuming and intensive years of parenting only represent a small slice of your entire life and in your entire relationship as a couple. "In the grand scheme of things, this is a short time," says Katie, the mother of three school-aged boys. Good thing, she adds, because "maintaining your relationship while you're raising kids is friggin' hard."

Modelling Healthy Conflict Resolution Skills for Your Kids

Don't feel like you have to hide all evidence of conflict from your kids. You don't want them to grow up with the weirdly warped idea that healthy relationships are 100 percent conflict-free all of the time. If you think about it, it makes a lot more sense to teach them about conflict resolution skills by showing them how people who love one another work things out. (Of course, there are some conversations that are best left to times when the kids are safely out of earshot. Clearly, you'll want to use your discretion here.)

It's an approach that Renee, the mother of two school-aged children, applauds. In fact, she's chosen to go this route with her partner. "We fight in front of our kids. We actually do it very consciously. We're both loud talkers, so we have to remind the kids that we're not yelling at one another; we're just talking loudly and emphatically! But we did it very deliberately because I want them to know how to argue with people they love. I tell them, "There are ways of doing it. You can fight, but you can't hurt. It's about learning how to argue respectfully."

What does it mean to argue respectfully? According to couple relationship experts, being able to express empathy toward your partner in the heat of the moment is key. It's a powerful way to signal to your partner that you're deeply invested in the relationship and willing to work through the hard stuff together. Arguing respectfully also means remaining calm and treating one another with respect, solving the problem together, and being able to demonstrate through your subsequent interactions that the issue has been resolved and the relationship is still on track—an important message to telegraph to one another as well as your kids.

You'll also want to help your kids understand that not all relationship fixes happen in a flash; there can be a bit of a process involved: "Your mom and I disagree about this, but we're working on finding a solution together." Likewise, you can signal that there's a good time—and a bad time—to try to work through an issue with another person. Saying something like, "I'm still pretty upset about this, so I'm not quite ready to talk about it right now" helps kids to recognize that it's okay to turn on your emotional four-way flashers if you need a bit of time to regain your cool. It's about acknowledging and taking responsibility for managing your own emotions and in a way that contributes to healthy relationships with those you love.

On the other hand, witnessing conflicts between parents can be harmful to kids if the arguments become heated and hostile, the parents treat one another with contempt, poor conflict resolution skills are modelled, such as verbal insults, raised voices, physical aggression, or giving the other person the silent treatment, the conflict itself centres around the child (in which case, the child may blame himself), or the conflict is serious enough to make the child worry about its effect on the family. Those are the kinds of situations you want to avoid. If that has become your default way of communicating with your partner or your ex-partner, the two of you may want to consider seeking help from a therapist who can help you learn healthier ways of working through conflicts together—ways that are beneficial, and not harmful, to your child.

It may be particularly beneficial to seek support as a couple if you and a new partner are working through the challenges of co-parenting in a blended family. Blended family relationships can be challenging. They can require a lot of work. And one way to motivate yourself and your partner to do that hard work is by reminding yourself how much harder it all is for your kids. Serena, who is the step-parent of twin girls in their twenties, as well as the biological parent of two boys in their teens, explains, "The kids are the ones who are being asked to switch houses and bedrooms and to adjust to different parenting styles. They're the ones who are being asked to share holidays with up to four different extended families, depending on how many sets of grandparents are involved. They might even be asked to share their siblings with another family. So do what you can to make it easy—or at least easier—for them. Ask yourself how you want them to remember the role you played in their childhood and then act accordingly. This is one of those situations where it can be helpful to remind yourself that it's the adults' job to make things okay, not the kids' job."

What does this mean in practical terms, if you're the step-parent? It means putting your stepchildren first some of the time, in recognition of the fact that they may be feeling displaced. It means feeling liberated—not limited—by the fact that your stepchild's biological parents need to be the key decision-makers in that child's life, because this frees you up to be more of a mentor and a guide. (Or, as Loren describes it, a "step-friend." Loren ended a conflict-ridden relationship with a former partner when he was unable to forge healthy relationships with the two children she brought into the relationship.) It means recognizing that your stepchildren see bits of themselves in both of their biological parents and that it will be deeply wounding to them to watch you and their parent disparage their other parent, and that they will feel a need to come to that parent's defence. The good news, according to Serena, is that it is possible to find a way to navigate these challenging issues, both as a couple and as a family: "While I 'mothered' the girls, it felt more like I was being invited to be an awesome aunt. This isn't everyone's story, but it's my story, and it worked well. I can't imagine my family without the girls."

Going Solo

Sometimes, what's broken in a relationship simply can't be fixed. In that case, it may be time to move on. It's a fact of life for the estimated 1.2 million Canadian parents who are no longer in a spousal or common-law relationship with their child's mother or father.

Margaret knew it was time to end her marriage when differences in parenting philosophies became irreconcilable. "We had agreed that our teenage son could not have any drug paraphernalia on the premises, but then my husband relented without my consent, agreeing to allow him to store this stuff in the garage." On the surface, the point of conflict was her son's drug use, but it actually ran much deeper than that. The fact was that Margaret felt like her husband was undercutting her authority as a parent. "This was the deciding event for me. Our marriage had drifted apart, we had less in common than we used to, and it seemed futile to stay together in the wake of such disrespect. I didn't want my two sons to grow up believing that it's perfectly okay for a husband to overrule his wife." And so they separated.

Cathy, the mother of a teenager and a young adult, separated from her children's father when their two girls were four and eight, and initially struggled with the decision to leave her marriage. She wanted to do whatever was in the best interests of her children, but she wasn't completely sure what that meant. In the end, she decided that she had reached the point of no return and that it was time to end her marriage to a man "who did not spend much time with the children and who could not intuitively understand when I needed support." Two decades later, she has no regrets. "Now that my girls are grown up, I have no doubt that I made the right decision. My girls have seen me become very independent and happy, and I think this has made them strong young women," she says.

The research seems to back her up. A 2016 study published in *Developmental Psychology* highlighted the fact that staying in a loveless marriage for the sake of the kids can, in fact, be harmful to the kids. The researchers involved in the study found that living with parents who are in a loveless marriage contributes to adolescent mental-health problems independent of the quality of parent–child relationships and the amount of conflict between parents.

It's a fact that buoys Breanne, the single mother of four school-aged children, and validates her decision to exit an abusive marriage: "In some situations, making the decision to leave an abusive relationship is the ultimate act of self-care. I knew something wasn't right. I knew my marriage was different than other people's marriages. I knew other people didn't fight as much. I knew other people got support from their partners." She knew something needed to change, and she resented the message she kept getting from other people: she just needed to try a little harder. She explains, "As women, we're told 'marriage takes work' and 'it takes time for people to grow together,' but sometimes, this kind of advice does women a disservice. Sometimes, the healthiest thing a woman can do for herself and her kids is to leave an unhealthy marriage." While the prospect of becoming the single parent of four children might be daunting to some, for Breanne, it was a relief. Because she no longer had to feel like she was walking on eggshells, she found it was less work to parent on her own than it had been to parent alongside her ex. "Besides, I was a single parent long before I was single," she says.

A key challenge of single parenthood is figuring out how to parent effectively with your ex. Children benefit when they are able to maintain healthy relationships with both parents—when that is possible. Rebecca, the mother of a ten-year-old son who has special needs, feels fortunate to have such a positive co-parenting relationship with her son's father. They might not have been able to make things work as a couple, but they're definitely making things work as co-parents. The two of them decided early on that "whatever happened between the two of us was going to stay between the two of us—that we were going to leave Michael out of it. And we've been pretty good about that."

For Breanne, the situation has been a lot more difficult. She's had to learn how to choose her battles in order to minimize conflict with her ex. She says, "They eat a lot of junk food at his house. They play video games. He buys them new toys every time they come over because he wants his house to be the super-fun house. And his parenting techniques are less than stellar. The discipline is really inconsistent. But I have to let a lot of things go, because if he wasn't willing to listen to me back when we were married, he certainly isn't going to listen to me now. So, I just tell my kids, 'Different houses, different rules," and we leave it at that. As long as what's happening isn't harmful to my kids, I let it go."

Tapping into support from other people is key to thriving as a single parent. "Being married in itself is not necessarily protective; what benefits women more is that they feel loved and comforted when in need—whoever the source of those feelings," noted psychologists Suniya S. Luthar and Lucia Ciciolla in a 2015 study.

Late in her journey as a single parent, Loren stumbled upon an incredible source of support: other single moms who were simultaneously scrambling to keep all the balls in the air. "All of a sudden, I had somebody to pick up my daughter at school if I was running late at a meeting," she recalls. "And, likewise, my friends had someone to pick up their kids because I worked at home and was closer to the school, so I could get there if it didn't work for them. If they had to go away for a weekend, I would take my daughter to stay at their house so their kids could be in their own beds. And they didn't have to worry so much about travelling for work or even going out on a date because our kids were friends or, at a minimum, knew one another very well. We could really be there for each other. When one of us got sick, the other could swing by Safeway and pick up stuff to make chicken soup. It really changed my life. The idea that you can be useful to another person and committed to one another in ways that don't involve a romantic relationship was revolutionary to me. I remember thinking, 'Oh, wow. This is how community works. This is what they mean when they say it takes a village.'"

The other mothers became her village.

CHAPTER 10

Parenting Strategies That Work for You and Your Child

I have been practising trying to be calm, patient, and non-reactive; understanding how things work from another being's perspective and developmental stage; being a "bigger person"; being the adult; believing in myself and my ability to use my intelligence and creativity to find solutions that are in everyone's best interest, especially theirs; and, most importantly, acknowledging and working through my own feelings so I don't get stuck making everything about me.

—Ginette, mother of two young children

There's no doubt about it: most of us are holding ourselves up to a higher parenting standard than ever before. Parenting has changed a lot over the years. "*Parenting* wasn't even a verb when I was growing up," says Loren, the mother of two young adults. And now that simple verb has pretty much taken on a life of its own, often fuelling anxiety, guilt, and feelings of being overwhelmed. There's this ever-present sense that you're being judged and found guilty of any number of parenting crimes: the crime of being too lenient, the crime of being too controlling, and perhaps both crimes simultaneously if you happen to be having a particularly bad day.

This chapter is about escaping all those feelings of guilt and judgment and becoming a more confident and competent parent. It's about feeling better *about* your parenting and doing better *with* your parenting at the same time. Because here's the thing: you can learn how to parent in a way that actually makes things better for you and your child, as opposed to making things harder or more stressful for both of you. Better for you means reducing the stress and increasing the joy of parenting. Better for your child means allowing him or her to thrive. And your relationship with one another will be better because the strategies that we're going to talk about emphasize the parent-child connection above all else.

As you're about to discover, this is the shortest chapter in the book by far. And there's a good reason for that. So much of what constitutes "good parenting" is stuff that has little or nothing to do with your child. I'm referring, of course, to all the things we talked about in earlier chapters: the thinking part of parenting, managing your emotions, treating yourself with self-compassion, and prioritizing self-care. Once you have those fundamentals in place, parenting is relatively easy. You've already done the hard work of getting to a happier, healthier place yourself.

How Understanding Child Development Can Make You a Better Parent

Apparently, the Rolling Stones got it wrong when they sang about "mother's little helper"—or at a minimum, they got the "helper" part wrong. The miracle fix that so many moms (and dads) are craving may, in fact, be a crash course in child development. That knowledge is what makes it easier to get through the long days and sometimes even longer nights of parenting.

Learning about child development certainly proved to be a game-changer for Mary, the mother of a seven-year-old boy. "It makes it so much easier to understand my son and respond to him effectively. It has completely changed how I see challenging behaviour," she explains. Learning about child development allows you to see things from a different perspective—from your child's perspective, to be precise. Instead of treating your toddler as an incomplete adult—a tiny person who's pretty bad at behaving like he's thirty-five—you begin to understand and appreciate him for who he is right now: someone who's actually pretty great at being two. And that, in turn, changes everything, both in terms of how you feel and how you choose to respond to him.

You'll feel more confident in your ability to nurture and guide your child's development along. You'll have a better understanding of what's happening right now with your child, and you'll have a better sense of how things will change as your child continues to learn and grow. Not only does this knowledge increase your enjoyment of parenting: it also eliminates a lot of the worry, guilt, and second-guessing that only serves to make parenting harder.

You won't take your child's annoying behaviours quite so personally. Instead of treating your child's totally annoying—but completely age-appropriate—behaviour as a problem to be solved (or, worse, attributing it to bad parenting), you'll be able to put that behaviour in context. You'll be able to see that behaviour for what it is: a perfectly reasonable behaviour for a child his age, given the skills and abilities he has right now. And because understanding child development makes it easier to recognize the fact that those skills and abilities aren't fixed—your child can build and improve on those skills over time—you'll feel less pressured to rush in to try to fix a problem that may not even be a problem at all. You'll understand that your two-year-old is having a meltdown because she's a two-year-old, not because you're a bad parent and not because she's a bad kid. The two of you are simply spending some time in Toddler World. Recognizing that simple yet all-important fact makes parenting less stressful for you and being a kid more enjoyable for her. Everybody wins!

You'll be inspired to shift from the "what" to the "why." Instead of narrowly focusing on what you *should* be doing to react to your child's behaviour because you feel pressured to fix a particular behavioural issue right now, you'll become curious about what you *could* be doing, based on your growing understanding of and intuition about your child. It's about allowing yourself to become curious about your child's underlying needs and intentions as opposed to merely reacting to his surface behaviours—something that's easier to do, of course, if you're able to parent from the place of calm we talked about back in Chapter 5. Once you've taken the time to consider your options, you'll be ready to choose how to respond—or whether, in fact, you need to respond at all. This slower and more thoughtful approach to parenting helps to take the pressure off you to respond instantly in the moment, increasing the likelihood that you'll be able to parent in a way that you can actually feel good about and that takes into account what's healthy for your relationship and what's possible for your child right now.

You'll parent with greater empathy. You'll find it easier to recognize that you and your child are in this thing together and to celebrate the fact that neither of you has to be perfect. "I try to keep in mind that everyone is doing their best," says Sarah, the mother of seventeen-year-old triplets. Parenting is, after all, ultimately about empathy—about recognizing that it's hard to be the parent *and* it's hard to be the kid. As philosophers John Kaag and Clancy Martin put it in an essay for *Aeon*, "Childhood is often terrifying. So is parenthood."

What Children Want and Need from Their Parents at Every Stage of Their Development

I've spent the last three decades researching all things parenting. A lot has changed during that time, but what hasn't changed is what actually encourages children to thrive. Yes, this advice tends to get sliced and diced in all kinds of different ways, but ultimately, good parenting boils down to doing three simple yet all-important things:

1. Giving your child the gift of unconditional love and approval
2. Providing the kind of warm, sensitive, and responsive parenting that fosters a loving connection between you and your child
3. Celebrating your child's growing independence and supporting your child's emerging abilities

Good parenting is about providing kids a safe place to grow—with that safe place being the security of your loving relationship. And it's about recognizing that your job as a parent is to nurture and protect, as opposed to shape and mould, your child. As developmental psychologist Alison Gopnik explains in her book *The Gardener and the Carpenter,* "Our job is not to make a particular kind of child but to provide a protected space of love, safety, and stability in which children of many unpredictable kinds can flourish."

Now, let's talk about the three key parenting strategies that combine to create that nutrient-rich parenting soil—the kind of environment that allows children to thrive and that makes parenting so much less stressful.

UNCONDITIONAL LOVE AND APPROVAL

Experiencing unconditional love and approval from another person means feeling safe and secure and benefiting from a truly no-strings-attached relationship. You don't have to do a single thing to earn that person's love. You've already earned it, just by being you. A child who is raised in an atmosphere of unconditional love and approval ends up receiving some really important messages: "You are worthy of love." "I will always be a safe place for you to land." "I love you just the way you are." Very Mr. Rogers, I know! These are extremely powerful messages to give to a child—ones that Sarah and her partner work hard at conveying to their three teenagers through their parenting: "We try to emphasize that there is nothing the kids could do that would make us stop loving them. We might be disappointed by something that happened—a mistake that was made or a pattern of behaviour that is causing frustration for someone else—but that doesn't affect how we feel about the person."

Being served a regular diet of these messages of unconditional love and acceptance—what psychologists call "unconditional parental regard"—allows your child to grow up feeling good about herself and confident in her abilities. This, in turn, gives her the courage to try new things and to dare to be the person she was meant to be. What you're providing your child with when you choose to parent in this particular way is a secure foundation upon which to build a life. Lara, the mother of a ten-year-old boy, says, "Just the other day, my son gave us the best compliment. He said, 'I always feel safe when I'm with you and Dad.' I want him to always feel safe: safe to make mistakes, safe to be silly, safe to tell us anything."

Emotional safety is key. Children need to feel that all of their emotions are acceptable—including the messy ones. "It's important for your child to feel that you're the one person in their lives that they can come to with anything—and that they don't have to worry about being judged or making you upset," says Melanie, the mother of two young children. Your child will find it easier to come to you with these messy emotions if you give your child the message that you can handle anything, including the tough stuff. She adds, "Children are very conscious of their parents' emotions. If they think something might hurt your feelings or make you angry, they will hesitate to bring you their concerns."

That's why it's so important to acknowledge and accept all emotions and to give kids a blanket permission slip to feel all the feelings. Trying to talk kids out of their feelings or doing your best to ignore those feelings gives kids the message that certain kinds of feelings are unacceptable—and that they are unacceptable too, because, after all, they are the owners of those feelings. Shutting down a child's feelings doesn't magically make the feelings go away. It simply drives the emotion underground or causes the emotion to get expressed in other ways that could make things harder for you and your child. Being willing to accept and talk about their feelings directly makes it possible for children to learn how to accept, cope with, and manage their feelings and to recognize that it's okay to turn to other people for support in handling emotions that are simply too big for them to handle on their own—a critically important message for children to receive. (We talked about becoming comfortable with uncomfortable emotions and helping your child to do the same in Chapter 7.)

What happens when children don't grow up hearing these messages and instead experience what psychologists call "conditional parental regard"?

They grow up worrying that they aren't, in fact, worthy of love. The messages that they receive from their parents are, after all, both crystal-clear and devastating: "Only certain types of thoughts, behaviours, and actions are acceptable. Step outside those limits and you are no longer worthy of my love." As a group of psychologists from the University of Houston explained in an article in the *International Journal of Adolescence and Youth*, "Conditional parental regard may lead the child to believe that love from the parent is unstable and unreliable, which may then form the foundation for a view of the self as unworthy of love."

They feel less connected to their parents. The child learns that the parent's love can never be taken for granted. It has to be earned repeatedly, which means it can disappear at any time. This not only causes the child to feel emotionally distant from the parent, but it can also lead to deep-rooted feelings of resentment toward that parent because the child has to work so hard to earn that parent's love.

They grow up craving constant validation from others—the result of learning early on that they need to seek such validation from their parents. It's an unhealthy pattern that can result in a shaky sense of self and fuel a tendency toward perfectionism. As Thomas Curran of the University of Bath and his co-authors noted in a thought-provoking article that connected the dots between conditional parental regard and adolescent perfectionism, published in *Personality and Individual Differences*, "Parental conditional regard is an intrusive interpersonal style that is used to manipulate self-conscious affect (e.g., guilt and shame) with the aim of eliciting desired behavior. It works by connecting children's perceptions of self-worth with the attainment of parent expectations. . . . It promotes a sense that children's own standards are irrelevant, superseded instead by those of the parent. . . . Children adopt extremely high standards, and strive for perfection, to both gain parental approval and avoid the guilt and shame that follow love withdrawal."

As you can see from everything we've talked about in this section, it's so much healthier for kids—and so much less stressful for parents—to simply focus on conveying your unconditional love and acceptance to your child. It's the kind of parenting gift that just keeps on giving, reaping immeasurable dividends throughout the lifetime of your child and resulting in a warm and caring relationship between the two of you. Let's talk now about another key parenting strategy that builds on that bond.

Warm, Sensitive, and Responsive Parenting

Warm, sensitive, and responsive parenting means picking up on a child's cues, being curious about his intentions, and responding to his needs in a warm and loving manner, based on what you think he needs in that moment. It's about parenting in a way that tells your child, "I am here for you," "You matter to me," and "You are worthy of my time and attention."

It's about being tuned in. You are curious about what the world looks like from your child's point of view (what he's seeing, thinking, and feeling) and you find yourself wondering about his goals and intentions—and how you might support those goals and intentions. When Julia looks back on the earliest months of her daughter's life, she's struck by how much time she spent simply studying her daughter. "My biggest strategy—and I think I started doing this fairly early on, when she was just a couple of weeks old—was to really try to get to know her as an individual, spending every single second with her and paying attention to every little thing."

It's about being ready to respond. This can be something as simple as smiling and nodding to indicate that you're paying attention, which gives your child the message that her goals and intentions have been seen and understood—a pretty powerful message to give to another human being. Child development experts use the term "serve and return" parenting to describe this really tuned-in and attentive form of parenting. It's a term that brings to mind the idea of a tennis game, with each player being intensely focused on and ready to respond to his opponent's actions and reactions. It's the interactive element that's key, both in terms of supercharging the parent-child relationship and serving as a launching pad for learning. When a parent responds to a child's needs in a sensitive and responsive manner—in a way that recognizes and meets the child's needs as those needs emerge—the child learns that she can count on that parent. And because human beings are designed to learn by watching other people, the child picks up all kinds of valuable information, simply by observing the parent's actions and reactions. This is critical to the development of social-emotional skills. In fact, it's been said that the family is a learning lab for empathy—the place where we learn how to interact with other people and how to decode their behaviours and intentions. Not only is the family the place where we learn to make sense of other people; it's the place where we learn about ourselves too. A parent helps you to calm your emotions and then you begin to figure out how to get to this place of calm on your own; a parent helps you to focus your attention and then you begin to learn how to focus your own attention.

This doesn't mean that parents need to be tuned-in and responsive 100 percent of the time—good news for most of us mere mortals with finite reserves of patience and attention and countless other demands on our time. In fact, there's some evidence to show that variations in parental responses, meaning that a parent responds to a child's bids for attention most but not all of the time, can actually be beneficial to child development in that it helps a very young child to puzzle out the fact that they are separate and distinct from the parent, as opposed to part of the same person. But having a parent who is consistently inattentive—who doesn't tune back in when a child repeatedly or urgently signals his need for attention, perhaps because that parent is distracted by other worries—can be confusing and even distressing to a child.

This brings to mind a classic experiment that is referred to as the "still face" experiment, which was pioneered by developmental psychologist Edward Tronick. In this experiment, mothers were instructed to remain completely unresponsive to their babies' bids for attention and to exhibit a completely emotionless (or "still") face. After running through every trick in the baby playbook, such as being adorable, making cute noises, and generally doing anything they could to get their parents to engage with them, the babies simply fell apart. And the entire process, from happy baby to wailing baby, took just ninety seconds—something that speaks to the power of the parent-child connection.

AUTONOMY-SUPPORTIVE PARENTING

Autonomy-supportive parenting is about parenting in a way that celebrates your child's growing independence and supports your child's emerging abilities. It's about giving your child these kinds of important messages: "I trust you," "I believe in you," and "You can count on me for help."

The challenge, of course, is to find ways to support and guide your child in a non-intrusive way—a way that acknowledges and helps your toddler to achieve her goal of putting on her boots herself ("Try turning your boots around so that the toes on your boots are pointing this way") without completely taking over ("Here, give me that boot"). It's about letting learning unfold in a natural and unscripted way—the way that actually works best for human beings. You're not rushing in to take charge of the learning process, but you're available to offer moral support or hands-on help if your child needs it. In other words, you're letting your child take the lead.

It can feel like a bit of a tightrope act, figuring out "when to let them do their own thing and trust that they're going to be okay" and "when to say okay, this is too far and now we need to intervene," notes Rebecca, the mother of a ten-year-old who has special needs. "That's the balance—and I don't know where that balance lies."

Most of us struggle to figure this out (and to keep figuring it out) as our children continue to learn and grow. At certain points, it's about playing cheerleader. You encourage your child's growth by offering support and encouragement. "If there's anything that my son is finding difficult—something he doesn't want to do because it's hard—I'll say, 'Hey, remember that time when you were learning to ski? How it seemed impossible, but then within two days, you were bombing down a mountain?'" says Brian, the father of two school-aged boys.

At other times, it's about providing feedback. The best kind of feedback is highly specific; it's directly relevant to the child's goals or intentions and narrowly focused on the specific task he's trying to master right now. You want your child to be able to figure out what's working, what's not, and what else he might want to try. This not only helps your child to acquire important problem-solving skills, but it also encourages your child to develop what psychologists refer to as a "growth mindset," which is the idea that people can learn and grow and that challenges can be rewarding. When you're paying attention enough to be able to provide that specific feedback, you have the opportunity to supercharge your child's learning by boosting both his competence and his confidence. We're talking pretty powerful stuff.

As children become more independent, you'll find yourself playing more of a consulting role. "Your role as a parent changes over time—from 'director' to 'producer,'" explains Shannon, the mother of two preteens. "We direct them less as they get older. We're more focused on trying to support the decisions that they make." Of course, it's also important to know when to be the grown-up, adds Loren, the mother of two young adults. "I remember one time when my son was about ten, I'd asked him to make a decision about something and he said, 'Mom! You're the mom. *You* decide.'"

Now that we've talked about the three things that children need at every stage of development—unconditional love and approval; warm, sensitive, and responsive parenting; and support for their growing autonomy—let's zoom in and consider what kids need at specific stages of their development and what this means for us, as their parents.

What Children Need from Parents at Specific Stages of Their Development

Children are constantly changing, which means you constantly have to change your parenting game plan too. Here are the key things to think about as your child moves from stage to stage.

BABIES, TODDLERS, AND PRESCHOOLERS

The early years are all about lessons in trust. A healthy parent-child relationship teaches young children that they can trust in other people and turn to them for help. At the same time, you also want to encourage your child's growing quest for independence and support his emerging abilities, so that he can grow up feeling competent and confident. Finally, it's important to recognize that your child has strong feelings but few tools for managing those feelings. He hasn't had a chance to acquire those skills quite yet. This means he's going to need help from you in managing feelings that are simply too big to handle on his own—a process that begins by your acknowledging and accepting those feelings.

SCHOOL-AGED CHILDREN

The primary school years are all about helping your child to develop the types of skills that will allow her to function well in all areas of her life: how to focus her attention, how to make sense of her thoughts and emotions and gain insight into what other people are thinking and feeling, how to think critically, and how to solve problems. In fact, you'll be busy supporting all areas of her development: physical, social-emotional, and cognitive. Your child will be spending a lot of time making friends and building relationships with other caring adults, including teachers, but her connection to you will continue to provide the foundation of her world.

ADOLESCENCE

The adolescent years are all about coming to terms with your preteen or teen's growing quest for independence and trying to find a way not to take that too personally. Sometimes, parents retreat when kids head into the adolescent years, mistaking their need for greater autonomy for a desire for decreased connection. Or parents take the increased desire for independence as personal rejection, which triggers feelings of hurt, anger, or loss.

It's important to understand that you still matter to your teen. In fact, you matter a lot. You might feel like you're becoming obsolete, but nothing could be further from the truth. Your teen still wants you to be around, available as an on-call resource that he can turn to as needed—but on his terms rather than yours. Remember how your toddler used to treat your lap like "home base"—a safe place to return to for comfort and reassurance after venturing out into the world, which at that point, likely meant venturing across the room? What we're talking about here is the adolescent equivalent, but in this case, your teenager wants you to turn yourself into wallpaper—ever-present, non-intrusive wallpaper.

Just as you need to know that you still matter to your teenager, your teenager needs to know that he still matters to you. How do you show him how much he matters? By spending time with him. A 2014 study published in *Developmental Psychology* concluded that "time spent with parents appears to become more important as adolescents age" and that "the relationship between time spent together and perceived mattering was stronger . . . for fathers than for mothers." The key takeaway message from this study is clear: "Decreased amounts of interaction with either parent were associated . . . with adolescents' perceptions that they mattered less to that parent." So, you'll definitely want to make that time.

EMERGING ADULTHOOD

Developmental psychologist Jeffrey Jensen Arnett has coined the phrase "emerging adulthood" to describe the years between eighteen and twenty-nine, when young people are well on the way to becoming adults, but they aren't quite there yet. They're in the process of launching themselves into the world, but they're not quite ready to launch.

Navigating this in-between stage can be tricky for parents and kids alike. What's key to maintaining your connection during these sometimes-tumultuous years is to acknowledge your emerging adult's autonomy and to recognize that she's more of a roommate than a kid if and when she happens to "boomerang" back home. It's also important to resist the temptation to rush in and offer truckloads of unsolicited advice, notes Rob, the father of a twenty-year-old daughter: "When Madison wants to talk to me about something, I always ask, 'Are you looking for advice or are you just looking for someone to listen?' Probably about 70 percent of the time, she says, 'I just want you to listen.' And that's my cue to just sit back and listen as opposed to always jumping in with a solution or advice. This simple rule has helped a lot. I find we communicate a lot more, because she feels safe knowing we have that rule to guide us."

It's all about letting go in stages while maintaining connection and allowing the relationship to evolve in a natural, healthy way. This is something Margaret is already thinking about, even though her three children are still quite young: "On the one hand, it's inconceivable that my kids will grow up and leave someday. On the other hand, I feel like every little step that they've taken along the way—the first time I left them at kindergarten, the first time they slept over at someone's house—has been preparing them and me for that inevitable departure. Because it's not just about the child separating from the parent; it's a two-way street."

CHAPTER 11

Finding Your Village

You really need that one parent you can call—someone who will drop everything to help you. We're not meant to parent alone.

—Janette, mother of three young children

Janette has it right: we *aren't* meant to parent on our own. We really aren't.

It's a simple truth recognized by every exhausted and overwhelmed parent—and that's backed by a hefty amount of science too. Consider the work of primatologist and evolutionary theorist Sarah Blaffer Hrdy, for example. She makes the case that social support is critical to parenting success and that we're meant to turn to others for help in raising our children. According to Hrdy, it takes roughly two decades for a child to become "nutritionally independent," meaning that the child has finally become capable of generating the income needed to feed himself. Getting to that point requires an investment of roughly 13 million calories—far more than any individual mother or even any individual mother and her partner are capable of providing on their own. That's why parents need support from "the village"—because they need a little help shouldering that load.

As it turns out, tapping into support from others is an essential part of being human. We not only crave this kind of support, but our bodies have actually learned to anticipate it—to factor the amount of social support available into our tally of biological resources. As the authors of a 2015 study published in *Current Opinion in Psychology* explained, the human brain treats social relationships as a resource that can be relied upon to achieve goals. The brain "*expects* access to relationships" and if it finds that this kind of support is missing, it "prepares the body to either conserve or more heavily invest in its own energy." This is because "the brain construes *social* resources as *bioenergetic* resources, much like oxygen or glucose." This helps to explain why socially isolated individuals tend to consume more sugar (to make up for the reduced number of social resources available to them) and why hills don't appear quite as steep when you're standing next to a friend—a key finding from a much-cited series of studies at the University of Virginia and the University of Plymouth. The impact of social support, or its absence, can be that far-reaching.

It turns out that even imagining a supportive significant other standing beside you can significantly lighten the load. Just knowing that you have people who care about you—even if they aren't actually with you right now—makes difficult things seem more possible. *Parenting* becomes more possible, in other words.

In this chapter, we're going to talk about the many benefits of tapping into support from the village, and how parenting becomes so much easier and less stressful when other people are sharing the load. Then, I'll wrap up the chapter and the book by talking about why the village needs to do a much better job of supporting parents and children—why it's time for the village to step up.

Why Parents Need Support

Being a parent is all about investing in an intense and demanding relationship. It's about endless giving to another person and not expecting to receive the same kind of reciprocal investment in return (well, not for a couple of decades anyway). It's easy to become depleted when you're doing all this giving, unless you have other people who are working just as hard to replenish you.

FRIENDSHIPS ARE ESSENTIAL, NOT A LUXURY

Behind-the-scenes support and replenishment is particularly important for mothers, who continue to shoulder the heaviest load when it comes to child care. Arizona State University researchers Suniya S. Luthar and Lucia Ciciolla have identified four key factors that contribute to well-being in mothers, and not surprisingly, being able to tap into support from friends is key. Their research has demonstrated that mothers are more likely to thrive as individuals and function well as parents when:

- they feel unconditionally loved (when they're "seen and loved for their 'core' selves," as Luthar and Ciciolla put it);

- they feel comforted in times of distress (as a result of having a source of "reliable comfort" to turn to);

- they are able to be authentic in their relationships (by virtue of being seen and loved for who they truly are); and

- they feel satisfied with the quality of their friendships.

It turns out that having high-quality friendships are essential. Luthar and Ciciolla stress that mothers must "deliberately cultivate and maintain close, authentic relationships with friends as well as family" and treat these friendships as "essential buffers against the redoubtable challenges of sustaining 'good enough' mothering across two decades or more." In other words, lunch with your best friend isn't a luxury; it's a necessity—an essential investment in your own well-being and one that also benefits your kids.

PARENTS NEED SUPPORT AT EVERY STAGE OF PARENTING

Becoming a parent is a major life transition. Yes, most of us manage to weather this transition, but that doesn't necessarily mean we do so quickly or automatically. There can be times of significant struggle. It's important to acknowledge this fact so you don't find yourself feeling like you're doing it wrong if you're feeling unsure or scared by the magnitude of the task you've taken on. It is daunting, and you have to find your own path, which takes time. In the meantime, you can tread in the footsteps of other parents who've at least helped to forge the way for you.

Being able to compare notes with someone who is years ahead of you on the path can be particularly helpful and reassuring. They can provide you with a quick pep talk and reassure you that you will make it through to the other side. That's important, because when you're stuck in the midst of a really tough stage, it can be easy to lose sight of the fact that things will eventually get better—that it won't be this hard forever. "You don't believe this is just a phase when you're in it," explains Janette, the mother of three young girls. "You can't see that until you're past it. And that makes it really hard, because there are so many different phases to get through."

Most of us recognize the need for support when our children are really little because their need for care is so round-the-clock and intense. As Courtney E. Martin put it rather memorably in a 2017 article for the blog *On Being,* "A newborn baby is a barnacle. An appendage. The cutest possible parasite you can imagine." But what we fail to recognize is that tapping into support from the village is essential at each and every stage of parenting, particularly during our kids' preteen and teen years. There's a lot going on for both mothers and their children during the middle school years, note Luthar and Ciciolla: "Just as middle school encompasses the most trying developmental period for children, our findings suggest that this is also the most challenging time for mothers." Not only are preteens extremely moody and increasingly independent, they're also struggling with increased academic pressures that can spill over into their relationships with their parents. As luck would have it, this is a tough developmental stage for moms as well. It's the point at which marital satisfaction is at its lowest and marital conflict is at its highest, which can cause moms to do some serious soul-searching about their lives. The best way to weather these middle-school and mid-life storms is to connect with other moms who are weathering similar challenges, note Luthar and Ciciolla: "Mothers should treat it as an imperative, and not an option, to connect with supportive friends, and stick with this resolve especially during the middle school years." In other words, it may be time to reconvene the new-mom support group that got you through those rocky early days.

You'll probably want to keep that mom support group up and running through the high school years as well. Research conducted at the University of North Carolina at Chapel Hill highlighted the fact that moms of teens (as compared to dads of teens) really benefit from added social support during the often tumultuous teen years. This group of researchers found that when mothers have others to turn to for support and advice, they find it easier to maintain close and caring relationships with their teens. The reason? Being able to talk through tough problems with a supportive friend may help to normalize some of the more challenging aspects of parenting a teenager, giving those moms the message, "It's not just you!" This, in turn, may help mothers to feel calmer and more confident in their parenting abilities. Feeling support from the village makes it easier for you to be the parent you want to be. Mothers who benefit from greater amounts of social support (from people in general and from their spouses in particular) are less likely to resort to harsh, hostile, and controlling parenting. It starts with you, but it doesn't have to end with you. Other people can share the hard work and heavy-lifting of parenting.

What the Village Stands to Gain from Offering This Support

Up until now, we've been talking about what parents stand to gain by tapping into support from their village. Now let's consider what the village stands to gain by offering such support to parents, because it's anything but a one-way street.

In our culture, we have a tendency to treat parenting as a private problem we should be able to solve on our own—and to beat ourselves up when we can't. But here's the thing: the village has a vested interest in the health and well-being of its children because they represent the next generation of citizens. Other more collectivist cultures do a far better job of recognizing this simple yet all-important fact: each individual villager has an important role to play in nurturing the next generation along. They treat the birth of a child as a cause for celebration, as opposed to implying that the child is a burden or giving parents the message that they're the ones who are responsible for solving "the problem" that is that kid. "When someone has a child, there's an acknowledgement that they've brought something wonderful to the tribe; that they've enriched the community by having this child. And there's a real sense of joy about it," explains parenting author Teresa Pitman.

A shared commitment to nurturing all the children of the village makes life so much easier for parents—and not just because there are more hands available to help with the heavy lifting. The emotional load becomes correspondingly lighter as well. Parents are less likely to feel judged and blamed if a particular child is struggling. After all, if it's the entire village's responsibility to care for that child, it's the entire village's responsibility to shoulder the blame if things aren't going well. It's not about attempting to narrowly pin the blame on that child or his parents.

Ultimately, what it all comes down to is a willingness to allow ourselves to feel blessed, not burdened, by our interconnectedness, to treat that fundamental dependency as a source of strength, not weakness, and to build a society on that basis. Or, as economic researcher Lyman Stone likes to put it, it's about making a collective decision to support "those citizens who make the societally essential, forward-looking choice to become parents"—something that would prove to be a complete game-changer for ourselves and our kids.

Why It Can Be Tough to Access This Kind of Support

Of course, it's one thing to know that you'd benefit from support from the village—and that your fellow villagers would benefit from providing such support. It can be quite another thing to actually find a way to tap into it. Parenting can be a lonely, even isolating, activity. We get so swept up by the hurricane that is our extraordinarily busy lives that we find ourselves with little time or energy left to invest in relationships. "Everyone is so busy with their own lives that they don't have time to help others in need. It does take a village, but our modern village feels more like a caravan—from home to school to whatever extracurricular activity the kids are involved in that day, then back home for bath and bed," notes Melanie, the mother of two young children. Christina, the mother of an eleven-year-old son, echoes those sentiments: "I think the notion of a village is a great idea, but in my experience, many people are focused on cultivating their own garden." While connecting with the village is an increasing challenge for every parent, for some parents, it can be even tougher.

It's tougher if you're a dad. As Chris Routly of the National At-Home Dad Network noted in a 2017 article for *Fatherly*, "When a mom makes the decision to find community and support, it's generally easily accessible. If she doesn't fit in with one group of moms, there are others to choose from. Dads have it harder in that respect." The gap in the amount of support available to moms versus dads carries over into the online world as well. A 2015 Pew Research study found, for example, that moms were nearly twice as likely to have received support on a parenting issue from their online networks in the previous thirty days as compared to dads, with 50 percent of moms versus 28 percent of dads reporting that they had benefited from such support.

It can be tougher if you aren't able to access support from family members. It could be that you live at a considerable distance. It could be that you and your family are estranged. Or it could be that family members simply aren't as involved as you had hoped they would be in your children's lives. "Having actively involved, communicative, and supportive grandparents would have been such a game-changer," says Christina. "Especially in the early years. Someone to bring over a meal every now and again, or offer a night of babysitting or a hand with housekeeping, or some other type of help when I was struggling. That would have been tremendously helpful, both practically speaking and in terms of feeling that I, my son, and my family were valued."

It's tougher if you're living on a lower income. Pooja, the mother of a teenager and a young adult, recalls how isolated her family became when they first moved to Canada from India and found themselves living on a very tight budget. "Getting a driver's licence was too expensive for me, so I could not take my children to a lot of activities," she explains. Her oldest daughter, who was ten years old at the time, was particularly impacted by the experience. She struggled to understand why the family was less well off in Canada than they had been back in India and why they had far less money than other families in Canada. The explanation that the family was living frugally while Puja and her husband upgraded their skills so they could build a better life for their family in Canada simply didn't resonate with their ten-year-old, so she came up with a made-up explanation of her own—an explanation that was designed to make her feel a little less different and isolated. "She told her friends that we were living like this because we were taking part in a contest in which we were required to live a life of poverty for an entire year, and that there were secret cameras all around us, filming our entire life."

It's tougher if your children are dealing with significant challenges. This has certainly been Sandra's experience. She's the mother of ten-year-old twins who were born in Ethiopia but adopted at the age of one and who are still actively processing a number of earlier traumas. "What my kids go through is so invisible that people have no idea what's happening—like all the anxieties that they face about abandonment," she explains. Some people are afraid to get too close because they don't understand or aren't willing to invest the time to understand: "People either pass through at the speed of light or they sit on the sidelines forever trying to figure you out." She finds herself yearning for deeper and more lasting friendships, "the kind of thing where you don't even knock on your friend's front door. You just wander in. And if they're sick, you just start cleaning their kitchen. Isn't that the way it's supposed to be?" She remains hopeful that she will be able to establish those kinds of connections in her new community (she and her family recently moved), but she recognizes that those kinds of friendships don't pop up overnight, at least not with a family like hers: "We're weird and we're different and it takes a long time to cultivate supports."

So, what can you do if you find yourself dealing with extra-challenging circumstances—the kind of circumstances that may cause your fellow villagers to hesitate before knocking on your front door?

Take stock of your existing supports and invest in the relationships that replenish rather than deplete you. "Right now, my best supports are parents who have the same struggles, who are able to empathize without trying to one up me. I need solidarity, not competition," says Rebecca, the single parent of a preteen who struggles with mental illness. Her most helpful relationships are those with people who are willing to take the time to figure out what Rebecca actually needs at any given moment so that they can respond accordingly: "I need people who will take time to ask me whether I need strategy or empathy—who recognize that I've probably tried everything in the book," she explains.

Recognize that the community that you need at one stage in your life as a parent may be very different than the community that you need at another stage. And that you'll be drawn toward the type of community you need at the time. Sometimes, you have to let go of some relationships in order to make new ones. It's like pruning a tree to get rid of the dead branches in order to make room for new, healthy growth. You simply allow the less-nurturing relationships to quietly wither away. That's the way things have worked for Robin, the mother of two school-aged children, including a ten-year-old transgender daughter: "If someone in our circle wasn't onside with us, they just fell away quietly," she explains.

Connecting with Your Village

Some people are lucky enough to embark on the journey of parenting with a pre-existing village in their sights. They know where the village is and how to get there. It's simply a matter of showing up and asking their fellow villagers for support. That's how things played out for Christine. She was able to tap into an existing group of friends who had been getting together at her house on Friday night for years. The get-togethers started before she had kids, but they really ramped up once her kids arrived on the scene. And for at least the past ten years, she's been able to count on a particular group of people showing up on her doorstep every Friday night. She's deliberately kept things low-key so that she doesn't have to do a lot of thinking or prep work before people start to arrive: "I just put out some snacks and I probably sweep and clean the bathroom, but there's no guarantee. I've trained everyone to have low expectations." There's also no fixed agenda: "Sometimes, we watch YouTube videos together. Sometimes, we play a game. Sometimes, we just sit around and talk. But everyone knows that on Friday night, you can come and relax at Christine's. It's something we've been doing forever."

The support from her village spills out of her living room and into the rest of the week. And there's no sense of obligation—of ever owing anyone else any favours. "If someone starts talking like that, the other person will say something like, 'Unless you're friend-dumping me today, it will all come out in the wash. Unless we have to tally up because our relationship is over today, then there's nothing to worry about. Sooner or later, you'll end up doing something for me. This is our village. These are the people I feel most comfortable calling on because I'm not going to be in debt. There is no debt. This is a long-term thing.'"

Like Christine, Elizabeth, the mother of two young sons, recognized the importance of being able to tap into support from her village, but in her case, there was a bit of a problem: her village was a couple of hours away. Shortly after the birth of her second child, she and her husband decided that they needed to do something to change that, and they made the decision to uproot their family and move back to the community where they had grown up—a community where both sets of parents and a large number of other extended family members continued to reside. "Family is the most important thing to me," she explains. "We made the decision to move to be closer to family so that my children could see their grandparents, great-grandparents, cousins, and other family members regularly and build memories with them." It was all about tapping into support from her existing village, in other words.

Germaine also made the decision to move back home so that she and her young son could be closer to family. For her, it was a conscious decision to put the supports in place that she and her son would need to thrive. "One thing you definitely need [as a single parent] is a support system," she explains. "I didn't have one in Nova Scotia, and that is why I moved back home to Newfoundland. I don't know what I would have done without my mother and my father."

Building Your Village from Scratch

For other parents, accessing support from the village actually means building that village from scratch. They simply don't have an existing village to turn to for support. It could be that they are living at a distance from family members and don't have the option or the desire to relocate, or that support from family members is unavailable for any number of other possible reasons, such as a relationship is strained or severed, or a family member is unwell or maxed-out meeting other demands. As author and wellness expert Annabel Fitzsimmons puts it, it becomes a matter of "building that village a little bit more."

How do you go about building that village? "You find your groove. You find your tribe of moms—the people you can talk to, who get you. And those are the people you gravitate toward," says Lola, the mother of three children.

Margaret found that community in her workplace when her two sons were growing up. "We had no immediate family in Western Canada, so there were no grandparents, aunts, uncles, or cousins for our children to get together with on a regular basis," she explains. "We ended up aligning ourselves with co-workers who were in a parallel situation, and spent many holiday dinners, camping trips, and outings with their families. This provided support to us as parents and gave the kids surrogate cousins. We have fond memories of bringing up our children together."

Not quite sure how to get started in building this kind of village? Try looking for opportunities to join forces with other families in ways both big and small. That's something we used to do a lot more of a generation ago and something we definitely need to get back to doing again, says Alexa, the mother of a teen and a preteen: "I'd like to see more families thinking about other families and looking for opportunities to collaborate, pool resources, or offer support. I think that's something my parents did much more organically. They planned activities around opportunities for carpooling so that they could share that burden. That's something we don't do nearly as often these days."

Lisa, a single parent who is raising a preteen and a teen, would welcome more of that kind of load sharing. She's found that functioning as a single parent is every bit as difficult as she'd feared it would be: "I wish there was a more intentional collective of families making meals together, caring for one another's children, and helping out with maintenance and chores," she says. Anything that might help her to feel a little less stretched, in other words.

Of course, building a village is not just about tackling tasks together; it's also about creating community together and looking out for one another in small yet powerful ways. Karen, the mother of two preteens, explains, "It's about being there for other parents—running over to your next-door neighbour's house if they're having a bad day and a kid is sick. Seeing if you can drive the other kids to school." Her best advice? "Don't be afraid to offer to help somebody and don't be afraid to ask for help if you need it." This last bit of advice is key, says Rob, the father of one. "Yes, the village has a responsibility to reach out to parents, but the parent also has to be prepared to ask the village what's available," he insists.

That's exactly what Karen (another Karen) ended up doing when she found herself caught up in the perfect storm of new-parent misery. Not only was she still dealing with the physical fallout from a difficult pregnancy (she'd been suffering from pubic symphysis dysfunction), but her newborn son, Nicolas, was dealing with gastroesophageal reflux. What he needed to feel happier—to be carried around in an upright position—was the one thing she found difficult to provide while her body was trying to heal. She quickly realized that the challenge she was dealing with was too big to handle on her own, so she emailed four friends to see if they would be willing to take Nicolas for a walk in his baby carrier. They happily agreed, and Karen started posting pictures to Facebook of the members of what she called "Nico's Walking Club." Other people started asking if they could be part of the club too, without even knowing what had inspired the club or what a huge help they were being to both Karen and Nicolas. Over a two-month period, ten friends joined the club—the four friends she'd emailed initially plus six others who'd spotted the Facebook posts. "It really came down to not being afraid to ask for help," she recalls. "And to asking for help in a way that was very precise. I knew what we needed to make our days a bit easier, and it was something that so many people enjoyed doing. No one ever complains about getting to snuggle with a sleeping baby in a carrier!"

Not only did Karen give herself and her son the gift of much-needed support, she also gave her friends a gift as well: the gift of being able to make a real difference for a new family. Yes, it feels great to be on the receiving end of that kind of gift, but it feels pretty great to be on the giving end as well—one of the perks of being a villager.

Finding Support Online

There are times when parenting can feel particularly lonely and isolating, like on days when you're caring round-the-clock for a sick child or are temporarily stuck indoors in the wake of an ice storm. These are times when you badly need support and when that support can feel impossibly far away—unless, of course, you are able to find community online.

THE UPSIDE

Online support is the modern equivalent of the 1970s mom-to-mom phone call, during which stay-at-home moms found themselves holding on to the telephone receiver for dear life. In many ways, online support is better than that old-school landline connection, instantly connecting you to the entire world of mothers, or at least those who choose to congregate online. For one thing, there's the 24/7 nature of that support. As Janette, the mother of three young children, explains, "With social media, you can catch up in the middle of the night with groups of people who are feeling the same way that you are."

Then there's the fact that you can connect with parents who are grappling with the exact same issues as you are, even if those issues are anything but common or mainstream. Somewhere on the internet—and likely on Facebook—you'll be able to find a support group or discussion board devoted to your parenting challenge du jour, whether it's coping with postpartum depression, co-parenting with your ex, raising a child with a complex medical condition, or parenting a hard-to-parent kid. "The closed, carefully screened groups are especially valuable if you need to share personal stories and questions without your neighbours, co-workers, and mother-in-law reading about it," says Sarah, the mother of seventeen-year-old triplets.

Online support can make a real difference for parents who are struggling. A 2014 study conducted at Michigan State University found, for example, that people experience increased feelings of social support, a stronger sense of community, and increased life satisfaction after they have supportive interactions on social media. "Social media can be our village if we let it—if we're particular about how we use it," notes Lara, the mother of a ten-year-old son.

The challenge, of course, is that social media isn't universally positive. There are times when posting to, or scrolling through, your social media feed leaves you feeling worse, not better.

FEELING JUDGED

"Social media can be a nightmare," says Andrea, the mother of an eight-month-old daughter. "If I take a photo of my baby in her car seat, I'm really careful to check and double-check where her straps and snaps are. I need to make sure everything is perfect in order to prevent criticism on Facebook." Andrea isn't the only one to encounter the heavy hand of online judgment. Roughly a quarter of parents (27 percent) report similar experiences of being judged after sharing something about their children or their approach to parenting. That was one of the key takeaways from a 2016 study of a thousand Canadian parents conducted by *Today's Parent* magazine.

Certain parents are particularly vulnerable to such judgment: moms who hold themselves to impossibly high standards as parents and who attempt to feel better about their parenting by seeking validation for their parenting efforts via social media. It's pretty much a recipe for disaster, according to Ohio State University professor Sarah J. Schoppe-Sullivan. As she and her co-authors reported in a study published in *Sex Roles* in 2017, "These mothers may seek the readily available validation Facebook promises for their strong investment in the domestic sphere and confirmation they are meeting society's impossibly high standards for parenting. However, their dependence on external validation via Facebook activity, which will never bolster their fragile self-worth, ultimately undermines their well-being." They end up feeling less confident and more depressed.

FEELING LONELY

While heading online allows us to connect with others, connecting with someone online doesn't allow us to reap the same benefits as connecting with that person face-to-face. There's this disturbing sense of faux connection. You're connected, but you're not. Not really.

Too often, we have operated on the basis of a misguided expectation that tech will fill in the blanks in our relationships when we don't have time to invest in them. Want to know what's going on with me? Go check out my Facebook update. Who knows, maybe I'll read yours as well. It can feel like some sort of self-serve faux intimacy. As Sherry Turkle notes in her book *Reclaiming Conversation*, "Computers offer the illusion of companionship without the demands of friendship . . . the illusion of friendship without the demands of intimacy." Instead of nourishing ourselves with real connection, we settle for the relationship equivalent of fast food.

It's easy to have the illusion of connection when stories about family members and friends are flying by in your social media feed. You feel like you know what's going on in the lives of your nearest and dearest—until you don't. "I miss big things and then I feel awful," confesses Karen, the mother of two preteen girls. "I'll say to myself, 'Where was I when this person was going through that?'" Instead of seeing the entire movie of our friends' lives, all we have is the current snapshot. We lose the narrative thread that weaves together the entirety of our friends' lives. Because of the way our social media feeds work, serving up an endless diet of good news, bad news, random trivia, and memes, it's easy to skip over a post that asks more of you as a friend than you are willing or able to give at the moment. "Sometimes, I'll see things but I'll pretend that I didn't, because I know I just can't keep up with that particular crisis right now," says Karen. And she isn't the only one who is choosing to look the other way. A 2015 Pew Research study found, for example, that parents are much more likely to respond to social media posts sharing good news than bad news. While 88 percent of moms and 71 percent of dads reported that they responded to good-news posts, just 61 percent of moms and 53 percent of dads reported doing the same when the news was bad.

Feelings of Jealousy or Inadequacy

Ever have the sense when you're scrolling your Facebook feed that everyone else you know is leading a totally fabulous life and that they also have a lot more friends than you do? Apparently, it's a fairly common feeling, and it happens because we have a front row seat to our own lonely and miserable moments but no one else's. As a result, we end up with a pretty skewed picture.

Economist Seth Stephens-Davidowitz wrote about this phenomenon in a recent article for *The New York Times* and offered some wise advice. "Don't compare your Google searches with other people's Facebook posts," he urged. He then went on to make the case that the best way to get a sense of what ordinary people are actually struggling with in their lives, as opposed to what they are posting on Facebook, is to venture into the weird world of Google autocomplete. When you begin to search for something on Google, Google presents you with a series of autocomplete possibilities, based on similar searches conducted by other users. If, for example, you type in the phrase "my family is," it offers the following suggestions: "toxic / my everything / crazy / my life / boring / so negative / broken / special because." Clearly, families are a source of considerable anxiety—but you already knew that, right?

Danielle, the mother of two school-aged daughters, one of whom has autism, tries to remind herself that social media posts only tell part of the story. Still, there are days when a particular social media post ends up rubbing her the wrong way: "I see posts on social media from moms who cut their kids' sandwiches into fun shapes. Meanwhile, I'm over here silently grateful that my kid didn't wet her pants at school."

That's one of the reasons that Olivia, the mother of a toddler, chooses to keep it real on social media—because she doesn't want to make things harder for other parents. "I feel like I'm being more authentic if I post true accounts of my life on social media," she explains. "Don't get me wrong. I don't post everything. My 'friends' don't need to know everything about me.

But I have posted at times when I've had a bad day or when my son is sick or when life generally sucks. And I hope that doing so inspires others to do the same." It turns out that Olivia isn't just helping her friends by deciding to go this route; she's also improving her own social media experience at the same time. As a recent Michigan State University study revealed, people who choose to keep it real in their social media posts are more likely to perceive feelings of support from their social media friends than people who choose not to post about their struggles.

Of course, there's a fine line to be walked in terms of how much you decide to share, to say nothing of where and with whom. The internet never forgets, and yet children have "the right to be forgotten"—or at least the right to have a say in shaping the digital footprint that parents and others are creating on their behalf. It's an issue that government privacy agencies, children's rights advocates, and others are likely to continue to grapple with for quite some time. In the meantime, it's up to you to make conscious and deliberate choices about what you do and don't decide to share about your child online, and to guide your child through the process of making such decisions too.

MAKING ONLINE SUPPORT WORK FOR (NOT AGAINST) YOU

So online support, and social media in particular, isn't inherently good or bad. It's all about how you choose to use it. You want to use it in ways that leave you feeling more supported and connected, not less. For Julia, a first-time mother, that meant posting "Daily Jocelyn" photos of her infant daughter to her Instagram feed so that she could share her motherhood journey with far-flung friends and family members, and arranging to meet up at a nearby park with a group of moms she met on an online message board—using online connection as a springboard to real-world community, in other words. It's all about being more mindful about your use of technology and considering both what you stand to gain and what you stand to lose by spending a lot of time in the online world. If your goals are to make connections, feel supported, and create community, how well are you achieving that goal? Are there different avenues you might want to try, either in addition to or instead of heading online? And if you're craving that online connection, are there other ways of making it more intimate and interactive—perhaps by connecting via video conference call with a handful of your nearest and dearest?

Online support can be incredibly valuable, but we don't want to get in the habit of escaping into tech simply because it's easier to stare at a screen than to look deeply into the eyes of another human being. We need to spend face-to-face time with people we care about, or we risk having once-powerful friendships devolve into casual acquaintanceships. As Nancy Colier notes in *The Power of Off*, "Sadly, with technology, we risk winning the world but losing our village. We can be part of a community made up of people all over the world but not talk to the few people who share a bus stop with us every morning. Though *known about* by everyone, we are increasingly *known* by no one."

At the root of the problem is the fact that it can be difficult to connect with other people, even when you are in the same place. "Parents may sit together on the bench while their children swim or play hockey, but even then, how much of that time is spent checking our phones, and perhaps even talking on our phones, rather than talking to the person next to us?" asks Melanie, the mother of two young children. It's a poignant reminder to look up from our phones at least a little more often and challenge ourselves to dare to lock eyes with our fellow villagers.

An SOS to the Village

"Parents are in survival mode. We need support. We need help." That's what Lola, a mother of three, told me the day I interviewed her for this book. Her message was urgent and hard-hitting, and her words stayed with me for a very long time.

Lola's SOS message to the village was very much on my mind as my car pulled into the parking lot of Springfield Public School, a small, rural school in a tiny village of five hundred people in southwestern Ontario. I'd been thinking, on the drive up, about how overwhelmed and exhausted many parents feel, to say nothing of how guilty and how judged. And now I was about to do something I'd done countless times over the previous few years: speak to a group of parents congregated in a jam-packed school gymnasium about what they could do to try to make life a little bit easier for themselves and their kids.

Normally when I arrive at a school ahead of one of my presentations, the building is empty. Not until five minutes before I'm scheduled to speak, or even a few minutes *after* I start speaking, do parents begin to flood into the school gym. But this time, things were different. The gymnasium was already half full and I wasn't scheduled to start speaking for at least another half-hour. The parents who'd shown up early were using the time to enjoy one another's company, to share a laugh, and to catch up on one another's news. I felt like I'd stumbled into a family reunion—the best kind of family reunion where everyone feels both welcome and celebrated.

As it turned out, that was merely the first sign that things were going to be very different at this particular presentation. The spirit of caring that I'd detected from the moment I first stepped foot in the school continued to build over the course of the evening, with parents speaking openly and honestly about their struggles, and without any corresponding fear of judgment. They didn't feel the need to put on a falsely brave face and pretend that things were easier or better than they actually were. They didn't hold off on sharing a personal anecdote or asking a question about a problem that one of their children was facing until after the room had emptied and everyone else was safely out of earshot, which is the way things typically play out. This particular group of parents felt safe and supported, seen and understood. They knew they could count on their village to be "the village."

That's how things are supposed to work. We're *supposed* to feel supported by our fellow villagers. There are, after all, so many things the village can do to make things easier and better for parents and kids—and it's actually in the village's best interest to do so. The people of Springfield don't just understand this; they live it. And that spirit of community is contagious. I'd been so swept up by what I'd witnessed, in fact, that I'd told all the parents gathered in the gym that night that I was pretty much sold on the idea of moving to Springfield.

As you can imagine, I was feeling pretty euphoric as I pulled out of the parking lot to head back home, buoyed by all those villager-to-villager acts of caring. I was thinking about how different the world would be if every school community felt like that. And that's when I spotted the sign: a weather-worn, hand-painted red-and-white sign that read, "Save Springfield P.S."

A quick Google search confirmed my worst fears. Despite valiant attempts by the Springfield villagers to save their much-loved community school, it would be closing in another two years' time. It didn't matter how many school board meetings the parents attended or how vigorously they waved their hand-made protest signs declaring, "Rural schools matter" and "Our kids deserve to go to school in their own community"; Springfield Public School would be closing, along with four other local rural schools.

I was surprised by how deeply the news affected me. After all, I'd only known this particular group of parents for a couple of hours—albeit a pretty magical couple of hours. But then I realized that the anger and sadness I was feeling wasn't just about this particular group of parents and this particular wrecking ball, which outside forces had chosen to take to their village. It was also about the countless other short-sighted and misguided policy decisions I've witnessed time and time again—decisions that make life so much harder for parents.

And that, in a nutshell, is what happens when politicians and other policy-makers get it wrong, when society not only fails to step up and support parents, but the decisions it makes and the policies it puts in place actually end up making life more difficult for parents. Because the way things stand right now, parenting isn't just hard; it's almost impossibly hard—and for reasons that have little to do with parenting.

The issues that we're grappling with are so much bigger than any of us, which makes them all the more challenging to resolve. The fact is, it's going to take all of us pulling together to make the situation significantly better by making changes at the personal, political, and cultural level. It may start with you, but it can't end with you, not if we're actually going to fix things in a way that improves life for every child and every parent in the village.

It seems to me that this is the perfect time to be having this kind of conversation. We are, after all, in the midst of what can only be described as a cultural moment—a moment when settling for the status quo just isn't good enough. Why shouldn't things be better? Why shouldn't we dare to imagine a better world? Why shouldn't we encourage our kids to do the same?

Of course, making these kinds of shifts is going to require a lot of blue-sky thinking—time spent considering *what's possible* as opposed to merely *what is.* But if you happen to glance up at the sky at just the right moment, you might even be lucky enough to spot a flock of Canada geese winding their way across the sky in a classic V formation.

Why lucky, you ask? Because, as it turns out, we have so much to learn from those Canada geese: You don't have to go it alone. Someone else will take the lead if you grow tired and feel the need to drop back. You don't have to have all the answers. Someone else who's just a little ahead of you on this journey will help you to find your way. The load is so much lighter when we share it. That's what allows us to go the distance. And it's not about you; it's actually about us. Because that V stands for *village.*

Acknowledgements

It may have been my fingers clicking away on the keyboard during the two years it took to write this book, but the book was anything but a solo effort. A huge number of people supported me through the all-encompassing process of bringing this book into the world. They were my village, in other words.

I'd like to introduce you to the members of my book-writing village, starting with the largest group of villagers—the wise and caring moms and dads who opened up their hearts to me while I was researching this book. After all, this book wouldn't exist at all if it weren't for their wisdom and their stories. I am grateful to each and every one of those parents, who are Alison Armstrong, Robin Bacsfalvi, Lori Bamber, Steve Bennett, Edward Boose, Lisa Borden, Lindsay Brewda, Lola Augustine Brown, Mireille Brownhill, Danielle Christopher, Melanie Clark, Lisa Clarke, Rebecca Coleman, Lara Cooley, Lauren Dewar, Glenda Dominics, Danielle Donders, Elaine Dunphy, Ginette Ess, Anthony Floyd, Fran Fosberg, Nicole Gagliardi, Angie Gallop, Stephanie George, Michael Giasson, Sara Gold, Michelle Gordon, Brandi Gowan, Gordon Graham, Karen Green, Christine Hennebury, Denise Hennebury, Julia Horel, Nicole Johnson, Sandra Jordan, Cathy Kerr, Claire Kerr-Zlobin, Rebecca Lee, Veronica Leonard, Karen Leiva, Lisa MacColl, Isabelle MacNider, Shannon McCauley,

Michael McCauley, Amanda McEachern, Jillian McKay, Sarah McKay, Jenna Morton, Casey Palmer, Kerri Paquette, Johanna Parker, Michelle Parker, Andrea Paul, Kim Plumley, Patricia Reilly-King, Amanda Reimer, Kate Robson, Kelly Ross, Steve Slaunwhite, Laurie Smith, Evie Sykes, Janette Taylor, Mary Toth, Samantha L. Waters, Germaine Watson, Sandy Woolfrey-Fahey, and the other parents who chose to contribute anonymously.

I owe a huge debt of gratitude to another group of villagers: the numerous subject-matter experts I consulted while I was researching this book. They are Andrea Doucet (Brock University sociology professor and Canada Research Chair in Gender, Work, and Care), Annabel Fitzsimmons (author and fitness and meditation instructor), Stephanie George (Indigenous midwife and lactation consultant), Hugh MacMillan (social worker), Michele Landsberg (author and journalist), Brian Nichols (psychotherapist), Teresa Pitman (author), Wendy Priesnitz (author and education advocate), and Nora Spinks (CEO of The Vanier Institute of the Family). While your names may only pop up in the actual text from time to time, please know that the wisdom you shared with me during our phone calls or face-to-face meetings helped to guide my thinking from the first word to the last word of this book. Thank you.

Another group that deserves a major shout out is the book's technical review team: Michael Dickinson (pediatrician), Marla Good (parent and editorial consultant), Shelley Hermer (social worker and family therapist), and Cathy Kerr (early-childhood professional). Thank you for suggesting ways to make the text as relevant, helpful, and inclusive as possible. This book is immeasurably stronger because of your ever wise and always encouraging feedback.

Thank you also to my agent Hilary McMahon, vice-president of Westwood Creative Artists, for her usual wisdom and encouragement; and to all the people I have had the pleasure of working with since that lucky day when I became a HarperCollins Canada author: my editor Brad Wilson, for his unwavering commitment to this book and his superhuman determination to find just the right title—even when that meant carefully considering and painstakingly rejecting no fewer than fifty different author-supplied title possibilities; Iris Tupholme, for continuing to be a fierce champion of my books; Lola Landekic, for coming up with the perfect cover concept, one that brilliantly captures the spirit and flavour of the book; production editor Stephanie Conklin, for unwavering cheerfulness and professionalism; copy editor Stacey Cameron, for going above and beyond the call of duty in chasing down superfluous parentheses (like these); proofreader Angelika Glover; and the other unsung heroes in my HarperCollins Canada "village," for their countless contributions: Alan Jones, Zeena Baybayan, Leo MacDonald, Michael Guy-Haddock, Cory Beatty, Suman Seewat, and Deanna Norlock.

Last but not least, I need to thank my dear friends Lori Bamber and Christine Hennebury, who encouraged me to write the bravest and best book I was capable of writing; and my beloved family, for all the sacrifices they made while I was distracted and/or just plain unavailable during the writing of this book. I continue to be grateful for your love and support. You will always be the heart of my village. ♥

Notes for Readers Who Want to Know a Little More

Looking for a reason to actually read this set of notes, as opposed to just skipping over them? Here are two: (1) So you can dive into a carefully curated set of resources. Instead of overwhelming you with an exhaustive list of every book, article, and study I consulted while I was researching this book (which would have meant including the most tedious, annoying, and mundane), I've zeroed in on the best of the best: the resources that are actually worth your while tracking down. (2) So, you can be privy to a couple of brief but important side conversations—conversations that I really wanted to have with you back in the actual chapter, but that would have bogged everything down unnecessarily or taken us too deep into the policy weeds, or both.

So, there you go. I hope I've convinced you to at least take a peek and that these resource picks and bonus ideas add to your enjoyment of the book.

Chapter 1: Parenting in an Age of Anxiety

If you'd like to read Alex Usher's blog posts about the dip in starting salaries for university graduates, you'll find them in the *One Thought Blog*, which he hosts on the website for his consulting firm, Higher Education Strategy Associates. The two posts that I drew upon were "Field of Study: Oh the Humanities" (January 10, 2018) and "A More Nuanced Look at Graduate Incomes" (January 25, 2018).

If you'd like to learn more about the impact of precarious employment on the decision to have kids (to say nothing of the far-reaching impact of precarious employment in general), you might want to check out *Getting Left Behind: Who Gained and Who Didn't in an Improving Labour Market,* published by the Poverty and Employment Precarity in Southern Ontario (PEPSO) research group.

If you're curious about a possible link between sky-high housing prices and the fact that many millennials are choosing not to have kids, you might be intrigued by a 2018 Zillow Research study, which identified an association between rising housing prices and declining fertility rates. Every 10 percent increase in the cost of housing in a particular housing market is associated with a 1.5 percent drop in fertility rates in millennials in that same market, according to this study.

For more about the impact of recessions on family relationships, see "Recession Hurts Family Relationships," a November 5, 2016, post on the *Child and Family Blog.*

For a challenge to the idea that the current generation of young people is exceptionally narcissistic (an idea put forth by psychologist Jean Twenge), see this powerful takedown by Jeffrey Jensen Arnett and his co-authors, published in *Emerging Adulthood* in 2013: "The Dangers of Generational Myth-Making: Rejoinder to Twenge."

For more about the rise of perfectionism in young people, see Thomas Curran and Andrew P. Hill's article "Perfectionism Is

Increasing, and That's Not Good News" (*Harvard Business Review*, January 26, 2018) and their related 2017 study in the *Psychological Bulletin* ("Perfectionism Is Increasing Over Time: a Meta-Analysis of Birth Cohort Differences from 1989 to 2016").

Chapter 2: Work-Life Imbalance

Our family policy needs to make a couple of important pivots, if we're going to start to solve the problem of work-life imbalance. Specifically, we're going to have to solve the problem that is child care (and by that, I mean high-quality, affordable, and accessible child care), and we're going to have to deal with some deeply rooted structural issues that result in women carrying the bulk of the load when it comes to care. So, let's have two quick side-conversations about these two issues, starting with child care.

Child care is a big-ticket item, which is why most governments tend to shy away from making a significant investment in this area. But, along with that big ticket comes a potentially big opportunity. As it turns out, child care is a game-changer when it comes to easing work-life role conflicts, encouraging greater gender equity within couple relationships, and eliminating the so-called motherhood tax (the fact that mothers are penalized in the workplace for being the ones who typically take the lead on care) and the daddy bonus (fathers are actually rewarded in the workforce by virtue of the fact that they're seen as more reliable and committed workers). As Molly Redden wrote in *The Guardian*, "According to a recent comparison of policies across two dozen countries, it was access to affordable, reliable childcare, not flexible hours or new parent leave, that played the biggest role in closing the gender wage gap and ensuring that new mothers could remain in the workforce."

Sure, the upfront costs can be hefty, but investing in child care is actually a pretty savvy investment, because it pays for itself. In its pre-budget submission for the 2018 federal budget, the Child Care Advocacy Association of Canada crunched the numbers and concluded that the initial $8 billion investment required to subsidize parent fees by 40 percent would be offset by increased income tax revenue if more affordable child care made it possible for 150,000 well-educated mothers to re-enter the Canadian workforce, at which point, "The net cost to taxpayers would be zero." That wasn't just pie-in-the-sky economic forecasting, by the way. As Pierre Fortin, an economics professor at the University of Quebec at Montreal who has analyzed the economic impact of Quebec's $8.05-per-day child-care program, told the *Toronto Star* back in 2011, "The argument can no longer be that governments cannot afford it. This program is paying for itself."

Of course, that type of economic analysis only factors in dollars-and-cents benefits. If you want to get a true picture of the impact of accessible and affordable high-quality child care, you need to look at the longer-term impact on parents and kids—impacts that aren't easily captured in any line of a budget spreadsheet. As it turns out, good child care supports good parenting. It's a point that sociologist and demographer Kate C. Prickett made in her 2015 doctoral dissertation for the University of Texas at Austin ("The Work Lives and Parenting Behaviors of Mothers with Young Children"): "A number of studies have revealed that mothers are more likely to engage in sensitive and stimulating parenting when their children are in stable high-quality child care outside the home. The two most common explanations are that relationships with and support from care providers allow mothers to gain more self-efficacy and pleasure from their parenting and that high-quality caregiving promotes child behavior that elicits more sensitivity from parents." In other words, it's about the village helping parents to parent in a way that they can actually feel good about and that manages to benefit everyone as a result—the child, the parent, *and* the village.

Okay, enough about child care. Now let's talk about how workplace norms serve to entrench gendered ideas about work and care. Research conducted by Oxfam Canada and the Canadian Centre for Policy Alternatives indicates that women in Canada are three times as likely as men to work part-time and nineteen times as likely to cite "caring for children" as the reason they work part-time. While this is a popular strategy for making the work-life juggle a little bit more manageable for individual families, more flexible work arrangements come with some hidden costs, like lower wages, fewer opportunities for training or promotion, and considerably reduced lifetime earnings. What it all comes down to is a tendency for workplaces to disproportionately value certain patterns of work (full-time, standard hours) and certain types of workers (workers who conform with what sociologists call "ideal worker norms"—in other words, workers who are able to prioritize work above all else). As economist Claudia Goldin noted in a 2014 article for the *American Economic Review*, "The gender gap in pay would be considerably reduced and might vanish altogether if firms did not have an incentive to disproportionately reward individuals who labored long hours and worked particular hours." A better and more equitable approach would be to recognize that workers benefit from having greater flexibility at life stages when the work-family juggling act is particularly demanding, and to refuse to penalize workers for asserting their right to have a life outside of work.

That's it for the side conversations. Now here's a quick roundup of resources: If you'd like to delve more deeply into the issue of work-family guilt, you'll want to read "Bringing Work Home: Gender and Parenting Correlates of Work-Family Guilt among Parents of Toddlers" by Jessica L. Borelli and her co-authors (*Journal of Child and Family Studies*, June 2017) and "The Costs of Thinking about Work and Family: Mental Labor, Work-Family Spillover, and Gender Inequality in Dual-Earner Families" by Shira Offer (*Sociological Forum*, December 2014). For a related discussion on the impact of non-standard employment on work-family balance, see "Effects of Non-Standard Work on the Work-Family Balance: A Literature Review" by Magali Girard (*McGill Sociological Review*, January 2010).

For a discussion of how small business success rates are impacted by the number of children and by motherhood versus fatherhood, see "What Drives Self-Employment Survival for Women and Men: Evidence from Canada" by Kate Rybczynski (*Journal of Labor Research,* March 2015).

For some inspiring blue-sky thinking about policies that make it easier for moms and dads to share work and care responsibilities more equitably, see *State of the World's Fathers: Time for Action*, a 2017 report published by MenCare (a coalition of non-profits working on the issue of gender equality).

For strategies for making lengthy commutes a little less hellish, see *Commuting with a Plan: How Goal-Directed Prospection Can Offset the Strain of Commuting* by Jon. M. Jachimowicz and his co-authors (Harvard Business School Working Paper 16-077, 2016).

For more about what *actually* contributes to quality of life (as opposed to what we merely *assume* contributes to better quality of life), consult the Canadian Index of Wellbeing, which is hosted by the University of Waterloo.

Chapter 3: The Why of Distracted Parenting

If you're eager to learn more about how our lives, our relationships, and our brains are being transformed by technology, I highly recommend the following four books: *The Power of Off* by Nancy Colier (2016); *The Shallows: What the Internet Is Doing to Our Brains* by Nicholas Carr (2011); *Reclaiming Conversation: The Power of Talk in a Digital Age* by Sherry Turkle (2015); and *Irresistible: The Rise of Addictive Technology and the Business of Keeping Us Hooked* by Adam Alter (2017).

If you can't wait to learn more about inattentional blindness and unicycling clowns, the study you want is "Did You See the Unicycling Clown? Inattentional Blindness While Walking and Talking on a Cellphone," by Ira E. Hyman, Jr., and his co-authors (*Applied Cognitive Psychology*, July 2010).

If you'd like to read Yale University economist Craig Palsson's 2014 study linking the rise of smartphones with a rise in child injuries, you can read the final published version, "Smartphones and Child Injuries," in the December 2017 issue of the *Journal of Public Economics*.

If you're ready to do a deep dive into the whole issue of technoference (a.k.a. the impact of technology on our relationships), you'll want to track down these three studies by Brandon T. McDaniel and his various co-authors: "Technoference: Parent Distraction with Technology and Associations with Child Behavior Problems" (*Child Development*, January/February 2018); "Technology Interference in the Parenting of Young Children: Implications for Mothers' Perceptions of Coparenting" (*The Social Science Journal*, December 2016); "'Technoference': The Interference of Technology in Couple Relationships and Implications for Women's Personal and Relational Well-Being" (*Psychology of Popular Media Culture*, January 2016).

If you agree that it's time for technology companies to exercise greater social responsibility, you might want to read more about the precautionary principle, which emphasizes the importance of anticipating harm before it occurs as opposed to waiting until evidence of harm is indisputable or trying to fix problems after the fact. It is most often applied to environmental issues, but it has also been applied to the health and safety arena as well. For a crash course on the origins of the principle, see "The Precautionary Principle in Environmental Science" by David Kriebel and his co-authors (*Environmental Health Perspectives*, September 2001).

Chapter 4: The Truth about Parenting

The studies that were most helpful to me in making the case that parents aren't, in fact, universally miserable are as follows (listed in reverse chronological order according to date of publication): "Emotional Cost of Emotional Support? The Association Between Intensive Mothering and Psychological Well-Being in Midlife" by Justine Gunderson and Anne E. Barrett (*The Journal of Family Issues*, May 2017); "How Parents Fare: Mothers' and Fathers' Subjective Well-Being in Time with Children" by Kelly Musick and her co-authors (*American Sociological Review*, October 2016); "Lay Understanding of Happiness and the Experience of Well-Being: Are Some Conceptions of Happiness More Beneficial than Others?" by Agnieszka Bojanowska and Anna M. Zalewska (*Journal of Happiness Studies*, April 2016); "Who Mothers Mommy? Factors That Contribute to Mothers' Well-Being" by Suniya S. Luthar and Lucia Ciciolla (*Developmental Psychology*, December 2015); "The Price Mothers Pay, Even When They Are Not Buying It: Mental Health Consequences of Idealized Motherhood" by Angie Henderson and her co-authors (*Sex Roles*, September 2015); "The Pains and Pleasures of Parenting: When, Why, and How Is Parenthood Associated With More or Less Well-being?" by S. Katherine Nelson and her co-authors (*Psychological Bulletin*, May 2014); "Evaluative and Hedonic Well-being Amongst Those with and without Children at Home" by Angus Deaton and Arthur A. Stone (*Proceedings of the National Academy of Sciences*, January 2014); "Parents Reap What They Sow: Child-Centrism and Parental Well-Being" by Claire E. Ashton-James and her co-authors (*Social Psychology and Personality Science*, November 2013); "Positive and Negative Emotion in the Daily Life of Dual-Earner Couples with Children" by Belinda Campos and her co-authors (*Journal of Family Psychology*, February 2013); "In Defense of Parenthood: Children Are Associated with More Joy than Misery" by S. Katherine Nelson and her co-authors (*Psychological Science*, January 2013); and "Parenthood and Psychological Well-being: Clarifying the Role of Child Age and Parent-Child Relationship Quality" by Kei M. Nomaguchi (*Social Science Research*, March 2012).

If you'd like to read some of the emerging research on parent burnout, you'll want to track down these three studies: "Exhausted Parents: Sociodemographic, Child-Related, Parent-Related, Parenting and Family-Functioning Correlates of Parental Burnout" by Moïra Mikolajczak and her co-authors (*Journal of Child and Family Studies*, February 2018); "Exhausted Parents: Development and Preliminary Validation of the Parental Burnout Inventory" by Isabelle Roskam and her co-authors (*Frontiers in Psychology*, 2017); and "The Big Five Personality Traits and Parental Burnout: Protective and Risk Factors" by Sarah Le Vigouroux and her co-authors (*Personality and Individual Differences*, December 2017).

Chapter 5: The Thinking Part of Parenting

If you'd like to do some thinking about the thinking part of parenting (yes, very meta, I know), three books you'll want to scoop up are *Deep Work: Rules for Focused Success in a Distracted World* by Cal Newport (2016); *The Happiness Track: How to Apply the Science of Happiness to Accelerate Your Success* by Emma Sepalla (2016); and *Positivity* by Barbara L. Fredrickson (2009).

If you'd like to dig a little deeper into the research on solitude, creative thinking, and the wisdom of your future self, the following three studies may be of interest too: "Solitude as an Approach to Affective Self-Regulation" by Thuy-vy T. Nguyen and her co-authors (*Personality and Social Psychology Bulletin*, December 2017); "Time of Day Effects on Problem Solving: When the Non-Optimal Is Optimal" by Mareike B. Wieth and Rose T. Zacks (*Thinking & Reasoning*, 2011); "What Is the Optimal Way to Deliver a Positive Activity Intervention? The Case of Writing about One's Best Possible Selves" by Kristin Layous and her co-authors (*Journal of Happiness Studies*, April 2013).

If that last study triggers your curiosity about the power of writing as a tool for self-discovery, you might want to track down a copy of *Opening Up by Writing It Down: How Expressive Writing Improves Health and Emotional Pain* by James W. Pennebaker and Joshua M. Smyth (2016). Now in its third edition, it continues to be the definitive work on this subject.

Chapter 6: How to Boost Your Enjoyment of Parenting

I have a huge—and ever-growing—collection of books about happiness, but the book that provided the most help to me while I was researching this chapter was *How to Have a Good Day* by Caroline Webb (2016).

My thinking for this chapter was also influenced by the following four studies in particular: "Buying Time Promotes Happiness" by Ashley V. Whillans and her co-authors (*Proceedings of the National Academy of Sciences*, 2017); "Reframing the Ordinary: Imagining Time as Scarce Increases Well-Being" by Kristin Layous and her co-authors (*The Journal of Positive Psychology*, January 2017); "The Personal and Interpersonal Rewards of Communal Orientation" by Bonnie M. Le and her co-authors (*Journal of Social and Personal Relationships*, September 2013); "Sense of Control Predicts Depressive and Anxious Symptoms across the Transition to Parenthood" by Courtney Pierce Keeton and her co-authors (*Journal of Family Psychology*, May 2008).

Chapter 7: How to Tame the Anxiety, Guilt, and Feeling of Being Overwhelmed

For more about what it takes to make stress work for, and not against, you, see *The Upside of Stress: Why Stress Is Good for You and How to Get Good at It* by Kelly McGonigal (2015).

For more about managing uncomfortable emotions, see *Emotional Agility: Get Unstuck, Embrace Change, and Thrive in Work and Life* by Susan David (2016) and track down "Rethinking Rumination" by Susan Nolen-Hoeksema and co-authors (*Perspectives in Psychological Science*, September 2008).

If you'd like to read Eliann Carr's 2015 graduate thesis about parental apologies, you'll find it online by searching for *Healing Bridge: Exploring the Relationship between Parental Propensity to Apologize and Child Well-Being*.

Finally, if you think you'd benefit from learning more about self-compassion—and, to be frank, I think all of us would benefit from learning more about self-compassion—you'll want to get your hands on a copy of *Self-Compassion: Stop Beating Yourself Up and Leave Insecurity Behind* (2011) by Kristin Neff. I've purchased and given away countless copies of this book, and it's been a hit with every single person I've given it to.

Chapter 8: The Guilt-Free Guide to Healthier Living

For more on how becoming a parent can affect your overall health, see "Evaluation of a Physical Activity Intervention for New Parents: Protocol Paper for a Randomized Trial" by Alison Quinlan and her co-authors (*BMC Public Health*, November 2017); "Oh Baby! Motivation for Healthy Eating during Parenthood Transitions: A Longitudinal Examination with a Theory of Planned Behavior Perspective" by Rebecca L. Bassett-Gunter and her co-authors (*International Journal of Behavioral Nutrition and Physical Activity*, July 2013); "Understanding Parental Physical Activity: Meanings, Habits, and Social Role Influence" by Kyra Hamilton and Katherine M. White (*Psychology of Sports and Exercise*, July 2010).

For more on how your stress levels affect your kids' health, see "Stress: Personal Matter or Family Affair? Intra- and Inter-Individual Relationships between Stress, Physical Activity,

Sedentary Behavior, and Nutrition" by Miriam Reiner and her co-authors (*International Journal of Child, Youth, and Family Studies*, January 2015) and "Parenting Stress: A Cross-Sectional Analysis of Associations with Childhood Obesity, Physical Activity, and TV Viewing" by Kathryn Walton and her co-authors (*BMC Pediatrics*, October 2014).

For more on sleep and the impact of sleep deprivation on both parents and kids, see "Bedtime Use of Technology and Associated Sleep Problems in Children" by Caitlyn Fuller and her co-authors (*Global Pediatric Health*, 2017); "Do Parents' Support Behaviours Predict whether or Not Their Children Get Sufficient Sleep? A Cross-Sectional Study" by Evelyn Pyper and her co-authors (*BMC Public Health*, 2017); "Decreases in Self-Reported Sleep Duration among U.S. Adolescents 2009–2015 and Links to New Media Screen Time" by Jean M. Twenge and her co-authors (*Sleep Medicine*, 2017); "Association between Portable Screen-Based Media Device Access or Use and Sleep Outcomes: A Systematic Review and Meta-Analysis" by Ben Carter and co-authors (*JAMA Pediatrics*, December 2016); and "Overnight Therapy? The Role of Sleep in Emotional Brain Processing" by Els van der Helm and Matthew P. Walker (*Psychological Bulletin*, September 2009).

For more on how parents and kids affect one another's activity levels, see "Bidirectional Associations between Activity-Related Parenting Practices, and Child Physical Activity, Sedentary Screen-Based Behavior and Body Mass Index: A Longitudinal Analysis" by Ester F.C. Sleddens and her co-authors (*International Journal of Behavioral Nutrition*, July 2017); "Parent-Child Association in Physical Activity and Sedentary Behavior" by Didier Garriguet and his co-authors (Statistics Canada *Health Reports*, June 21, 2017); "Parental Physical Activity Associates with Offspring's Physical Activity until Middle Age: A 30-Year Study" by Taina Hintsa and her co-authors (*Journal of Physical Activity and Health*, March 2017); "The Impact of Different Types of Parental Support Behaviours on Child Physical Activity, Healthy

Eating, and Screen Time: A Cross-Sectional Study" by Evelyn Pyper and her co-authors (*BMC Public Health*, 2016); "Do Specific Parenting Practices and Related Parental Self-Efficacy Associate with Physical Activity and Screen Time among Primary Schoolchildren? A Cross-Sectional Study in Belgium" by Sara De Lepeleere and her co-authors (*BMJ Open*, 2015).

For more on screen time, see *Screen Time and Young Children: Promoting Health and Development in a Digital World* (Canadian Paediatric Society, June 1, 2017); *How Does the Time Children Spend Using Digital Technology Impact Their Mental Well-Being, Social Relationships and Physical Activity? An Evidence-Focused Literature Review* by Daniel Kardefelt-Winther (UNICEF Innocenti Discussion Paper, 2017); and "Effects of Instant Messaging on School Performance in Adolescents" by Karan Grover and his co-authors (*Journal of Child Neurology*, 2016).

If you'd like to read sociologist Tracy Bacon's 2015 doctoral thesis about family meals (and family meal guilt), you can track it down online by searching for its title: *Good Conversation, Healthy Food, and Hard Work: How Organizations and Parents Frame the Family Meal.*

For more on the science of habit change, see "Don't Think Too Positive" by Gabriele Oettingen (*Aeon*, July 25, 2016); "Motivating Healthy Diet Behaviors: The Self-as-Doer Identity" by Amanda M. Brouwer and Katie E. Mosack (*Self and Identity*, 2015); and "The Fresh Start Effect: Temporal Landmarks Motivate Aspirational Behavior" by Hengchen Dai and her co-authors (*Management Science*, October 2014); "Holding the Hunger Games Hostage at the Gym: An Evaluation of Temptation Bundling" by Katherine L. Milkman and her co-authors (*Management Science*, February 2014); "The Role of Self-Compassion in Women's Self-Determined Motives to Exercise and Exercise-Related Outcomes" by Cathy M. R. Magnus and her co-authors (*Self and Identity*, October 2010).

Chapter 9: Parenting as a Team Sport

For more on the impact of children on the couple relationship, you might want to treat yourself to copies of the following two books: *How Not to Hate Your Husband after Kids* by Jancee Dunn (2017), and *Balancing the Big Stuff: Finding Happiness in Work, Family, and Life* by Miriam Liss and Holly H. Schiffrin (Rowman & Littlefield, 2014). If you want to dig even deeper, you might want to track down the following articles and studies: "Try These 'Love Hacks' to Fix Your Marriage" by John Tierney (*The New York Times*, September 18, 2017); "It's the Motive That Counts: Perceived Sacrifice Motives and Gratitude in Romantic Relationships" by Mariko L. Visserman and her co-authors (*Emotion*, June 2017); "Self-Esteem and Relationship Satisfaction during the Transition to Motherhood" by Manon A. van Scheppingen and her co-authors (*Journal of Personality and Social Psychology*, May 2017); "More than Just Sex: Affection Mediates the Association between Sexual Activity and Well-Being" by Anik Debrot and her co-authors (*Personality and Social Psychology Bulletin*, January 2017); "Who Mothers Mommy? Factors That Contribute to Mothers' Well-Being" by Suniya S. Luthar and Lucia Ciciolla (*Developmental Psychology*, December 2015); "Sexual Frequency Predicts Greater Well-Being, but More Is Not Always Better" by Amy Muise and her co-authors (*Social Psychology and Personality Science*, November 2015); "Is It Good to Be Giving in the Bedroom? A Prosocial Perspective on Sexual Health and Well-Being in Romantic Relationships" by Amy Muise and her co-authors (*Current Sexual Health Reports*, September 2015); "Do You Get Where I'm Coming From? Perceived Understanding Buffers against the Negative Impact of Conflict on Relationship Satisfaction" by Amie M. Gordon and Serena Chen (*Journal of Personality and Social Psychology*, 2015); "Mothers' Work–Family Conflict and Enrichment: Associations with Parenting Quality and Couple Relationship" by Amanda R. Cooklin and her co-authors (*Child: Care, Health, and Development*, 2014); "Let's Talk about Sex: A Diary

Investigation of Couples' Intimacy Conflicts in the Home" by Lauren M. Papp and her co-authors (*Couple and Family Psychology*, March 2013); "The Effect of the Transition to Parenthood on Relationship Quality: An Eight-Year Prospective Study" by Brian D. Doss and his co-authors (*Journal of Personality and Social Psychology*, March 2009); "For Richer, for Poorer: Money as a Topic of Marital Conflict in the Home" by Lauren M. Papp and her co-authors (*Family Relations*, February 2009); "No Fun Anymore: Leisure and Marital Quality across the Transition to Parenthood" by Amy Claxton and Maureen Perry-Jenkins (*Journal of Marriage and the Family*, February 2008); "Marital Satisfaction across the Transition to Parenthood" by Erika Lawrence and her co-authors (*Journal of Family Psychology*, February 2008).

For more on functioning well as a parenting team (whether you're co-parenting with your partner or your ex or both), see the following two studies: "Effects of the Inter-Parental Relationship on Adolescents' Emotional Security and Adjustment: The Important Role of Fathers" by Go Woon Suh and her co-authors (*Developmental Psychology*, October 2016); and "Marital Problems, Maternal Gatekeeping Attitudes, and Father-Child Relationships in Adolescence" by Matthew M. Stevenson and his co-authors (*Developmental Psychology*, April 2014).

Chapter 10: Parenting Strategies That Work for You and Your Child

The two books that most influenced my thinking for this chapter are *Unconditional Parenting: Moving from Rewards and Punishments to Love and Reason* by Alfie Kohn (2005) and *Raising Human Beings: Creating a Collaborative Partnership with Your Child* by Ross W. Greene (2016).

For more on the science behind the parenting strategies discussed in this chapter, see "New Insights into Teen Risk-Taking—Their 'Hot' Inhibitory Control Is Poorer than

Children's" by Emma Young (British Psychological Society *Research Digest*, February 1, 2018); "Mother Still Knows Best: Maternal Influence Uniquely Modulates Adolescent Reward Sensitivity During Risk Taking" by João F. Fuassi Moreira and Eva H. Telzer (*Developmental Science*, January 2018); "How Do Emerging Adults Respond to Exercise Advice from Parents? A Test of Advice Response Theory" by Lisa M. Guntzviller and her co-authors (*Journal of Social and Personal Relationships*, September 2017); "Structural Relations between Sources of Parental Knowledge, Feelings of Being Overly Controlled, and Risk Behaviors in Early Adolescence" by Sabina Kapetanovic and her co-authors (*Journal of Family Studies*, August 2017); "The Role of Separation Anxiety in Mothers' Use of Autonomy Support: An Observational Study" by Dorien Wuyts (*Journal of Child and Family Studies*, April 2017); "I Know I Have to Earn Your Love: How the Family Environment Shapes Feelings of Worthiness of Love" by Camilla S. Øverup and her co-authors (*International Journal of Adolescence and Youth*, January 2017); "Does General Parenting Context Modify Adolescents' Appraisals and Coping with a Situation of Parental Regulation? The Case of Autonomy-Supportive Parenting" by Stijn Van Petegem and his co-authors (*Journal of Child and Family Studies*, 2017); "The Neurobiology of the Emotional Adolescent: From the Inside Out" by Amanda E. Guyera and her co-authors (*Neuroscience and Biobehavioral Reviews*, July 2016); "It's Worse when Dad, Rather than Mom, Yells at Teenagers" by Laura M. Padilla-Walker (*Child and Family Blog*, May 28, 2016); "What It Feels Like to Be a Mother: Variations by Children's Developmental Stages" by Suniya S. Luthar and Lucia Ciciolla (*Developmental Psychology*, January 2016); "Adolescents' Information Management: Comparing Ideas about Why Adolescents Disclose to or Keep Secrets from Their Parents" by Lauree Tilton-Weaver (*Journal of Youth and Adolescence*, May 2014).

Chapter 11: Finding Your Village

For an introduction to the work of primatologist and evolutionary theorist Sarah Blaffer Hrdy, see Eric Michael Johnson's two-part interview with her for *Scientific American*, published in March 2012.

For more on social baseline theory (the idea that our bodies treat social relationships as a biological resource), see "Social Baseline Theory: The Social Regulation of Risk and Effort" by James A. Coan and David A. Sbarra (*Current Opinion in Psychology*, February 2015); "Social Support and the Perception of Geographical Slant" by Simone Schnall and her co-authors (*Journal of Experimental Social Psychology*, September 2008).

For more on the important role "the village" has to play in the lives of parents and kids, see "A Radical Idea to Improve Family Life in America: Babysit Your Neighbor's Kids" by Lyman Stone (*Vox*, February 5, 2018) and "Why Mothers of Tweens— Not Babies—Are the Most Depressed" by Lucia Ciciolla and Suniya Luthar (*Aeon*, April 4, 2016).

Now, let's wrap up with one final side-conversation, about creating forward-thinking policies that actually make things better for parents and kids.

We need to do a better job of recognizing that the decisions that governments are making today will have a substantial impact on our children—and their children's children. We need to look for opportunities to ensure that our children's voices are heard and that their interests both now and into the future are factored in as well.

One way to do this is to force governments to be more responsive to the needs of future generations. In a recent essay for *Aeon*, Dutch philosopher Thomas Wells made the case for setting aside a block of "votes for the future." Specifically, he recommended that a designated group of non-governmental organizations (NGOs) be asked to function as "trustees of the generations to come" in policy-making. These NGOs would control a block of votes—10 percent of the votes—and vote with the interests of future generations in mind. Just as referencing the *Constitution of Canada* and the *Canadian Charter of Rights and Freedoms* allows us to tap into the wisdom of the past, "votes for the future" would allow us to connect with the wisdom of the future—or at least our best guess about what that wisdom might be.

Another way to do this is through active citizen engagement: designing public policies in collaboration with the very people whose lives will be most affected by those policies. It's an approach that's deeply rooted in optimism and empathy—in a belief that we can and must resolve the defining issues of our time together so that the entire village can thrive together.

Index

A

abuse
  childhood, 105–7
  in couple relationship, 230
achievement-focused parents, 14, 24, 25, 29–30
ADHD (attention deficit hyperactivity disorder), 15
adolescents and young adults
  academic performance, 178
  changing role of parents of, 85, 244,246–47
  myths about today's, 22–23
  parental anxiety regarding job prospects of, 25
  parental conflict over parenting of, 215
  parents' work hours, 42
  perfectionism of, 26–27, 240
  physical activity, 189, 191
  relationship skills, 62
  screen time, 195–99
  sleep deprivation in, 177–79, 182
  smartphone use, 59, 62, 178, 199
  social support for parents of, 253
adoption, 15, 156, 257

advice, unsolicited, 139, 247
alcohol, 180, 181, 203
allowance, child's, 29
alone time, 114–17
Alter, Adam, 66, 123, 179
Andrew-Gee, Eric, 59, 60, 65
anger, 108, 143, 147, 246
antioxidants, 200
anxiety
  about economy, 9–13
  effect on parenting of, 13–14, 29
  about future, 8
  about giving children competitive edge, 24–26, 123
  and feeling judged, 15–17, 139. See also parent shaming
  managing day-to-day level of, 27–28
  and poor-quality work, 44
  and sense of control, 137
  and sleep deprivation, 174
  and striving to be perfect parent, 139–40
  and technoference, 63–64
apology, parental, 154–55
Applied Cognitive Psychology, 60

apps. *See also* smartphone
  beneficial, 72, 181
  for children, 24
  organization of, 71
  for parents, 113
  teaching child how to use, 197
Ariely, Dan, 222
Arnett, Jeffrey Jensen, 23, 246
attention deficit hyperactivity disorder
  (ADHD), 15
attention span, and smartphone use,
  59–60, 66, 72, 132–33
automation, and future employment,
  11, 30
autonomy-supportive parents, 128,
  243–44

B

babies, 245
  asking for support, 252, 261–62
  and couple relationship, 209–11
  physical activity needs of, 191
  reliance on outside experts, 138
  and return to work, 40–41
  and screen time, 193–94
  "still-face" experiment with, 242–43
Bacon, Tracy, 201
Barrett, Anne E., 79
batch-cooking, 125–26, 202
bedtime. *See also* sleep
  rules for family, 182–83
  screen use at, 178–79, 180
behavioural issues, 42, 68, 74, 85, 195,
  202, 219, 235, 238
bidirectionality, 87–88, 188
blended family household, 228–29
body image, 207
boomer-generation parents, 12
boredom, 133–34, 139, 140–41
breakfast, 182
breastfeeding, 64

Breathnach, Sarah Ban, 142
Brooks, David, 99
Brown, Amy, 138
burnout. *See* parental burnout
Burstyn, Ellen, 151

C

caffeine, 108, 174, 180, 203
calm state of mind, achieving, 108,
  109–14, 115, 117–18, 134, 181, 204
Canadian Association of Optometrists,
  196
Canadian Federation of Independent
  Business (CFIB), 18
Canadian Fitness and Lifestyle Research
  Institute, 192
Canadian Ophthalmological Society, 196
Canadian Paediatric Society (CPS), 194,
  195
*Canadian 24-Hour Movement Guidelines
  for Children and Youth*, 177, 191
car accidents, sleep deprivation and, 175
carbohydrates, complex, 200, 201
career plans, 221–22
Carey, Benedict, 157
Carr, Eliann R., 154
Carr, Nicholas, 58, 66
Center on the Developing Child, 156
Child: Care, Health and Development, 218
child care
  lack of universal system in Canada, 34,
    39, 279–80
  parental sharing of, 34–35, 81
Child Care Advocacy Association of
  Canada, 280
child-centric parents, 78–79
child development
  children's needs at each stage of, 237–44
  children's need at specific stages of,
    245–47
  importance of understanding, 234–36

Child Development, 68
childhood
  abuse, 105–7
  fast-forwarding through child's, 29
  obesity, 172
child safety, 14, 68–69
choir, benefits of singing in, 169
chores. *See* household tasks
Chua, Amy, 78
"chunking" tasks, 152–53
Ciciolla, Lucia, 83, 225, 231, 251, 253
Cincinnati Zoo incident (2016), 21
circadian rhythms, 176, 181
Claxton, Amy, 220
cognitive reappraisal, 137, 149, 160
Cohen, Emma, 192
Colier, Nancy, 61, 116, 268
Common Sense Media, 199
community building, 261, 267–68.
   See also social support
commuting time, 37–38, 130
  as role-switching time, 50–51, 168
compassion
  self-, 146, 158–61, 206–7
  teaching children, 66, 155, 157
computer use. *See* screen time
conditional parental regard, 239–40
conflict, effect on children of parental,
  219, 226
conflict resolution skills, 226–29
connection, making room for moments
  of, 113, 121–22
control, boosting sense of, 136–37
conversation, impact of smartphones
  on, 61–62, 268
cooking. *See also* meals
  batch-, 125–26, 202
  with children, 202–3
co-parenting
  in blended family, 228–29
  with ex-partner, 230–31

coping strategies, 144–47
  helping child develop, 147, 156, 157
couple relationship
  abuse in, 230
  arguing respectfully, 226–27
  conflicts about money, 89, 217–18
  conflicts about parenting, 215
  conflicts about sex, 215–16, 225
  in first years of parenthood, 209–11
  long commutes and, 37
  mid-life, 253
  nurturing, 218–19, 220–26
  recession and, 13
  resentment and, 115, 166, 173, 184, 209
  self-compassion and, 159, 160–61, 214
  sleep deprivation and, 177
  staying in relationship for sake of kids,
   230
  technology use and, 73
  unshared workloads and, 212–15
  work-life conflict and, 40, 51, 218,
   279
couple's therapy, 216, 218, 225, 227–28
Cowan, Carolyn P., 209
Cowan, Philip A., 209
Coyne, Sarah M., 64, 67
creative thinking, 110
Crum, Alia, 145
cultural values, changing, 27, 35, 123
Curran, Thomas, 26–27, 240
Currant Opinion in Psychology, 250
curveballs, dealing with life's, 88–90,
  138, 141, 157–58, 160–61, 207

D

Daly, Kerry, 8, 123
"dandelion" children, 87
Davis, Arran, 192
decision fatigue, 126
deep work, concept of, 112–13
dehydration, 200

Deloitte, 11

Denis, Katie, 46

depression, 89, 92, 135, 137, 159, 203.
    See also anxiety

Dermott, Esther, 16

Developmental Psychology, 230, 246

developmental stages, 83–86, 253

Diener, Ed, 45

diet, 164, 172, 200–203

digital amnesia, 61

digital technology. *See* technology

dinner, family, 201–3

divorce, co-parenting after, 228–31

Doss, Brian D., 210

Doucet, Andrea, 221

downtime. *See* leisure time

dual-income households, 33–34, 217,
    218

E

eating habits, improving, 201–3

educational consultants, 24

emails, 51, 59, 72–73, 132–33

emotional safety, 238–39

emotions

    helping children manage, 147, 238–39,
        245

    negative, 57, 147–48, 159, 174

    positive, 108–9, 134

empathy

    parenting with greater, 236

    teaching children, 66, 155, 157, 194,
        226–27, 242

employment. *See also* work hours; work-
    life balance and automation, 11

    for future generations, 10–12, 25, 28

    income, 10, 14, 48

    precarious nature of, 9, 30, 44–45

    rates for recent graduates, 10

    self-, 43–44, 48

energy boosts

    healthy, 182, 203

    unhealthy, 108–9, 174

eulogy virtues, 99

European Working Conditions Survey,
    52

exercise. *See* physical activity

expectations, managing unrealistic, 26,
    29–30, 150–53

experts, reliance on outside, 138–39

extracurricular activities, 24, 122, 151,
    167

eye problems, screen time and, 196

F

Facebook, 29, 49, 71, 153, 168, 262–67.
    See also social media

family dinners, 201–3

fast food, 173, 202–3

fathers

    and alcohol and drugs, 40

    apologies from, 154–55

    eating habits of, 164

    and parenthood, 75, 78, 80–83

    physical activity decline in, 163, 184

    and relationship conflict, 210, 219

    and self-employment, 43, 48–49

    sleep deprivation in, 176

    societal expectations of, 81, 215

    as stay-at-home parent, 214, 256

    time spent on household tasks, 212

    time spent on parenting-related tasks,
        83, 212–13

    and work-life balance, 41, 45–46

feelings, helping children manage, 147,
    238–39, 245

finances, family

    and decision to have children, 13, 278

    and giving children competitive edge, 24

    impact on social support of, 256–57

stress about, 48, 217–18

and support of children into adulthood, 12

fitness. *See* physical activity

Fitzsimmons, Annabel, 167, 170, 260

Fonseca, Gabriela, 13

food choices, talking to children about, 201

forgiveness, in parent-child relationship, 154–58, 161

Fortin, Pierre, 280

Fredrickson, Barbara L., 98, 141, 148

Freed, Richard, 56

freelancing, 43–44

fresh-start effect, 205–6

friends, 167, 186, 202, 225–26, 231–32, 251–52

on Facebook, 265, 268

G

gender differences

in sports participation, 189

in time spent on household tasks, 201, 212

in time spent on parenting-related tasks, 83, 212–14

in wages, 279, 281

Global News, 24

goal(s)

approach vs. avoidance, 198

big-picture parenting, 98, 111

fitness, 187, 204, 205–6

importance of pursuing, 97, 124, 129–30

re-engagement, 207

setting achievable, 204, 205–6

WOOP strategy for setting, 206

goal culture, 123, 150

Goldin, Claudia, 281

Google, 266

Grabowski, Michael, 113

grandparents, 256, 259

gratitude, 141–42, 223

Graydon, Shari, 46

Great Recession, 10

growth mindset, encouraging children to develop, 244

The Guardian, 44

guilt

family dinners as source of, 201–2

goal culture and, 123, 150

gratitude, 141

reliance on outside experts and, 139

self-care and, 165–66

sex life and, 216

smartphone, 55–56, 63–65, 70

strategies for taming, 153–58

work-interfering-with-family, 39, 49

guide dogs, 20

Gunderson, Justine, 79

H

Hanson, Rick, 128

happiness. *See also* parental happiness

celebrating good news, 223

giving back and, 129, 135

goals and, 129–30

reclaiming misery time, 130–31

reducing boredom, 134

reducing multi-tasking, 132–33

rut, 129

savouring, 131–32

self-efficacy and, 136

Harmon, Sandra, 82

Harris, Malcolm, 9

Harris Interactive, 73

Hayward, Helen, 81

health. *See also* self-care

parenting's toll on, 163–65

stress and family's, 172–73

taking action to improve, 204–7

helicopter parents, 17–22, 78
Henderson, Angie, 82
Hill, Andrew P., 26–27
homework, 26
hopes and dreams, 96–103
Horne, Jim, 176
Hospital for Sick Children (Toronto), 193
household tasks
  "chunking" of, 152–53
  mealtime, 201
  optimizing, 125
  outsourcing, 36, 38, 127, 130, 217
  sharing of, 201, 212, 223
  and temptation bundling strategy,
    130–31
  time set aside to do, 151–52
Hrdy, Sarah Blaffer, 249
Human Resources Professionals
  Association, 11

I

immigrant experience, 256–57
immune system, 175
inattentional blindness, 60
income inequality, 14, 256–57
infants. *See* babies
injury
  child, 68–69, 191
  sleep deprivation and, 175
Instagram, 197, 267. *See also* social media
instincts, trusting, 116–17, 137–38
International Journal of Behavioral
  Nutrition and Physical Activity, 196
internet use. *See* smartphone; social media
intimacy, 225
iPhone, 36. *See also* smartphone

J

Jabr, Ferris, 110
jobs. *See* employment

journal, gratitude, 142
Journal of Child and Family Studies, 39, 91
Journal of Child Neurology, 178
Journal of Family Psychology, 76
Journal of Nutrition Education and Behavior,
  64
Journal of Social and Personal Relationships,
  135

K

Kaag, John, 236
Kahneman, Daniel, 130
Kelly, Dan, 18
Klass, Perri, 55, 69
Kohn, Alfie, 18
Kushlev, Kostadin, 67, 70

L

language development, 193–94
Lareau, Annette, 79, 82
Lawrence, Erika, 209
Layous, Kristin, 96, 131
leisure time
  hiring help, 36, 38, 127
  lack of, 35–36, 37, 38, 47
  of mothers vs. fathers, 81–82
  and screen time with children, 198
  with partner, 220–21
letter, gratitude, 142
life satisfaction, 75–78, 79, 80, 89–90,
  96–97
  predictors of, 141
life skills, 28, 155
Lincoln, Abraham, 69
loneliness, 262–63
love
  parenting with conditional, 239–40
  parenting with unconditional, 237–39
Luthar, Suniya S., 83, 225, 231, 251, 253
Lyubomirsky, Sonja, 96

M

MacDougall, Andrew, 55–56
MacMillan, Hugh, 105, 106
Marois, René, 132
Making Women Count, 212
Martin, Clancy, 236
Martin, Courtney E., 114, 121, 252
McDaniel, Brandon T., 64, 67, 69
meals
  breakfast, 182
  dinner, 199, 201–3
  preparation of, 125–26, 202
  timing of, 201
media, stories about parenting in, 17–23,
  77, 78
Meer, Jenn, 55
Mehrabian, Albert, 62
melatonin suppression, 178, 180
memories
  childhood, 46, 104
  recording rather than experiencing, 61
  sleep deprivation and negative, 174
mental illness, parenting child with, 86,
  258
#MeToo movement, 22
middle school years, 253
Miller, Lisa, 192
mobile devices, 36. *See also* smartphone
mothers
  apologies from, 154
  eating habits of, 164
  employed in tech industry, 47–48
  leisure time of, 81–82, 212–13
  living with terminal diagnosis, 102–3,
    158
  parental satisfaction of, 80
  perfectionism of, 82–83, 92, 94
  physical activity decline in, 163
  and self-blame, 93, 107
  self-employed, 43–44

  sleep quality of, 82, 176
  societal expectations of, 81, 82–83, 214
  stress levels of, 173
  support from friends, 251–52, 253
  time spent on household tasks, 201, 212
  time spent on parenting-related tasks,
    83, 212
  work-interfering-with-family guilt
    of, 39
motivational strategies, 130–31
multi-tasking, 124, 125, 132–33, 140, 176
Musick, Kelly, 80–81, 83
myopia, in children, 196

N

napping, 180
narcissistic kids, 23, 278
National At-Home Dad Network, 256
nature vs. nurture, 87
negative thinking, 148–49
neighbourhoods, and parenting style, 14
Nelson, S. Katherine, 77, 96
neoliberalism, 26–27
Nesi, Jacqueline, 62
Newman, Harmony, 82
Newport, Cal, 112, 113, 149
Nomaguchi, Kei M., 84–85
Norway, 112

O

obesity, child, 172, 195, 196
Oettingen, Gabriele, 206
Offer, Shira, 41
O'Hanlon, Bill, 206
online support, 262–63, 267–68
"orchid" children, 87
Organisation for Economic Co-operation
  and Development (OECD), 44
outdoors, benefits of time spent, 192, 196
outsourcing tasks, 36, 38, 127, 130, 217

P

Palsson, Craig, 68
Papp, Lauren M., 215, 216, 217
parental burnout, 90–93
  risk factors, 93–94, 174
parental happiness, 119–20, 127–28
  being present with child, 121–22, 134, 172
  making better use of time, 124–27
  resisting goal culture, 123
  self-care and, 172
  strategies to achieve, 128–42
  understanding child development and, 235
parental illness, 102–3
parental leave, 30, 40–41
parent-child relationship
  abusive, 105–6
  being authentic and, 140–41, 156, 157
  bidirectionality in, 87–88
  child-centric parenting and improved, 78–79
  deep connection in, 113
  developmental stages and, 85, 245–47
  distracted parenting and, 65–68
  exercising together and, 192
  repairing, 154–55
  screen time and, 194
  uniqueness of each, 86, 87–88
  warm and caring, 237–39, 240
  work-life imbalance and, 40–45, 47
parenting
  boosting enjoyment of. See parental happiness
  cognitive demands of, 113, 117, 132
  effect of recession on, 13–14
  and emotional depletion, 89, 91, 92–93
  emotional labour of, 213–14
  hard work of, 89–90, 135, 136, 252, 271
  with hopes for future in mind, 96–103, 108, 109–10
  and life satisfaction, 75–78, 79, 80, 89–90, 96–97
  as limited time offer, 132
  and making peace with past, 104–7
  and physical depletion, 91, 92, 93, 108
  serve and return, 241–42
  support. See social support
  stages, 83–86, 253
  styles. See parenting styles
  today vs. past, 2–3, 7–8, 11–12, 34, 56–57, 82–83, 233, 261
  while terminally ill, 102–3, 158
  with unconditional love and approval, 237–40
parenting style, 14, 15, 78–79
  achievement-focused, 14, 24, 25, 29–30
  autonomy-supportive, 128, 243–44
  child-centric, 78–79
  concerted cultivation, 79, 82
  distracted, 55–74, 111, 132
  helicopter, 17–22, 78
  parental conflict about, 215
  permissive, 39
  Tiger Mom, 78
  "tough is better," 19–20, 104, 254
parent shaming, 2–3, 15–17, 21
Park, Ryan, 29
Pediatric Exercise Science, 189
perfectionism
  as a result of conditional parental regard, 240
  rising rates of, 26–27, 123, 278
Perry-Jenkins, Maureen, 220
Personality and Social Psychology Bulletin, 115
Pew Research, 90, 256, 265
physical activity
  body image and, 207

children's, 172, 188–92

decline after becoming parent, 163–64,
183–85

as family resource, 186

fitness goals, 187, 204, 205–6

health benefits of, 38, 163, 181, 182,
183, 191

mindset about, 186–88, 204–5

outdoors, 192

planning workouts, 185–86, 187

Pieper, Josef, 35

Pickett, Kate C., 42, 43

Pitman, Teresa, 40–41, 138, 254

planning fallacy, 151–52

playtime

active, 191, 192

and parental boredom, 133–34,
140–41

and smartphone use, 67, 194

PLOS One, 60

Pluess, Michael, 87

positive psychology, 128, 129–30, 141

pregnancy, 88, 222

preschoolers, 122, 137, 164, 245

and family dinner, 202

physical activity, 191

and screen time, 193–95

smartphone apps for, 24

and technoference, 64–68

trusting instincts in caring for, 137–38

and work-life balance, 52, 85

preteens, 253

Prickett, Kate C., 280

primary school-age children, 85, 88,
245

and family dinner, 202

physical activity, 189, 191

and screen time, 193–96

and work-life balance, 52

private schools, 24

problem-solving skills, teaching child,
244, 245

*Proceedings of the National Academy of
Sciences*, 20, 79

productivity

hacks, 51–52

and sleep, 174–75

Project: Time Off, 46

Psychological Bulletin, 90

Psychology of Sports and Exercise, 184

Public Health Ontario, 177, 182 198

Q

quality of life, improving, 28, 47, 96–97

Quebec's child-care program, 280

R

Raising Arizona, 96

recession, impact on families, 13–14,
45, 278

recreation facilities, 190

Redden, Molly, 279

relaxation techniques, 146

relocation, and work-life balance, 47

resilience, child's, 156, 157

retirement savings, 12

Robert Wood Johnson Foundation, 16

role conflict, 48–53

Roshi, Shunryu Suzuki, 96

Routly, Chris, 256

rumination, 148–50, 159

Rybezynski, Kate, 43

S

Sallie Mae, 12

Samuel, Alexandra, 73, 196

*Sanity Savers: The Canadian Working
Woman's Guide to Almost Having It All*,
31–32

Sax, David, 74

Scheiber, Noam, 18

school-age children. *See* primary
    school-age children

Schoppe-Sullivan, Sarah J., 264

screen time. *See also* smartphone
  at bedtime, 178–79, 180
  helping children manage, 73–74, 182,
    193–99
  and parental stress, 172

second-guessing, avoidance of, 137–38,
    139

seijaku (serenity in midst of chaos), 112

self-blame, 93, 107, 159

self-care. *See also* health
  benefits of, 106, 116, 170, 171–72
  definition of, 167–68
  fitting in to daily routine, 168–69
  guilt and, 165–66, 168, 170
  modelling for children, 169–70, 204

self-compassion, 149, 158–61, 206–7

self-efficacy, 136

self-employment, 43–44, 48

self-esteem, 53, 135, 136, 160

self-reflection, 148–50

Seppälä, Emma, 109

sex, 215–16, 225

shared gaze, 67

"should-free" day, 151

siblings, 87–88, 102, 197, 228

single-parent households, 34, 48, 91–93,
    127, 151, 154, 157, 229–32, 260–61

sleep
  and alcohol, 203, 204
  "architecture," 176
  children's, 177–79, 182
  clocking more hours of, 180–81
  deprivation, 82, 164, 174–76
  fixating on lack of, 182
  hygiene, 180
  and protein-heavy meals, 201

slow TV, 112

smartphone. *See also* apps; screen time;
    social media
  and child injury, 68–69
  and child misbehaviour, 68
  and cognitive drain, 59–61
  daily usage, 60, 72
  and enjoyment of parenting, 69–70
  as escape from hard work of parenting,
    57–58, 63
  and face-to-face conversations, 61–62
  family ground rules, 73, 198–99
  and language development, 193–94
  and memory, 61
  and playtime, 67
  and sleep quality, 178–79, 180
  reducing use of, 70–73, 182, 197–99
  as repository for memories, 61
  and sleep quality, 178–79, 180
  and work-life balance, 36, 49

snacks, healthy, 201

snowflake kids, 22–23, 27

social baseline theory, 250

social media
  apps, 71
  comparing self to others on, 153, 266
  feeling judged on, 17, 264
  feeling lonely and, 264–65
  feelings of jealousy or inadequacy on,
    266–67
  inauthentic memes on parenting, 89
  online support, 262–63, 267–68
  privacy issues, 267
  unplugging from, 55–56, 68, 72, 114,
    197

social policy, 39, 270–71

Social Psychological & Personality Science, 78

social skills, 66, 242

social support
  asking for help, 261–62

biological need for, 250

connecting with your village, 258–60, 268–69

from co-workers, 260–61

load sharing, 261

at each stage of parenting, 222, 252–54, 258

from family members, 256, 259–60

from friends, 92, 251–52, 257, 258–59

online, 262–63

and parenting success, 249

from parents with similar problems, 258, 263

societal lack of support for parents, 30, 34–35, 39, 254–55, 270–71

solitude, 114–16

sperm count quality, 176

Spinks, Nora, 74, 125

sports participation, children's, 189

Springfield, Ontario, 269–70

Stadlen, Naomi, 139

Statistics Canada, 12, 33, 36, 37, 39, 164, 189, 190, 212

Stephens-Davidowitz, Seth, 266

step-parenting, 228

Stone, Lyman, 255

Strazdins, Lyndall, 41–42

stress. *See also* anxiety; time stress

and food cravings, 200

and gender norms, 81

levels of mothers, 173

physical activity and, 183

reframing response to, 144–47

as source of energy, 108–9, 110, 118, 144

Sullivan, Andrew, 66

support system. *See* social support

T

Taylor, Jacob, 192

TD Wealth Financial Planning, 12

technoference, 64–69

technology. *See also* smartphone; social media companies, and social responsibility, 74, 283

disengaging from, 55–56, 68, 72, 114

impact of, 58–63, 178

teenagers. *See* adolescents and young adults

The Telegraph, 75

temptation bundling strategy, 130–31

text messaging, 62

after lights out, 178

Thinking & Reasoning, 110

Thoreau, Henry David, 121

Tiger Mom parenting style, 78

time stress, 36–37, 81, 124

effects of, 40–42, 47–48, 121, 172

strategies for managing, 125–27, 151–52

Time Well Spent, 71

Today's Parent, 264

toddlers, 110–11, 242, 243, 245

meltdowns, 235–36

physical activity, 191

and screen time, 193–94

to-do list, 181

Toronto (GTA), Ontario, 44

"total work," 35–36

pushing back against culture of, 45–46

in tech industry, 47

transgender children, 100

trauma, childhood, 105–6, 157

Tronick, Edward, 242

"tulip" children, 87

Turkle, Sherry, 62, 116, 265

tutoring services, 24

TV viewing
    at bedtime, 178
    effect on children of parents', 198
Twenge, Jean, 23
Twitter, 29

U

unconditional parental regard, 238
unemployment, 44–45
UNICEF, 198
universal child-care system, 34
university admissions, 24, 25
Usher, Alex, 10, 278

V

vacations, 46, 68
Vanier Institute of the Family, 8
video games, 178
village, connecting with your, 258–62,
    269–71
vision board, 97
visualization, 97–98

W

Walker, Matthew, 181
Webb, Caroline, 73, 151, 175
weight gain, 175, 203
White, Nancy, 81
WOOP goal-setting strategy, 206
work hours. *See also* time stress
    extreme. *See* "total work"
    maintaining focus and productivity
        during, 49
    non-standard, 42, 43
    part-time, 43, 281

self-employment, 43
work-life balance, 31–33. *See also* "total
    work"
    dissatisfaction with, 36–37, 45
    dual-income households, 33–34, 218,
        222
    and guilt, 38–40, 41, 49, 53
    and non-standard work hours, 42, 43
    resolving problems with, 46–53,
        132–33
    and self-employment, 43–44, 48–49
    single-parent households, 34, 48
    talking to employer about, 52–53
    and working remotely from home, 42
    and workplace norms, 34–35
*Work-Life Balance in Times of Recession,
    Austerity and Beyond*, 45
workplace norms, outdated, 30, 34–35,
    39, 281

Y

yoga, 146, 169
YouTube, 112, 197

Z

Zeigarnik effect, 132–33
ZERO TO THREE, 16
Zilibotti, Fabrizio, 14